Fairness in
Accounting

FAIRNESS IN ACCOUNTING

Janice Monti-Belkaoui
and
Ahmed Riahi-Belkaoui

Q

Quorum Books
Westport, Connecticut • London

Library of Congress Cataloging-in-Publication Data

Monti-Belkaoui, Janice.
    Fairness in accounting / Janice Monti-Belkaoui, Ahmed Riahi-
Belkaoui
      p.   cm.
    Includes bibliographical references and index.
    ISBN 1-56720-018-4 (alk. paper)
    1. Financial statements—Quality control 2. Disclosure in
accounting. 3. Fairness. I. Riahi-Belkaoui, Ahmed.
II. Title.
HF5681.B2M59   1996
657'.3—dc20   95-38764

British Library Cataloguing in Publication Data is available.

Library of Congress Catalog Card Number: 95-38764
ISBN: 1-56720-018-4

First published in 1996

Quorum Books, 88 Post Road West, Westport, CT 06881
An imprint of Greenwood Publishing Group, Inc.

Printed in the United States of America

The paper used in this book complies with the
Permanent Paper Standard issued by the National
Information Standards Organization (Z39.48-1984).

10 9 8 7 6 5 4 3 2

To Hedi

Contents

Exhibits   ix

Preface   xi

1. Fairness in Presentation   1

    Appendix 1.A: A European True and Fair View?   27

    Appendix 1.B: Income Smoothing   49

    Appendix 1.C: Fraud Cases Resulting from Fairness in
    Presentation   51

2. Fairness in Distribution   57

3. Fairness in Disclosure   71

    Appendix 3.A: FauxCom Inc.   106

    Appendix 3.B: Costs and Benefits of Business Information
    Disclosure   141

4. Entitlements, Rights, and Fairness in Intrafirm Resource
   Allocation   159

Selected Readings   175

Index   177

Exhibits

1.1 Generally Accepted Auditing Standards   19

3.1 Scope of Disclosures   73

3.2 Purposes of Required Financial Statement Disclosures   79

3.3 Deriving the Value Added Statement   82

3.4 The Characteristics of the Various Component Parts of
     Social Accounting   87

4.1 Results of the Analysis of Variance on the Greed Index   168

4.2 Greed Index Measures, Means and Standard Deviation by
     Fairness Treatment   169

Preface

Fairness has an important place in the practice of accounting. It is stated in the auditor's report that the financial statements fairly present the results of operations and cash flows for the year and end in conformity with generally accepted accounting principles. This statement presents to the users and the market the guarantee that the accountants (as preparers) and the auditors (as attestors) have strived to be fair. This conventional nature of the concept of fairness is fairness in presentation, connoting an idea of neutrality in the preparation and presentation of financial reports and the idea of justice in outcome. This view of fairness in accounting as fairness in presentation is rather limited, calling for expansion of the notion of fairness to deal with distribution, disclosure, and resource allocation considerations. Accordingly, the main objective of this book is to explain the conventional notion of fairness in presentation before elaborating on the more interesting notions of fairness in distribution, fairness in disclosure, and fairness in resource allocation. Each of these concepts is presented in a separate chapter.

1. Chapter 1, "Fairness in Presentation," will cover the conventional treatment of fairness in accounting as well as the resulting limitations and consequences.
2. Chapter 2, "Fairness in Distribution," will cover the contributions of various theories of justice (Rawls, Nozick, and Gerwith in particular) to different interpretations of fairness in accounting.

3. Chapter 3, "Fairness in Disclosure," will cover the avenues available for better disclosure to users in general that meet the interests of all the stakeholders.

4. Chapter 4, "Entitlements, Rights, and Fairness in Intrafirm Resource Allocation," will show how a moral authority espousing different theories of justice can reduce self-interest as it affects intrafirm distribution and disclosure.

The book may be used as a guide to understanding the concept of fairness as fairness in presentation and to the expansion of the concept to deal with the more crucial issues of distribution, disclosure, and resource allocation. It should be of interest to members of the accounting profession and to accounting students and researchers.

No book can be written without the help of numerous individuals and organizations. A special note of appreciation to my teaching and research assistant, Claire Howard, for her cheerful and intelligent assistance. A special note of appreciation is also extended to all the organizations, authors, and editors that have given permission to reprint portions of their work in this book. The help, encouragement, and professionalism of Mr. Eric Valentine, Ms. Bridget Austiguy, and the Greenwood Publishing Group are appreciated.

Finally, to Hedi, thanks again.

1

Fairness in Presentation

Fairness occupies an important role in accounting as it presents to the users and the market the guarantee that the accountant (as preparer) and the auditor (as attestor) have strived to be fair. The conventional nature of the concept of fairness is fairness in presentation, a guarantee that the diligence and care in the preparation and attestation of financial statements are to ensure an adequate presentation of the financial affairs of the firm. Because the central meaning of fairness is fairness in presentation, this chapter explicates the concept, understood in the United States as the fairness doctrine and in Europe as the "True and Fair" doctrine, and pinpoints some of the consequences of its application.

FAIRNESS IN ACCOUNTING

Fairness as Neutrality in Presentation

Fairness is best understood in the professional accounting literature and pronouncements as an expression of neutrality of the accountant in the preparation of financial reports.[1] The first suggestion of the use of fairness in accounting was made by D. R. Scott in 1941 when he listed it as a principle of accounting and stated: "Accounting rules, procedures, and techniques should be fair, unbiased and impartial. They should not serve a special interest."[2] Since then fairness became a value statement that is variously applied to accounting. Arthur Andersen & Co., in 1960 published a monograph on the subject that states the following:

Thus, the one basic accounting postulate underlying accounting principles may be stated as that of fairness—fairness to all segments of the business community (management, labor, stockholders, creditors, customers, and the public), determined and measured in the light of the economic and political environment and the modes of thought and customs of all such segments—to the end that the accounting principles based upon this postulate shall produce financial accounting for the lawfully established economic rights and interests that is fair to all segments.[3]

James Patillo followed by making fairness the subject of a book and ranking it as a basic standard to be used in the evaluation of other standards because it is the only standard that implies "ethical considerations."[4] He states:

> From these observations on the relation between accounting and the current social concepts and attitudes, it is concluded that accounting is essentially social in nature and has significant responsibilities to society. Furthermore, relating these ideas to the objective of financial accounting results in an emphasis on the communication of economic interests of the economy segments. Finally, from contrasting the connotations of justice, truth, and fairness, the current social concept of fairness is selected as the basic standard by which to measure the propriety of accounting principles and rules which purport to be means of attaining the objective. Fairness to all parties, therefore, is formulated to be the single basic standard of accounting, that criterion or test which all accounting propositions must reflect before being included into the accounting structure.[5]

The importance of fairness was also in evidence when C. T. Devine gave preserving equity among conflicting groups a central place among accounting concerns.[6]

Historically, fairness or the "fairness doctrine" evolved from the application of the concept of conservatism. The evolution went from a concern with liquidity and credit granting, generally associated with conservatism, to the idea that financial statement presentations should be fair to all users.[7] Fairness is then basically an extension of the user set from creditors to stockholders. This attempt was doomed to fail. As stated by Chatfield: "But what was fair (or conservative) for credit granters might not be for stockholders. The concept of conservatism in its corporate context required specifying the financial statement audience, which the doctrine itself was not helpful in doing."[8]

Having failed at producing useful information, some accounting writers put more emphasis on fairness in presentation. As explained by Skinner:

"This test extends the concept of usefulness, since it is conceivable that a distorted presentation would be more useful to some parties (using the word 'useful' in a narrow, selfish sense) than would an unbiased presentation."[9]

Fairness is generally associated with the measurement and reporting of information in an objective and neutral way. Information is fair if it is objective and neutral. As stated by Lee: "It must be based on firm, verifiable evidence (whenever possible), and it must not be such as to tend to benefit a particular user (or group of users) to the relative detriment of others."[10]

Fairness is much more achievable in managerial and cost accounting where any hint of impartiality or bias may distort the decision-making processes that rely heavily on managerial accounting data. Fairness becomes a necessary criterion of information in managerial accounting to ensure the integrity and accuracy of decision making. As stated by Flegm:

> In practice, managerial accountants continually strive to "call them as they see them" since it is essential that top management have faith that the comparative analyses of actual results with budget and forecast data are as impartial and free from bias as is humanly possible. The reason for this objectivity seems obvious since any other course would have the effect of influencing and perhaps misleading the decisions of management. Of course, public accountants too are striving for this same objectivity.[11]

In spite of contentions that fairness is subjective, ambiguous, and therefore cannot serve as a basis for developing accounting theory, it has become one of the basic objectives of accounting. A first evidence of this importance is the reference by the American Institute of Certified Public Accountants' (AICPA) Committee on Auditing Procedures to the criteria of "fairness of presentation" as conformity with generally accepted accounting principles, disclosure, consistency, and comparability. In an unqualified report, "present fairly" connotes compliance with generally accepted accounting principles and generally accepted auditing standards.

Since then, the fairness concept has become an implicit ethical norm. In general, the fairness concept implies that accounting statements have not been subject to undue influence or bias. Fairness implies that the preparers of accounting information have acted in good faith and employed ethical business practices and some accounting judgment in the presentation, production, and auditing of accounting results. The professional interpretation is now restricted to fairness in presentation.

"True and Fair" Doctrine

Financial statements of British companies are required by law to present a true and fair view of the state of affairs, making it the ultimate foundation of financial reporting in Great Britain.[12] A history of the concept is provided by Chastney.[13] It has been, however, a concept in continuous search for comprehensive definition, along with a reasonable consensus that more than a single presentation may satisfy the true and fair doctrine.[14,15] The lack of a clear explication is best illustrated in the following quotation:

> On the surface the true and fair view towers over British accounting but with the curious characteristics that no-one knows what it means, and very little academic analysis has been done on its role in accounting. As regards its meaning it is a legal term in origin and yet the Companies Acts have never defined it (nor has the Fourth Directive, of course) and there is little jurisprudence which bears upon it. There is no definition of it in accounting standards, auditing standards or other professional pronouncements. Most tellingly, a television broadcast in 1992 included interviews with senior British accountants: when asked to define the true and fair view, one (partner in Ernst and Young) laughed, another (senior partner of a major non big 6 firm) would say nothing and a third, the finance director of an Anglo-American multinational, asked for time to think about the question.[16]

Academic accountants were not successful either. Witness the following two attempts at defining true and fair:

> It is generally understood to mean a presentation of accounts, drawn up according to accepted accounting principles, using accurate figures as far as possible, and reasonable estimates otherwise; and arranging them to show, within the limits of current accounting practice, as objective a picture as possible, free from willful bias, distortion, manipulation, or concealment of material facts.[17]

> True means that the accounting information contained in the financial statements has been quantified and communicated in such a way as to correspond to the economic events, activities and transactions it is intended to describe. . . . Fair means that the accounting information has been measured and disclosed in a manner which is objective and without prejudice to any particular sectional interests in the company.[18]

The two definitions link "true and fair" basically to accurate and free from bias. This noble attempt does not, however, detract from the professional and legal implied definitions of true and fair as a technical term implying a compliance with sound accounting principles.

The problem was not solved even with the Fourth Directive, which required that all financial statements of limited liability companies subject to

European Economic Community company law should present a true and fair view as follows:

1. The annual accounts shall comprise the balance sheet, the profit and loss account and the notes on the accounts. These documents shall constitute a composite whole.

2. They shall be drawn up clearly and in accordance with the provisions of this Directive.

3. The annual accounts shall give a true and fair view of the company's assets, liabilities, financial position and profit or loss.

4. Where the application of the provisions of the Directive would not be sufficient to give a true and fair view within the meaning of paragraph 3, additional information must be given.

5. Where in exceptional cases the application of a provision of this Directive is incompatible with the obligation laid down in paragraph 3, that provision must be departed from in order to give a true and fair view within the meaning of paragraph 3. Any such departure must be disclosed in the notes on the accounts together with an explanation of the reasons for it and a statement of its effects on the assets, liabilities, financial position and profit or loss. The Member States may define the exceptional cases in question and lay down the relevant special rules.[19]

No clear definition of the true and fair doctrine was provided, leading to different interpretations by the members of the European Community and a tendency to interpret it in the context of national culture, national accounting tradition, and national generally accepted accounting principles.[20]

In addition to the lack of a comprehensive definition, there is definitely much confusion among producers and users of accounting information on the exact meaning of true and fair.[21,22,23,24] The interpretation of the word "true" and the word "fair" by the technical partners of the top twenty U.K. audit firms provided for *true:* based on fact, undistorted facts, correct, complies with rules, not in conflict with facts, objective, correct within material, adherence to events, and factual accuracy; and for *fair:* not misleading, substance over form, proper reflection, putting in right context, consistent with underlying reality, ability to understand what has really gone on, in accordance with rules in context, reasonable, give right impression, and whether reader receives the right message.[25]

FAIRNESS IN THE AUDITOR'S REPORT

The Auditor's Standard Report: Past, Present, and Future

The audit report is the only formal means to communicate the results of the audit function to the users of financial statements. Over the years its format, content, and importance have changed in various attempts to increase or change its educational and informational value.

Its origins were in England, where its contents were prescribed by the English Companies Act of 1990 and were introduced as such in the United States. Until 1948 auditors were required to state whether, in their opinion, the balance sheet presented a true and correct view of the financial condition of the company after a detailed examination of the books was made. No standard report existed. An example is the following unaddressed certificate in the 1907 Sears, Roebuck and Company financial statement: "We have attended at Chicago, Illinois, and audited the accounts of the company for the year ended June 30, 1907, and certify that the balance sheet, in our opinion, correctly sets forth the position of the company as shown in the books of accounts. Deloitte, Plender, Griffiths & Co., Auditors, 49 Wall Street, New York City, September 7, 1907."

Another good example is the following report from the first annual report of the United States Steel Corporation:

New York
March 12, 1903

To the Stockholders of the United States Steel Corporation:

We have examined the books of the U.S. Steel Corporation and its Subsidiary Companies for the year ending December 31, 1902, and certify that the Balance Sheet at that date and the Relative Income Account are correctly prepared therefrom.

We have satisfied ourselves that during the year only actual additions and extensions have been charged to Property Account; that ample provision has been made for Depreciation and Extinguishment, and that the item of "Deferred Charges" represents expenditures reasonably and properly carried forward to the operations of subsequent years.

Full provision has been made for bad and doubtful accounts receivable and for all ascertainable liabilities.

We have verified the cash and securities by actual inspection or by certificates from the Depositories, and are of opinion that the Stocks and bonds are fully worth the values at which they are stated in the Balance Sheet.

And we certify that in our opinion the Balance Sheet is properly drawn up so as to show the true financial position of the Corporation and its Subsidiary Companies, and that the Relative Income Account is a fair and correct statement of the net earnings for the fiscal year ending at that date.

Price Waterhouse & Co.

Following World War I, the *Ultramares* case in 1931, the stock market crash in 1929, the *McKesson and Robbins* case in 1938, the passage of the securities acts of 1933 and 1934, and the release of Statement on Auditing Practices (SAP) no. 5 and no. 6 in February 1940 and March 1941, both titled "The Revised SEC Rule on 'Accountants' Certificates,' " the audit report was subjected to various changes in format and content. Finally, in October 1948 the American Institute of Public Accountants issued SAP no. 24, "Revision in Short-form Accountant's Report or Certificate." It amended the scope paragraph to read: "We have examined the balance sheet of X Company as of _____, and the related statements of income and surplus for the year then ended. Our examination was made in accordance with generally accepted auditing standards, and accordingly included such tests of the accounting records and such other auditing procedures as we considered necessary in the circumstances." Other changes followed in 1963 with the substitution of the word *surplus* by the phrase *retained earnings* and in 1971 with the addition of *statement of changes in financial position.* As a result the form of the auditor's standard report reads as follows:

We have examined the balance sheet of X Company as of (at) December 31, 19XX, and the related statements of income, retained earnings and changes in financial position for the year then ended. Our examination was made in accordance with generally accepted auditing standards and, accordingly, included such tests of the accounting records and such other auditing procedures as we considered necessary in the circumstances. In our opinion, the financial statements referred to above present fairly the financial position of X Company as of (at) December 31, 19XX, and the results of its operations and the changes in its financial position for the year then ended in conformity with generally accepted accounting principles applied on a basis consistent with that of the preceding year.

Although it has stood the test of time, the present form of audit report has been criticized for its failure to describe the auditor's function adequately. It gives the false impression that all is well financially for those firms receiving unqualified opinions and that the whole truth is being disclosed in the annual reports. What is in fact happening is that the financial statements are prepared by management and reflect only management's version of the truth. In addition, the audit report not only appears to the general public as a guarantee that is far from correct but is becoming more of a symbol than an important indicator. The Cohen Commission alerted the profession to the situation. It called for the profession to indicate explicitly that (a) the financial statements are representations of management, (b) the accounting principles deemed appropriate were used, and (c) the auditor's opinion is the result of judgments exercised by the auditor in his or her work. The commission thought that the present auditor's standard report is unsatisfactory and requires a thorough revision to clarify the present intended meaning and to add important aspects of the audit function not presently covered explicitly. The commission also gave the following example of tomorrow's auditor report:

Report of Independent Auditors

The accompanying consolidated balance sheet of XYZ Company as of December 31, 19XX, and the related statements of consolidated income and changes in consolidated financial positions for the year ended, including the notes, were prepared by XYZ Company's management, as explained in the report by management.

In our opinion, those financial statements in all material respects present the financial position of XYZ Company at December 31, 19XX, and the results of its operations and changes in financial position for the year then ended in conformity with generally accepted accounting principles appropriate in the circumstances.

We audited the financial statements and the accounting records and documents supporting them in accordance with generally accepted auditing standards. Our audit included a study and evaluation of the company's accounting system and the controls over it. We obtained sufficient evidence through a sample of the transactions and other events reflected in the financial statement amounts and an analytical review of the information presented in the statements. We believe our auditing procedures were adequate in the circumstances to support our opinion.

Based on our study and evaluation of the accounting system and the controls over it, we concur with the description of the system and controls in the report by management (or, based on our study and evaluation of the accounting system and controls believe the system and controls over it, we have the following uncorrected material weaknesses not described in the report by management . . .) (or other disagreements with the description of the system and controls in the report by management) (or a description of uncorrected material weaknesses found if there is no report by management). Nevertheless, in the performance of most control procedures, errors can result from personal factors. Also, control procedures can be circumvented by collusion or override. Furthermore, projection of any evaluation of internal accounting control to future periods is subject to the risk that changes in conditions may cause procedures to become inadequate and the degree of compliance with them to deteriorate.

We reviewed the process used by the company to prepare the quarterly information released during the year. Our reviews were conducted each quarter (or times as explained). (Any other information reviewed, such as replacement cost data, would be identified.) Our review consisted primarily of inquiries of management, analysis of financial information, and comparisons of that information to information and knowledge about the company obtained during our audits and were based on our reliance on the company's internal accounting control system. Any adjustments or additional disclosures we recommended have been reflected in the information.

We reviewed the Company's policy statement on employee conduct, described in the report by management, and reviewed and tested the related controls and internal audit procedures. While no controls or procedures can prevent or detect all individual misconduct, we believe the controls and internal audit procedures have been appropriately designed and applied.

We met with the audit committee (or the board of directors) or XYZ Company sufficiently often to inform it of the scope of our audit and to discuss any significant accounting or auditing problems encountered and any other services provided to the company (or indication of failure to meet or insufficient meetings or failure to discuss pertinent problems).

Test Check & Co.
Certified Public Accountants

Following the publication of the Cohen Report, the Auditing Standards Executive Committee (now called the Auditing Standards Board) of the AICPA formed a task force to examine possible revisions of the auditor's report. It agonized for three years before concluding that the report, the primary means of communication between the auditor and the users of his or her work, should be modified to clarify the character of the audit and the extent of the auditor's responsibility. The proposed changes were disclosed in September 1980 in a proposed Statement on Auditing Standards (SAS) titled "The Auditor's Report." The proposed form of the independent auditor's standard report will be as follows:

The accompanying balance sheet of X Company as of (at) December 31, 19XX, and the related statement of income, retained earnings and changes in financial position for the year ended are management's representations. An audit is intended to provide reasonable, but no absolute, assurance as to whether financial statements taken as a whole are free of material misstatements. We have audited the financial statements referred to above in accordance with generally accepted auditing standards. Application of those standards required judgment in determining the nature, timing and extent of testing and other procedures, and in evaluating the results of those procedures.

In our opinion, the financial statements referred to above present the financial position of X Company as of (at) December 31, 19XX, and the results of its operations and the changes in its financial position for the year then ended in conformity with generally accepted accounting principles.

The following seven changes in the wording of the report were made. The first change was the proposed deletion of the word *fairly* from the opinion paragraph. The word *fairly* has always generated some controversy; in 1964 an AICPA committee, the Seidman Committee, asserted in its 1965 report that:

In the standard report of the auditor, he generally says that financial statements "present fairly" in conformity with generally accepted accounting principles. What does the auditor mean by the quoted words? Is he saying: (1) that the statements are fair *and* in accordance with generally accepted accounting principles; or (2) that they are fair *because* they are in accordance with generally accepted accounting principles; or (3) that they are fair only *to the extent* that generally accepted accounting principles are fair; or (4) that whatever the generally accepted accounting may be, the *presentation* of them is fair?

The challenge to the profession did not go unanswered. In 1975 the AICPA Auditing Standards Executive Committee issued SAS no. 5 on the "meaning of 'Present Fairly' in conformity with Generally Accepted Accounting Principles in the Independent Auditor's Report." In it, the idea of fairness was stated as follows (paragraph 4):

a. The accounting principles selected and applied have general acceptance . . . ;
b. The . . . principles are appropriate in the circumstances . . . ;
c. The financial statements, including the related notes, are informative of matters that may affect their use, understanding, and interpretation . . . ;
d. The information presented in the financial statements is classified and summarized in a reasonable manner, that is, neither too detailed nor too condensed . . . ;
e. The financial statements reflect the underlying events and transactions . . . within a range of acceptable limits, that is, limits that are reasonable and practicable to attain in financial statements.

In spite of these clarifications, the debate on the usefulness of "present fairly" continues today. Those in favor of its deletion argue that (a) it is wrongly interpreted as an opinion on the fairness of financial statements rather than an opinion about their conformity with generally accepted accounting practices (GAAP), and (b) it is subjective and unnecessary, given that fairness is already embodied in the GAAP. Those in favor of its inclusion argue that (a) it may indicate to the nonsophisticated users of financial statements that the auditors are reneging on their responsibilities, (b) it is an overriding principle of accounting recognized by both the profession and the users, and (c) it acts as a "modifier" without which the audit process might appear more exact than it really is.

The second change was the assertion that financial statements are management's representations. This change is believed to give a true picture of the relationships between management and the auditors. Management prepares or finds somebody to prepare the financial statements to be verified by the auditors. Those arguing against the deletion maintain that (a) it may be more confusing to the users, (b) it may give the idea that the statements are used by management to present less than a factual picture of the financial condition of the company, and (c) it may give the impression that the auditors are backing away from any responsibility to find "material misstatements." The most relevant argument against the change is that it would be redundant given the usual presence of a management report in the annual report.

The third change was the deletion of the reference to consistency. The deletion is justifiable, because Accounting Principles Board (APB) Opinion no. 20 requires disclosure of changes in accounting principles. Therefore, reference to consistency is redundant in view of the requirements of APB Opinion no. 20. Those arguing against the deletion maintain that most users may not be aware of APB Opinion no. 20 and therefore need the reference to consistency.

The fourth change was the addition of the word *independent* to comply with the standard of independence and as a reminder to auditors, management, and users.

The fifth change was the replacement of the word *examined* with the word *audited* to emphasize the exhaustive work accomplished in an audit. Some think, however, that either word may be confusing to users and may mean anything from a perusal to a probe.

The sixth change is a statement in the scope paragraph that the application of generally accepted auditing standards (GAAS) requires judgment in determining the nature, timing, and extent of testing and other procedures and in evaluating the results of those procedures. Such change was expected to give a better picture of the nature of the opinion and help users in their interpretation of the opinion. It admits that audits do not guarantee complete accuracy, much less any firm protection against fraud. Some think, however, that the change is redundant, since the judgmental nature of the opinion is reflected in the current report wording: "included such tests . . . as we considered necessary in the circumstances." Others believe that the change sounds as if the accountants are trying to retreat even further and take even less responsibility; they appear to be doing less than the users thought they were.

The seventh change is the statement that an audit is intended to provide reasonable, but not absolute, assurance about whether financial statements as a whole are free of material misstatements. It is clearly a confession that an audit is only an audit and not a guarantee.

All of these changes, however, proved to be politically and practically difficult to accept, and the proposed SAS was shelved.

The Auditor's Standard Report: The Meaning of "Present Fairly . . . in Conformity with GAAP"

A current form of the auditor's standard report reads as follows:

We have examined the balance sheet of X Company as of (at) December 31, 19XX, and the related statements of income, retained earnings and changes in financial position for the year then ended. Our examination was made in accordance with generally accepted auditing standards and, accordingly, included such tests of the accounting records and such auditing procedures as we considered necessary in the circumstances.

In our opinion, the financial statements referred to above present fairly the financial position for the year then ended in conformity with generally accepted accounting principles applied on a basis consistent with that of the preceding year.

For more than forty years, the second part of the auditor's report has expressed the auditor's opinion that financial statements "present fairly . . . in conformity with generally accepted accounting principles." The meaning of "present fairly" and the relationship between that phrase and "in conformity with generally accepted accounting principles" are not, however, clear and have been the subject of various interpretations. Each of the meanings and interpretations gives a view of what the responsibility of the auditor *should be* in reporting on financial statements. The situation is confusing enough to create three interpretations of the auditor's responsibility in expressing an opinion.

Opinion on Fairness

The first interpretation is that the auditor is expressing an *opinion on fairness*. This view maintains that the auditor can express an opinion on fairness based on his own private standard completely apart from the GAAP. It calls for every auditor to formulate his or her own view of fairness in auditing financial statements. But this view may lead to a very chaotic and highly subjective situation. A framework is needed to attain a high level of quality and comparability. The GAAP provide such a framework.

Those who maintain that the auditor can express an *opinion on fairness* based on his or her own private standards have either misunderstood or misinterpreted the *Continental Vending* case (*U.S. v. Simon,* 425 F. 2d 706 [2d Cir. 1969], Cert. den. 397 U.S. 1006 [1970]). This case concerned a footnote that was alleged to be affirmatively misleading. More precisely, the court found that the financial statements omitted material facts, principally because they did not state (a) that a receivable from a company controlled by a major stockholder of Continental Vending was essentially a loan to the stockholder who used the other company as a conduit for the loan and was unable to repay it, and (2) that the "marketable securities" that served as collateral for the receivable consisted of stocks and bonds of Continental Vending. The defendant auditors contended that they had followed the GAAS in their examination and concluded that the financial statements conformed with the GAAP. The trial judge instructed the jury, however, that the "critical test" was whether the financial statement fairly presented the financial condition and to consider proof of compliance with professional standards as "evidence which may be persuasive but not necessarily conclusive" that the financial statements "were not materially false or misleading." Given these instructions, the jury found the defendants guilty. The appeals court heard the case and refused to reverse the decision. In its decision the appeals court considered the issue of whether the auditors had acted in good faith in not disclosing information that they were aware of but were not required by the GAAP—essentially in the form of published authoritative standards—to be disclosed:

> We do not think the jury was . . . required to accept the accountants' evaluation whether a given fact was material to overall fair presentation, at least not when the accountants' testimony was not based on specific rules or prohibitions which they could point out, but only on the need for the auditor to make an honest judgment and their conclusion that nothing in the financial statements themselves negated the conclusion that an honest judgment had been made. Such evidence may be highly persuasive, but it is not conclusive, and so the trial judge correctly charged.[26]

The decision of the court simply held that conformity with the GAAP, if established, does not by itself preclude a jury from inferring criminal intent from other evidence of the auditor's conduct, especially if the GAAP are silent on the subject. The court was calling the auditors to exercise individual judgments in areas in which no GAAP exist to determine that the statements are not misleading. It provided the following guidelines:

Generally accepted accounting principles instruct an accountant what to do in the usual case where he has no reason to doubt that the affairs of the corporation are being honestly conducted. Once he has reason that this basic assumption is false, an entirely different situation confronts him. Then . . . he must "extend his procedures to determine whether or not such suspicions are justified." If as a result of such extension or, as here, without it, he finds his suspicions to be confirmed, full disclosure must be the rule.[27]

A similar interpretation was expressed in the AICPA booklet titled *The Auditor's Report:*

> Accounting for business transactions requires approximations and estimates. Unlike certain fields of science where a specific result can be achieved by the combination of certain elements, the amounts of many items in the financial statement cannot be measured with exactness but are subject to the application of professional judgment on an informed basis.
> Therefore, when the auditor refers to fairness of presentation, no claim is being made as to precise exactness. Rather, the auditor is saying that unlike a reasonable range of materiality, the financial statements have been presented on a basis which is fair to all segments of the financial community.[28]

The above guideline does not ask auditors to appraise presentations based on their own private standards completely apart from the GAAP. In short, the *Continental Vending* decision has been misinterpreted by those interpreting the auditor's responsibility in expressing an opinion on fairness based on his or her private standards. In any case, if that would ever become a fact, the situation would be incredibly confusing, with auditors presenting and arguing their own brands of accounting theory to support their own opinions about fairness. The accounting world can do without such a situation.

Dual Opinion

The second interpretation is that the auditor is expressing dual opinions, one on fairness and one on conformity to the GAAP. This would lead the auditor to draw one of four possible conclusions:

1. The presentations conform with the GAAP and are fair.
2. The presentations conform with the GAAP and are not fair.
3. The presentations do not conform with the GAAP and are fair.
4. The presentations do not conform with the GAAP and are not fair.

The opinions about fairness rest on conformity with the auditor's private standard of fair presentation. The dual opinion is explicitly stated by the Canadian Institute of Public Accountants (CICA). In the *CICA Handbook* (Section 5500.08), the Canadian Institute requires auditors to fulfill the following responsibilities:

> The auditors should express an opinion, or report that they are unable to express an opinion, as to whether:
>
> a. the financial statements present fairly the financial position of the enterprise, the results of its operations and, where applicable, the source and application of its funds, and
>
> b. the financial statements were prepared in accordance with generally accepted accounting principles applied on a basis consistent with that of the preceding period.

The Canadian position implies that the auditor is responsible for appraising financial statement presentations based on his or her own private standard completely apart from the GAAP in addition to appraising conformity with the GAAP. In fact, to make sure that the auditor got the point, a letter dated May 16, 1972, to the members of the CICA from G. Mulcahy, then director of research, stated that a departure from the GAAP required a qualified opinion but only as to conformity with the GAAP. "This does not mean that auditors must necessarily qualify their opinion as to whether the financial statements present fairly the financial position of the enterprise, the results of operations and, where applicable, the source and application of its funds. That decision is a separate matter of professional judgment on the part of auditors."

Although the dual opinion seems to be acceptable to the Canadian profession, it is anathema for the U.S. counterpart. Again, the opinion on fairness above is perceived to undermine the GAAP and confidence in financial statements and to lead to a chaotic situation. For example, accounting firms may start competing on the basis of whose ideas on accounting theory agreed most with clients' situations.

Opinion on Conformity with GAAP

The third interpretation is that the auditor is only expressing an opinion on conformity with the GAAP. Therefore, the GAAP are regarded as the only standard of reference to be used by the auditor in judging the quality of the audited financial statements. This interpretation can be inferred from the AICPA official pronouncements. Thus in its Statement no. 4 (paragraph 189), the AICPA Accounting Principles Board discussed fair presentation in conformity with the GAAP:

The qualitative standard of *fair presentation in conformity with generally accepted* principles of financial position and results of operations is particularly important in evaluating financial presentations. This standard guides preparers of financial statements and is the subjective benchmark against which independent public accountants judge the propriety of the financial accounting information communicated. Financial statements "present fairly in conformity with generally accepted accounting principles" if a number of conditions are met: (1) generally accepted accounting principles applicable in the circumstances have been applied in accumulating and processing the financial accounting information, (2) changes from period to period in generally accepted accounting principles have been appropriately described in the financial statements in conformity with generally accepted accounting principles, and (3) a proper balance has been achieved between the conflicting needs to disclose important aspects of financial position and results of operations in accordance with conventional concepts and to summarize the voluminous underlying data in a limited number of financial statement captions and supporting notes.

In the statement it appears that conformity to the GAAP and application of the GAAP are the center of the auditor's responsibility in expressing an opinion. The GAAP appeared then as a rule book to be followed without the exercise of personal judgment by the individual auditor, a body of principles and techniques agreed upon by authoritative professional studies. As such they constitute an ideal collective standard to be used to appraise financial statements. The auditor's opinion is a personal approval of financial statements because they meet the standard adopted by the profession. For this interpretation to be valid, however, the GAAP need to be strengthened by a narrowing of the range of choices in accounting principles and a better identification of the circumstances in which a specific accounting principle is to be used.

Fairly or Exact Statements

The profession has struggled with the meaning attached to the phrase "present fairly . . . in conformity with GAAP." The acceptable meaning was that adherence to professional standards—both accounting and auditing—cannot ensure absolute accuracy, given the nature of the financial statements. It meant that although the GAAP governed the preparation of the financial statement, and the GAAS governed their audit, the auditor's report does not connote absolute accuracy. The GAAP and GAAS rest on estimations, evaluations, and judgments to both prepare and audit the financial statements, which precludes the use of words such as *true* or *correct* but calls for the use of a word such as *fairly*. This interpretation of "present fairly" as meaning that the GAAP require estimations, evaluations, and judgments in their application and cannot lead to "exact" financial statements was suppressed first in the AICPA booklet *Forty Questions and Answers about Audit Reports:*

> What is the significance of the expression "present fairly" in the CPA's report? . . . No one can be in a position to state that a company's financial statements "exactly present" financial position or results of operations. Accordingly, the CPA usually states that the financial statements "present fairly" in the sense that he believes they are substantially correct. For the same reason, his findings are expressed in the form of an opinion. However, it should be borne in mind that the judgment involved is an informed one, and is guided by generally accepted accounting principles."[29]

The Final Meaning of "Present Fairly"

After the shelving of SAS no. 5, the AICPA issued SAS no. 69: "The Meaning of Present Fairly in Conformity with Generally Accepted Accounting Principles in the Independent Auditor's Report."[30] The statement was intended to explain the meaning of the phrase "present fairly . . . in conformity with generally accepted accounting principles" in the independent auditor's report. The auditor's judgment concerning fairness in the presentation of financial statements is to be applied within the framework of generally accepted accounting principles, a term that encompasses the conventions, rules, and procedures necessary to define accepted accounting practice at a particular time. The fairness judgment is therefore a judgment as to whether (a) the accounting principles selected and applied have general acceptance; (b) the accounting principles are appropriate in the circumstances; (c) the financial statements, including the related notes, are informative of matters that may affect their use, understanding, and interpretation; (d) the information presented in the financial statements is classified and summarized in a reasonable manner, that is, it is neither too detailed nor too condensed; and (e) the financial statements reflect the underlying transactions and events in a manner that presents the financial position, results of operations, and cash flows stated within a range of acceptable limits, that is, limits that are reasonable and practical to attain the financial statements.

The Auditor's Standard Report: Content and Nature of the Opinion

Content of the Report

The auditor's process is not random. It is guided by the profession. Since 1972 the AICPA has issued SASs to serve as the most authoritative references available to auditors. These statements, however, provide less direction to auditors than may be assumed. They are used by practitioners as minimum rather than ideal standards of performance. They do not provide defined and detailed guidelines for determining the specific auditing procedures and the extent of evidence to be accumulated. They do, however, specify that a report must be issued any time a CPA firm is associated with financial statements. If the CPA is providing help in the preparation of the financial statements, a compilation or review report is required. If the CPA is conducting an audit, an audit report is required. It is this auditor's standard report that is the most important to the users of financial statements' information. To aid auditors in fulfilling their professional responsibilities, the accounting profession issued in 1947 ten *generally accepted auditing standards.* These standards, summarized in Exhibit 1.1, have not drastically changed since 1947. The last standard requires explicitly that the auditor express an opinion about the overall financial statements or a specific statement that an overall opinion is not possible, along with the reasons for not expressing an opinion. This opinion is communicated as the final phase of an audit in what is known as the auditor's report. The language of the auditor's report is standardized to cover specific points. The basic elements of the report are the following:

a. A title that includes the word *independent.*

b. A statement that the financial statements identified in the report were audited.

c. A statement that the financial statements are the responsibility of the Company's management and that the auditor's responsibility is to express an opinion on the financial statements based on his audit.

d. A statement that the audit was conducted in accordance with generally accepted auditing standards.

e. A statement that generally accepted auditing standards require that the auditor plan and perform the audit to obtain reasonable assurance about whether the financial statements are free of material misstatement.

f. A statement that an audit includes—

1. Examining, on a test basis, evidence supporting the amounts and disclosures in the financial statements

2. Assessing the accounting principles used and significant estimates made by management

3. Evaluating the overall financial statement presentation

g. A statement that the auditor believes that his audit provides a reasonable basis for his opinion.

h. An opinion as to whether the financial statements present fairly, in all

Exhibit 1.1
Generally Accepted Auditing Standards

GENERAL STANDARDS

1. The examination is to be performed by a person or persons having adequate technical training and proficiency as an auditor.
2. In all matters relating to the assignment, an independence in mental attitude is to be maintained by the auditor or auditors.
3. Due professional care is to be exercised in the performance of the examination and the preparation of the report.

STANDARDS OF FIELD WORK

1. The work is to be adequately planned, and assistants, if any, are to be supervised properly.
2. There is to be a proper study and evaluation of the existing internal control as a basis for reliance thereon and for the determination of the resultant extent of the tests to which auditing procedures are to be restricted.
3. Sufficient competent evidential matter is to be obtained through inspection, observation, inquiries, and conformations to afford a reasonable basis for an opinion regarding the financial statements under examination.

STANDARDS OF REPORTING

1. The report shall state whether the financial statements are presented in accordance with generally accepted accounting principles.
2. The report shall state whether such principles have been consistently observed in the current period in relation to the preceding period.
3. Informative disclosures in the financial statements are to be regarded as reasonably adequate unless otherwise stated in the report.
4. The report shall either contain an expression of opinion regarding the financial statements, taken as a whole, or an assertion to the effect that an opinion cannot be expressed. When an overall opinion cannot be expressed, the reasons therefore should be stated. In all cases where an auditor's name is associated with financial statements, the report should contain a clearcut indication of the character of the auditor's examination, if any, and the degree of responsbility he or she is taking.

material respects, the financial position of the Company as of the balance sheet date and the results of its operations and its cash flows for the period then ended in conformity with generally accepted accounting principles.

i. The manual or printed signature of the auditor's firm.

j. The date of the audit report.[31]

Unqualified Report

The most common type of audit report is one in which the auditor expresses an *unqualified opinion.* It is used when the financial statements have been presented in accordance with generally accepted accounting principles. It implies the belief that the financial statements have the following qualities:

1. The accounting principles selected and applied have general acceptance;

2. The accounting principles are appropriate in the circumstances;

3. The financial statements, including the related notes, are informative of matters that may affect their use, understanding, and interpretations;

4. The information presented in the financial statements is classified and summarized in a reasonable manner, that is, neither too detailed nor too condensed; and

5. The financial statements reflect the underlying events and transactions in a manner that presents financial position, results of operations, and changes in financial position stated within a range of acceptable limits, that is, limits that are reasonable and practicable to attain financial statements.[32]

Wording of an unqualified opinion covers (a) the address of the auditee, (b) the *involuntary paragraph,* (c) the *scope paragraph,* (d) the *opinion paragraph,* (e) the name of the CPA firm conducting the audit, and (g) the audit report date. It generally appears as follows:

Monti and DeAngelo, CPAs
1255 Campbell Avenue
Chicago Heights, IL 60680

We have audited the accompanying balance sheet of X Company as of [at] December 31, 19XX, and the related statements of income, retained earnings, and cash flows for the year then ended. These financial statements are the responsibility of the Company's management. Our responsibility is to express an opinion on these financial statements based on our audit.

We conducted our audit in accordance with generally accepted auditing standards. Those standards require that we plan and perform the audit to obtain reasonable assurance about whether the financial statements are free of material misstatement. An audit includes examining, on a test basis, evidence supporting the amounts and disclosures in the financial statements. An audit also includes assessing the accounting principles used and significant estimates made by management, as well as evaluating the overall financial statement presentation. We believe that our audit provides a reasonable basis for our opinion.

In our opinion, the financial statements referred to above present fairly, in all material respects, the financial position of X Company as of [at] December 31, 1996, and the results of its operations and its cash flows for the year then ended in conformity with generally accepted accounting principles.

Monti and DeAngelo, CPAs
February 15, 1996.

The introductory paragraph identifies the audited financial statements and highlights the separate and distinct responsibilities of management (the production of financial statements) and the auditor (the expression of an opinion on the fairness of the financial statements). The auditor's responsibility is strictly to conduct an audit and express an opinion.

The scope paragraph describes the nature and scope of the audit using generally accepted auditing standards as the point of reference to assure the user of the quality of the audit job. The audit requires (a) planning and performing the audit to obtain reasonable assurance that statements are free of material misstatements, (b) examining evidence on a test basis, (c) assessing accounting principles used and significant estimates made by management, and (d) evaluating the overall financial statement presentation. In addition, the scope paragraph states the auditor's belief that the audit provides reasonable basis for the opinion.

The opinion paragraph communicates the results of the audit and the best judgment of the auditor as to the fairness of the financial statements as measured by generally accepted accounting principles. Basically, the paragraph expresses the auditor's opinion as to whether the financial statements present fairly, in all material respects, the firm's financial position at a balance sheet date and the statement of operations and cash flows for the period and in conformity with GAAP.

Audit Reports Other Than Qualified

Occasionally, the auditor will not be able to give an unqualified opinion on the financial statements and may find it necessary to render a *qualified opinion,* an *adverse opinion,* or *disclaimer.* The auditor may conclude that a qualified opinion is not required when one of the following five conditions seems to prevail:

1. The scope of the auditor's examination is restricted by the client or by circumstances beyond either the client's or auditor's control.
2. The financial statements have not been prepared in accordance with the generally accepted accounting principles.
3. The accounting principles used in the financial statements have not been consistently applied.
4. There are material uncertainties affecting the financial statements that cannot be reasonably estimated at the date of the auditor's report.
5. The auditor is not independent.

A *disclaimer of opinion* is issued when the auditor is unable to arrive at a judgment on fairness for some pervasive reason such as financial precariousness, limitation of scope of the engagement, or nonindependent relationship. The disclaimer of opinion arises because of the lack of knowledge necessary to form *any* opinion on the financial statement, and that can occur only under the three situations described above. All the other types of opinions indicate that the auditor has sufficient knowledge to form an opinion.

An *adverse opinion* states that the auditor has concluded that the financial statements deviate materially from the GAAP in some specified manner or are otherwise so materially misstated or misleading that they do not present fairly the financial position or results of operations in conformity with the generally accepted accounting principles.

A *qualified opinion* states that the auditor believes that the overall financial statements are fairly stated "excluding" the effect of a specified matter.

What Does an Emphasis Paragraph Mean?

Sometimes when the problem is estimated to be solvable, the CPA firm does not issue a qualified opinion but instead puts a less severe warning that auditors call an "emphasis paragraph." Emphasis paragraphs are, however, applied differently from one CPA firm to another. Some auditors use emphasis paragraphs to signal that the company may not be in immediate trouble, but if things are not improved, they will be given a qualified report. That naturally causes skeptics to ask the fundamental question: Does an emphasis paragraph mean it is a cheap, clean opinion? Or is it a cheap, qualified opinion?

From the companies' point of view, an emphasis paragraph is preferable to a qualified opinion. The word *qualification* is an emotional word to the CPA firm, the firm audited, and the market. To the CPA firm, qualification is a delicate decision that involves subjective judgments and threatens auditors' fees and reputations. To the firm audited, qualification means a cloud hanging over its operations and the performance of management as well as various negative consequences. To the market, qualification triggers an immediate stampede by the investors, with stock prices dropping and confidence shattered. But qualified opinions are on the increase; at the same time the number of publicly held firms firing their auditors in 1982 jumped 48 percent, to 442 from 298 the year before. Given this situation, one may expect to see an increase in "emphasis paragraphs."

CONSEQUENCES OF FAIRNESS IN PRESENTATION

The perception and application of fairness in presentation as the production and presentation of financial statements in conformity with generally accepted accounting principles results sometimes in some unfortunate consequences.

1. A first consequence of fairness in presentation is the failure to rely on concepts of justice that dictate instead a fairness in distribution. This interpretation of fairness is presented in Chapter 2.

2. A second consequence of fairness in presentation is the failure to expand the scope of the disclosure in financial statements beyond conventional financial accounting information toward a fairness in disclosure. This interpretation of fairness is presented in Chapter 3.

3. A third consequence of fairness in presentation is the flexibility it creates in the management of earnings and income smoothing. This concept is explained in Appendix 1.B.

4. A fourth consequence of fairness in presentation is the climate it creates for fraudulent practices. Examples of notorious fraud cases are presented in Appendix 1.C.

CONCLUSIONS

This chapter has elaborated on the concept of fairness as fairness in presentation. The general perception of fairness in presentation as meaning conformity with generally accepted accounting principles is viewed as leading to consequences in disclosure, distribution, fraudulent practices, and income smoothing.

NOTES

1. Financial Accounting Standards Board, *Statement of Financial Accounting Concepts No. 1: Objectives of Financial Reporting of Business Enterprises* (Stamford, Conn.: FASB, 1978), 11.

2. Scott, D. R., "The Basis of Accounting Principles," *The Accounting Review* (December 1941): 341.

3. Arthur Andersen & Co., *The Postulate of Accounting* (New York, 1960), 31.

4. Patillo, James W., *The Foundation of Financial Accounting* (Baton Rouge, La.: Louisiana State University Press, 1965), 60–61.

5. Ibid.

6. Devine, C. T., "Research Methodology and Accounting Theory Formation," *The Accounting Review* (July 1960): 387–399.

7. Devine, Carl T., "The Rules of Conservatism Reexamined," *Journal of Accounting Research* (Autumn 1963): 129–130.

8. Chatfield, Michael, *A History of Accounting Thought* (Hinsdale, N.J.: The Dryden Press, 1974), 275.

9. Skinner, R. M., *Accounting Principles: A Canadian Viewpoint* (Toronto: The Canadian Institute of Chartered Accountants, 1972), 33.

10. Lee, T. A., *Company Financial Reporting: Issues and Analyses* (London: Nelson, 1976), 61.

11. Flegm, E. H., *Accounting: How to Meet the Challenges of Relevance and Regulation* (New York: John Wiley & Sons, 1984), 47.

12. Leach, R., "The Birth of British Accounting Standards," in R. Leach and E. Stamp, eds., *British Accounting Standards: The First Ten Years* (Cambridge: Woodhead-Faulkener, 1981), 7.

13. Chastney, J. G., *True and Fair View: History, Meaning and the Impact of the Fourth Directive*, Institute of Chartered Accountants in England and Wales Research Committee Occasional Paper No. 6 (London: Institute of Chartered Accountants in England and Wales, 1975).

14. Carpenter, David, "Some Approaches to a 'True and Fair View': A Review," *Irish Accounting Review* (Spring 1994): 49–64.

15. Rutherford, B. A., "The True and Fair View Doctrine: A Search for Explication," *Journal of Business Finance and Accounting* (Winter 1985): 483–494.

16. Walton, P. J., "The True and Fair View in British Accounting," *European Accounting Review* 2, no. 1 (1993): 49.

17. Lee, T. A., *Modern Financial Accounting,* 3rd ed. (Walton-on-Thames, Surrey: Nelson, 1981), 270.

18. Lee, T. A., *Company Auditing,* 2nd ed. (Wokingham, Berkshire: Van Nostrand Reinhold for the Institute of Chartered Accountants of Scotland, 1981), 50.

19. European Community Commission, *Fourth Directive* (ECC: Brussels, 1978).

20. Alexander, David, "A European True and Fair View?" *European Accounting Review* 2, no. 1 (1993): 59–80.

21. Boys, P. G., and B. A. Rutherford, "The Most Universal Quality: Some Nineteenth Century Audit Reports," *Accounting History* (September 1982): 13.

22. Nobes, C. W., and R. H. Parker, " 'True and Fair': A Survey of U.K. Financial Directors," *Journal of Business Finance and Accounting* (April 1981): 359–376.

23. Houghton, K. A., "True and Fair View: An Empirical Study of Connotative Meaning," *Accounting, Organizations and Society* 12, no. 2 (1987): 143–152.

24. Parker, R. H., and C. W. Nobes, " 'True and Fair': U.K. Auditors' Views," *Accounting and Business Research* (Autumn 1991): 349–362.

25. Ibid.

26. *U.S. v. Simon,* 425 F. 2d 706 (2d Cir. 1969), Cert. den. 397 U.S. 1006 (1970).
27. Ibid.
28. American Institute of Certified Public Accountants, *The Auditor's Report* (New York: AICPA, 1967), 12–13.
29. American Institute of Certified Public Accountants, *Forty Questions about Audit Reports* (New York: AICPA, 1989), 12.
30. American Institute of Certified Public Accountants, *Forty Questions about Audit Reports* (New York: AICPA, 1986), 11.
31. Ibid.
32. American Institute of Certified Public Accountants, *Statement on Auditing Standards No. 58, Report on Audited Financial Statements* (New York: AICPA, 1988), 9.

REFERENCES

Alexander, David. "A European True and Fair View?" *European Accounting Review* 2, no. 1 (1993): 59–80.

Alves, W. M., and P. H. Rossi. "Who Should Get What? Fairness Judgments of the Distribution of Earnings." *American Journal of Sociology* (November 1978): 541–564.

American Institute of Certified Public Accountants. *The Auditor's Report.* New York: AICPA, 1967.

———. *Forty Questions about Audit Reports.* New York: AICPA, 1986.

———. *Statement on Auditing Standards No. 58: Report on Audited Financial Statements.* New York: AICPA, 1988.

Arnett, Harold E. "The Concept of Fairness." *The Accounting Review* (April 1967): 251–297.

Arthur Andersen & Co. *The Postulate of Accounting* (New York, 1960).

Behrman, Jere R., and Mark R. Rosenzweig. "Labor Force—Caveat Emptor: Cross-Country Data on Education and Labor Force." *Journal of Development Economics* 44, no. 1 (1994): 22–35.

Belkaoui, Ahmed. *Socio-Economic Accounting.* Westport, Conn.: Greenwood Press, 1984.

Boys, P. G., and B. A. Rutherford. "The Most Universal Quality: Some Nineteenth Century Audit Reports." *Accounting History* (September 1982): 13.

Carpenter, David. "Some Approaches to a 'True and Fair View': A Review." *Irish Accounting Review* (Spring 1994): 45–64.

Chastney, J. G. *True and Fair View: History, Meaning and the Impact of the Fourth Directive,* Institute of Chartered Accountants in England and Wales Research Committee Occasional Paper No. 6. London: Institute of Chartered Accountants in England and Wales, 1975.

Chatfield, Michael. *A History of Accounting Thought.* Hinsdale, N.J.: The Dryden Press, 1974.

Cowan, Tom K. "Are Truth and Fairness Generally Acceptable?" *The Accounting Review* (October 1965): 788–794.

Devine, Carl T. "Research Methodology and Accounting Theory Formation." *The Accounting Review* (July 1960): 387–399.

————. "The Rules of Conservatism Reexamined." *Journal of Accounting Research* (Autumn 1963): 129–30.

European Community Commission. *Fourth Directive.* ECC: Brussels, 1978.

Financial Accounting Standards Board. *Statement of Financial Accounting Concepts No. 1: Objectives of Financial Reporting of Business Enterprises.* Stamford, Conn.: FASB, 1978.

Flegm, E. H. *Accounting: How to Meet the Challenges of Relevance and Regulation.* New York: John Wiley & Sons, 1984.

Houghton, K. A. "True and Fair View: An Empirical Study of Connotative Meaning." *Accounting, Organizations and Society* 12, no. 2 (1987): 143–152.

Leach, R. "The Birth of British Accounting Standards." In R. Leach and E. Stamp, eds., *British Accounting Standards: The First Ten Years.* Cambridge: Woodhead-Faulkener, 1981, pp. 15–32.

Lee, T. A. *Company Auditing,* 2nd ed. Wokingham, Berkshire: Van Nostrand Reinhold for the Institute of Chartered Accountants of Scotland, 1981.

————. *Company Financial Reporting: Issues and Analyses.* London: Nelson, 1976.

————. *Modern Financial Accounting,* 3rd ed. Walton-on-Thames, Surrey: Nelson, 1981.

Nobes, C. W., and R. H. Parker. " 'True and Fair': A Survey of U.K. Financial Directors'." *Journal of Business Finance and Accounting* (April 1981): 359–376.

Ordelheide, D. "True and Fair View: A European and A German Perspective." *European Accounting Review* 2, no. 1 (1993): 81–90.

Parker, R. H., and C. W. Nobes. " 'True and Fair': U.K. Auditors' View." *Accounting and Business Research* (Autumn 1991): 349–362.

Patillo, James W. *The Foundation of Financial Accounting.* Baton Rouge, La.: Louisiana State University Press, 1965.

Rutherford, B. A. "The True and Fair View Doctrine: A Search for Explication." *Journal of Business Finance and Accounting* (Winter 1985): 483–494.

Scott, D. R. "The Basis of Accounting Principles." *The Accounting Review* (December 1941): 341.

Skinner, R. M. *Accounting Principles: A Canadian Viewpoint.* Toronto: The Canadian Institute of Chartered Accountants, 1972.

United States v. Simon, 425 F. 2d 706 (2d Cir. 1969), Cert. den. 397 U.S. 1006 (1970).

Van Hulle, K. "Truth and Untruth about True and Fair." *European Accounting Review* 2 no. 1 (1993): 99–104.

Walton, P. J. "The True and Fair View in British Accounting." *European Accounting Review* 2, no. 1 (1993): 49.

William, Paul F. "The Legitimate Concern with Fairness." *Accounting, Organizations and Society* (March 1987): 165–189.

APPENDIX 1.A:
A EUROPEAN TRUE AND FAIR VIEW?

David Alexander
University of Hull

ABSTRACT

After a brief historical introduction, the paper examines the true and fair view (TFV) requirement in the Fourth Directive, and in the corresponding company legislation in UK, France and Germany. Differences and nuances are explored from a language and translation viewpoint and also related to pre-Fourth Directive requirements and culture. The extent of true harmonization is questionable.

Recent experience and usage of TFV in the UK is critically described and related to the broader European context. The general drift of the argument is that countries are tending to interpret TFV in the context of national culture, national accounting tradition and national GAAP. From a properly European perspective there is a need for changes in attitude from all concerned. TFV and GAAP are living and dynamic concepts. They are affected by the cultures within which they are used. Homogeneous attitudes to such concepts imply homogeneous cultural contexts, and this raises questions of a most fundamental nature.

NOTE ON TRANSLATIONS

There has been considerable discussion about the extent to which the French and German extracts and quotations in this paper should be translated into English. It is fundamental to the argument of the paper that vital nuances and shadings of meaning are not capable of translation. This implies that any translation would be misleading, and therefore that no translation should be given.

However, it is recognized that English may be the only effective means of communication from author to reader, not only for the British, but also for those whose native tongue is none of the three languages used here. Approximate paraphrases are therefore given on a number of occasions,

Address for correspondence
David Alexander, Director of Research, Centre for International Accounting Research, Department of Accounting and Finance, University of Hull, Hull HU6 7RX, UK

Source: Alexander, David, "A European True and Fair View?" *European Accounting Review* 1, no. 1 (1993): 59–80. Reprinted with permission of Routledge.

in square brackets. They should be interpreted as vague indications. They are emphatically not part of the argument of the paper.

INTRODUCTION

The Fédération des Experts Comptables Européens held its first conference in Brussels in October 1989. At one point in the programme delegates divided into a number of separate discussion groups and the French-speaking group soon found itself discussing the true and fair view (hereafter TFV) concept and its meaning and implications. No clear conclusions emerged, but the suggestion which seemed to find most favour was: *Il faut demander aux Anglais* [we must ask the English].

This is an unsatisfactory and even dangerous attitude. Certainly the greatest experience of operating the concept is in English-speaking countries, and this experience must not be ignored. But of course all attitudes – and many actions – are culturally based and a concept developed in one culture *cannot* simply be transferred or extended to another without alteration in its implications. An essential requirement for successful harmonization, in accounting as in other fields, is a trans-national exploration (i.e. a *European* exploration!) of such issues. Only through this process can we hope to move towards an understanding consistent with European thinking.

All this implies a major and long-term task. This paper seeks to make a small contribution from an accounting perspective.

ORIGINS

The origins of TFV can be studied in some detail in Chastney (1975) and are summarized in Rutherford (1985). Prior to 1900 an astonishingly wide variety of legal requirements came and went in the UK. Words frequently used in this kaleidoscope included true, correct, full, fair and just, either alone or in combination. Rutherford suggests that the frequent changes in wording of the required legal standard had little if any significance or practical effect. In 1900 the requirement to 'exhibit a true and correct view of the state of the company's affairs' appeared in the UK Companies Act, and this requirement lasted until after the Second World War.

The Committee on Company Law Amendment (The Cohen Committee) in its report (1945) recommended that Company Laws should require a true and fair view rather than a true and correct view. Examination of the report and of the detailed evidence given to the committee suggests, according to Rutherford, that the change was not regarded as particularly significant – just, perhaps, a little more honest. TFV wording was suggested to the committee in a memorandum from the Institute of Chartered Accountants in England and Wales. Nobody objected, so in it went.

The crucial point is that, not only is TFV undefined in law, but a study of its origins does not help us in deciding its precise operational significance.

THE FOURTH DIRECTIVE

Three major drafts of the Fourth Directive appeared. Article 2, which contains the central requirement for the role of annual accounts, differs significantly between each of the three versions. The first, in 1971, was based on the 1965 German *Aktiengesetz* [company law], and TFV was not mentioned. The second in 1974, after the UK joined the EC, does include TFV, and gives it equal importance with the requirement to follow 'the provisions of this Directive'. The final version in 1978 gives TFV, as we know, an over-riding importance, over and above 'the provisions of this Directive'. Appendix 1 shows the major alterations through the 1971 and 1974 drafts, in English, followed by the final 1978 version of Article 2, as officially published in English, French and German. It should be remembered that these different language publications have identical standing. It is not acceptable under EC philosophy to regard any one of them as original and therefore the other two as translations.

We now explore the application of this requirement in national company law, using the UK, Germany and France as exemplars.

UK COMPANY LAW

The UK Company Law requirement corresponding to Article 2 is Section 228, Companies Act 1985. This is reproduced in Appendix 2.[1]

There are clearly a number of differences between Article 2 of the EC Directive and S228 of the Companies Act. One is of particular significance. Article 2 states that, where the application of a particular provision is incompatible with TFV, then

> that provision must be departed from in order to give a true and fair view within the meaning of paragraph 3. Any such departure must be disclosed in the notes.

What exactly is meant by 'must be departed from'? We take this to mean that the figures in the income statement and/or the balance sheet must be altered *from* those that result from following 'the requirements of this Act' *to* those deemed necessary to give a TFV. Additionally, the evidence and quantification of this change must be disclosed in the notes.

Article 2 does not explicitly say in so many words that the income statement and balance sheet must themselves be altered. But, if we substitute the definition from Article 2 paragraph 1 into the statement in Article 2, paragraph 3, then we arrive at the requirement that the annual accounts (which comprise the balance sheet, the profit and loss account and the notes on the accounts, and which constitute a composite whole) shall give a true and fair view. It is clear from Article 2 paragraph 5 that, where a provision of the Directive (where provisions relate to the balance sheet, the profit and loss account and the notes) is incompatible with this requirement, then 'that provision must be departed from'. Since

a) the provision affects balance sheet, income statement and notes, and
b) balance sheet, income statement and notes are a composite whole, then
c) a departure from a provision must also be carried consistently through balance sheet, income statement and notes.

As an additional argument here, if Article 2 (5) means that the 'departure from a provision' need be 'disclosed in the notes' *only*, and the profit and loss account and balance sheet not altered, then Article 2 (5) would appear to be identical in meaning to Article 2 (4). It is submitted that Article 2 (5) must mean something different from and additional to Article 2 (4).

So we conclude that Article 2 does *require*, though it is not put in the clearest possible manner, that the income statement, the balance sheet and the notes as necessary, must each and all be prepared under the alternative methodologies, departing from specific provisions of the Directive, when Article 2, paragraph 5 applies. Section 228 of the UK Companies Act certainly does interpret and express this point in the clearest possible manner. In such circumstances 'the directors shall depart from that requirement in preparing the balance sheet or profit and loss account'.

BRD COMPANY LAW

The Fourth Directive Article 2(3) in the German version reads:

> Der Jahresabschluß hat ein den tatsächlichen Verhältnissen entsprechendes Bild der Vermögens-. Finanz- und Ertragslage der Gesellschaft zu vermitteln.

We are of course theoretically entitled to presume that the 'proper' translation of this is given by Article 2 (3) in the published English version. It is instructive to attempt a literal translation from the German. This might be something like:

> The annual accounts must show a picture of the assets, financing and profits position of the company that compares with the facts.

Comparison of this literal translation with the published English version, making allowance for some alternative wordings, suggests that:

– viewed word by word, the German version and the English version are in no way direct translations;
– viewed as a whole, with appropriate stylistic licence, from this

author's British perspective, the two versions do not appear to say or mean the same thing.

It is of course possible that the Anglo-Saxon mental interpretation of the English version, and the Teutonic mental interpretation of the German version, amount in the end to identical subjective meanings. Such a proposition is extremely hard positively to disprove, but it seems a priori unlikely, and there is ample anecdotal evidence that it does not seem to be the case in fact.

Taking the German language version as given (which of course the German parliament was certainly entitled to do), how does it appear in German Company Law?

A subordinate clause was added (in addition to some rewording) in the first sentence of Section 264 (2) of the 1986 HGB.

> Der Jahresabschluß der Kapitalgesellschaft hat unter Beachtung der Grundsätze ordnungsmäßiger Buchführung in den tatsächlichen Verhältnissen entsprechendes Bild der Vermögens-, Finanz- und Ertragslage der Kapitalgesellschaft zu vermitteln. Führen besondere Umstände dazu, daß der Jahresabschluß ein den tatsächlichen Verhältnissen entsprechendes Bild im Sinne des Satzes 1 nicht vermittelt, so sind im Anhang zuzätzliche Angaben zu machen. [A translation appears below.]

This extra phrase: *unter Beachtung der Grundsätze ordnungsmäßiger Buchführung*, is not exactly a brand new concept, as it is closely based on Section 149 of the 1965 Aktiengesetz:

> Der Jahresabschluß hat den Grundsätzen ordnungsmäßiger Buchführung zu entsprechen.

The second sentence of Section 264(2) of the 1986 HGB, quoted above, incorporates the essence of Article 2(4) of the Directive. Notice that it requires additional information *im Anhang* [in the notes], not additional information, full stop, as in the Directive.

Ordelheide (1990) translates Section 264(2) of the 1986 HGB as follows:

> The financial statements of the company must, in compliance with required accounting principles, present a true and fair view of the net worth, financial position and results of the company. If special circumstances result in the financial statements not showing a true and fair view within the meaning of sentence 1, then additional disclosures are required in the notes.

Two points emerge from this. First, it can be argued from the HGB text, and as Ordelheide reports is being argued by many German commentators, that it is *only the notes to the accounts* that have to be altered from 'the provisions of this Act' in order to show a TFV. The income statement and balance sheet can, according to this argument, be left as they were (Ordelheide 1990):

> (Some) commentators are advocating the so-called separation or uncoupling

thesis. According to their opinion the true and fair view basically has a bearing on the notes only whereas balance sheet and profit and loss account have to be set up in accordance with the individual rules and the German GAAP (see above: '. . . In compliance. . . .'). Since judges of the German supreme fiscal court – the BFH – are among these commentators and as they are the ones who finally determine what is to be understood as accounting principle in Germany, a corporation draws up its financial statement quite correctly if it refers to these commentators and makes use of the separation thesis.

This approach seems to us to be simply unacceptable. It is not in accordance with Article 2 of the Directive.

It has been put to the author that this approach (the separation or uncoupling thesis) is, however, fully in accordance with German Company Law as expressed in Section 264 (2) 1986 HGB. The point is accepted. This leads to the clear conclusion that Section 264 fails properly to enact the Fourth Directive.

Further, what is the significance of the additional subordinate clause in Section 264(2) of the 1986 HGB? Ordelheide's translation ('in compliance with required accounting principles') is one of several distinctly different ones we have heard, including 'within the principles of orderly book-keeping' and 'in accordance with Generally Accepted Accounting Principles (GAAP)'. What is surely clear is that a TFV, and a TFV *Unter Beachtung der Grundsätze ordnungsmäßiger Buchführung*, are not likely to mean the same thing! Notice incidentally that Ordelheide's commas round the subordinate clause in his English translation are not in the German original.

There is another very important difference between Article 2 of the Directive and Section 264 of the HGB. We have discussed at some length the differences between Article 2 (3) and Article 2(4), and the HGB equivalent. We have not discussed the differences between Article 2(5) and the HGB equivalent. This is for a very simple reason: there *is* no HGB equivalent! Ordelheide (1990):

> A transformation akin to those of Section 228(5) of Schedule 4 of the Companies Act 1985 in Britain, according to which provisions can [the Act says shall] be departed (from) in order to give a TFV, does not exist in German law.

What price harmonization?

It is worth noting in passing the persistent rumours that a (confidential) minute was passed by the EC Council of Ministers prior to the finalization of the Fourth Directive, at the request of German representatives, to the effect that the Directive could be interpreted as meaning that following the detailed regulations therein would lead to a TFV. Rutherford (private correspondence, 1991) failed in his attempts to obtain sight of such a minute. If this is indeed true then it seems absurd in logic, and, suggesting as it does that a formal agreement between Nation States can be undermined for the benefit of one state by secret but binding agreement, quite horrendous in law. The issue is worth further investigation.

The best we can offer here is a reference by Horst Kaminski in the *UEC Journal* for April 1979 (Kaminski, 1979).

> The Council and the Commission have declared that compliance with the provision(s of the Directive) is normally sufficient to achieve the stated objective (to give a TFV).

Kaminski gives as his source for this statement:

> See explanations to the record on the meeting of the Council, in the course of which the Directive was approved.

Kaminski's article, as published, was translated anonymously from his German original. If Kaminski's English language quotation above is correct (which is unproven) then it clearly supports the Anglo-Saxon view of TFV, rather than the legalistic view. If compliance with the provisions is 'normally sufficient' to give a TFV, then circumstances may obviously exist, abnormally, where following the provisions would fail to give a TFV.

FRENCH COMPANY LAW

Article 9 of the Code de Commerce (1983) contains the requirements arising from Article 2 of the EC Directive.

> L'annexe complète et commente l'information donnée par le bilan et le compte de résultat.

> Les comptes annuels doivent être réguliers, sincères et donner une image fidèle du patrimoine, de la situation financière et du résultat de l'entreprise.

> Lorsque l'application d'une prescription comptable ne suffit pas pour donner l'image fidèle mentionnée au présent article, des informations complémentaires doivent être fournies dans l'annexe.

> Si, dans un cas exceptionnel, l'application d'une prescription comptable se révèle impropre à donner une image fidèle du patrimoine, de la situation financière ou du résultat, il doit y être dérogé; cette dérogation est mentionnée à l'annexe et dûment motivée, avec l'indication de son influence sur le patrimoine, la situation financière et le résultat de l'entreprise.

> [The notes complete and comment on the information in the balance sheet and profit and loss account.

> The annual accounts must be regular, sincere and give a true and fair view of the wealth of the enterprise, of its financial position and of its results.

> Should the application of an accounting requirement not suffice to give a true and fair view, additional information is to be shown in the notes.

> If, in an exceptional circumstance, the application of an accounting requirement

is inappropriate for presentation of a true and fair view, it is to be departed from; such departure is to be mentioned in the notes, together with reasons, with an indication of its effects on the annual accounts of the business.]

It is worth noting that a literal translation of *image fidèle* would almost certainly be a faithful image. *Image fidèle* and TFV are clearly no more direct translations than TFV and the German version. Neither, incidentally, is there any close relationship between the French and the German terms.

Some of the differences between the French text of Article 2 of the Directive and Article 9 of the Code de Commerce are minor variations in wording. Two points seem potentially more important. First, the Directive states in sub-paragraph 4 that, where the application of a provision of the Directive is not sufficient to give a TFV, then *des informations complémentaires doivent être fournies* [additional information must be given]. However, the Code de Commerce states that *des informations complémentaires doivent être fournies dans l'annexe* [additional information must be given in the notes] (as in HGB, *im Anhang*).

By far the most important distinction however concerns the treatment of sub-paragraph 3 of Article 2 of the Directive. The French Company Law of 1966 required financial reports to be *réguliers et sincères*. These concepts are retained in the 1983 Code de Commerce. The TFV requirement is simply added to them.

It follows from our earlier discussions that the precise relationship of TFV with these other requirements is of crucial importance. The key text is:

les comptes annuels doivent être réguliers, sincères et donner une image fidèle de . . .

It is clear to us that this represents a list of three *separate* requirements:

ils doivent être réguliers
ils doivent être sincères
ils doivent donner une image fidèle.

Since the law requires that three separate conditions must all be met, the legislators obviously believed that no two of these conditions would necessarily lead to the third. In particular, therefore, it is technically possible to be *réguliers*, and *sincères*, without giving an *image fidèle*. It is also clear to us that Article 9 requires that the income statement or balance sheet figures must be altered (rather than merely the notes to the accounts), when a requirement of law would not lead to a TVF.

Given our clear interpretation of Article 9 of the Code de Commerce as requiring, *inter alia*, that *les comptes doivent donner une image fidèle*, what are we to make of the following (*Mémento Pratique Lefevbre*

Comptable)?[2] This is referenced to Article 9, but is obviously not quoted from it.

Des comptes annuels *réguliers et sincères donnant une image fidèle* du patrimoine, de la situation financière et du résultat de l'entreprise doivent être établis (emphasis in original).

The infinitive, *ils doivent donner*, has been changed to the present participle, *donnant*. The version quoted above could conceivably be expressed in English as: accounts must be established which are in accordance with regulation (*réguliers*) and in good faith (*sincères*) *thus* giving a TFV. This interpretation would reduce the requirements listed above from three to two, implying that a TFV would arise naturally and automatically from producing accounts in accordance with stated regulations and in good faith.

From this questionable beginning, how does the discussion in *Mémento Pratique Lefevbre Comptable* proceed? Three conceptions are suggested.

A. L'image fidèle est obtenue par le respect sincère des règles. [TFV is obtained by a proper respect for the rules.]
   This is rejected as unrealistic:
   Il n'est pas possible qu'une règle puisse répondre à une multitude de situations possibles. [It is not possible that a rule should respond to every conceivable situation.]
B. L'image fidèle prime les règles, qui ne sont plus qu'indicatives. [TFV is above the rules, which are no more than indicative.]
   This is also firmly and quickly rejected:
   car les entreprises arrivaient à des solutions trop différentes. [for businesses would arrive at excessively different conclusions.]
   This rejection seems a priori not necessarily valid. If *les règles* are properly clear, and if most people follow the indications, then most enterprises will not arrive at *des solutions trop différentes*. We explore UK experience relating to this point later.
C. L'image fidèle constitue le principe à respecter lorsque la règle n'existe pas ou lorsque la règle est insuffisante pour traduire la réalité. [TFV is the principle to respect when no rule exists or when the rule is insufficient to represent reality.]
   This last conception is accepted as *la seule valable* [the only valuable one]. The TFV *ne jouerait que lorsque* [does not operate unless] (note the negative construction, which is highly significant):
   1. Il n'existe pas de règle fixée par la communauté financière pour résoudre tel problème, la loi ou les organismes compétents n'ayant pas défini le bon usage en la matière (on pourrait même dire le 'fair play').
   2. Il existe plusieurs règles applicables, par exemple plusieurs méthodes d'évaluation; un *choix* est donc nécessaire.

3. La règle existe mais que son application stricte serait tromp-
   euse; ce cas ne peut être qu'*exceptionnel*.
(emphases in original).
[TFV does not operate unless:
1. No rule exists from the financial community to resolve such a
   problem, the law or the competent authorities not having
   defined good practice in the matter (one could even say 'fair
   play').
2. Several applicable rules exist, for example several valuation
   methods; a choice is therefore necessary.
3. The rule exists but its strict application would be misleading;
   this case could only happen exceptionally.]

1 and 2 are simple enough. It is 3, which is both interesting and problem-
atic. The discussion which follows on this is too long to reproduce in full.
Three points are worthy of emphasis.

First, it is clear that *l'annexe* must not be inconsistent with the income
statement and balance sheet:

elle est destinée à compléter le bilan et le compte de résultat et *non* à s'y
substituer ou à justifier leurs insuffisances. (emphasis added)
[it is designed to complete the balance sheet and the profit and loss account,
and not to replace them or justify their inadequacies.]

Second, Lefevbre gives an interesting quotation from le tribunal de
commerce de Paris (4 ch. 19 October 1982: GP 18 to 20 September 1983,
p. 7).

Vue sous l'angle britannique l'image fidèle ne veut pas dire image détaillée. Ce
n'est pas, par exemple, en photographiant chaque arbre de la forêt que l'on peut
avoir une vue fidèle, claire, nette et d'ensemble. Une photographie aérienne est
bien préférable pour se fair une opinion quant à son étendue, sa consistance,
la densité des plantations, etc.
En essayant de se placer selon les modes de penser français, l'image fidèle
veut dire essentiellement que les comptes doivent être tenus dans le respect
des principes de prudence (afin de ne pas, par optimisme dangereux dans les
appréciations faites en matière d'évaluation des biens et des risques, ternir les
résultats à venir), de régularité (respect des règles et procédures en vigueur),
de sincérité (appréciation de bonne foi desdites règles et procédures) et de
continuité (le contenu des comptes est totalement différent lorsque l'entreprise
va disparaître).
[Viewed from a British perspective, TFV does not wish to give a detailed
image. It is not, for example, through photographing each tree in the forest that
one could have a faithful, clear, clean and general view. An aerial photograph is
much preferable to give an opinion as to its extent, consistency, density of
planting, etc.
In attempting to place it within the fashions of French thinking, TFV wishes
essentially to say that the accounts must follow the principles of prudence (in
order not to, by dangerous optimism with the evaluation of assets and risks,
tarnish the results to come), of regularity (following the rules and procedures

in force), of sincerity (appraising in good faith the said rules and procedures), and of continuity (the contents of the accounts are totally different when the enterprise is about to disappear).]

It is interesting that the quotation has to resort to concepts like '*Vue sous l'angle Britannique*' and '*les modes de penser français*'. Does TFV have a European meaning? It is also interesting that the attempt to explain TFV under the *modes de penser français* reduces itself to a list of concepts, sounding rather similar to the idea of *Grundsätze ordnungsmäßiger Buchführung* which we explored in the German context.

The third point to emphasize is a more detached and perhaps more cynical one. Given all of this, when, in French eyes, *is* TFV *actually* going to change a set of accounts?

TFV AND UK REGULATION

The British have had many years experience of applying, or attempting to apply, the TFV and its philosophy to specific issues. We now explore a few of the more interesting and revealing examples.

There are a number of instances where Statements of Standard Accounting Practice (hereafter SSAPs) invoke the TFV override as a reason for requiring, *as normal* practice, a departure from a particular requirement of Company Law. Note as normal practice, not as *un cas exceptionnel*. These include SSAP19, under which investment properties need not be depreciated, and SSAP20 on foreign currency translation. Under SSAP20 unrealized gains on long-term foreign currency exposure are required to be included in reported profits for the year. The arguments in SSAP20 are particularly interesting in their pseudo-logic, but the issues are complicated in detail and confusing in summary. For a full discussion see the relevant chapter in Alexander (1990). Here we will look briefly at SSAP19.

Under paragraph 18 Schedule 4, Companies Act 1985, depreciation of fixed assets is a legal requirement.

In the case of any fixed asset which has a limited useful economic life, the amount of:
(a) its purchase price or production cost, or
(b) where it is estimated that any such asset will have a residual value at the end of the period of its useful economic life, its purchase price or production cost less that estimated residual value;
shall be reduced by provisions for depreciation calculated to write off that amount systematically over the period of the asset's useful economic life.

The essential requirements of SSAP19 are that investment properties should usually be shown at valuation, but that revaluation differences should be taken to a revaluation reserve account, not to the income statement. Investment properties should not be depreciated.

The Accounting Standards Committee accepted without argument that

SSAP19 conflicts with paragraph 18 of Schedule 4 (and also with IAS4). (They do not appear to have considered the possibility of arguing that investment properties are not *fixed* assets.) This problem is cheerfully and quickly solved in paragraph 19 of the SSAP.

> The application of this Standard will usually be a departure, for the overriding purpose of giving a true and fair view, from the otherwise specific requirements of the law to provide a depreciation on any fixed asset which has a limited useful economic life. In this circumstance there will need to be given in the notes to the accounts 'particulars of that departure, the reasons for it, and its effect'.

There are two essential points to make from the above. The first is to underline the beautiful simplicity of the logical process. In essence the process is:

1. In circumstance X, the law says that Y is required.
2. In circumstance X, we think the law should say that Z is required.
3. A TFV is required above all else.
4. A TFV is what we (accountants) say it is.
5. Accountants say that in Circumstance X, a TFV requires Z.
6. In circumstance X, Z is required.

It is a formula capable of almost infinite application.

The second point is to emphasize that SSAP19 requires a certain treatment as normal practice. All companies will treat investment properties in a similar consistent manner. The *image fidèle* principle is clearly being applied, is clearly directly affecting the contents of financial statements, but it is *not* causing *les entreprises* to reach *des solutions trop différentes*.

At first sight SSAP9 on stocks and long-term contracts may seem to be another example similar to SSAP19. But it is not, and SSAP9 is worth exploring in some detail. The following quotation may be familiar to some (Walton, 1990, writing in French).

> La norme comptable (SSAP9, émise en 1975) permettait aux sociétés qui travaillaient sur des contrats à long terme de reconnaître des bénéfices avant d'avoir terminé travaux. Le bénéfice devait apparaître dans l'actif du bilan comme travaux en cours. La Commission a remarqué que l'inclusion d'un bénéfice non réalisé dans ce poste du bilan était une infraction aux règles d'évaluation de la Directive. Encore une fois les Britanniques utilisaient l'image fidèle pour autoriser une dérogation systématique de la Directive.
>
> [The accounting regulation (SSAP9, issued in 1975) permitted businesses working on long-term contracts to recognize some profits before completion of the work. The profit needed to appear among the balance sheet assets as work in progress. The Commission said that the inclusion of an unrealized profit under this heading was against the valuation rules of the Directive. Again the British used TFV to authorize a systematic departure from the Directive.]

The situation is rather more complicated than this implies. Remember first that SSAP9 was issued in 1975, before the Fourth Directive was even agreed in its final form (1978), and six years before the enactment of the Fourth Directive provisions in the UK Companies Act 1981. Second, consider the reference above to the remarks of the Commission. It may well indeed be that *la Commission a remarqué que l'inclusion d'un bénéfice non realisé dans travaux en cours était une infraction aux règles d'évaluation de la Directive*. We are unable to confirm or deny this statement. But if the Commission did say that then it missed the point.

Article 39 Paragraph 1(a) of the Directive reads:

> Current assets must be valued at purchase price or production cost, without prejudice to (b) and (c) below.

Subsection (b) and (c) allow the possibility of lower, but not higher, evaluation. There is obviously a mistake in the wording of the Directive itself. Debtors are current assets and debtors are not shown at purchase price or production cost! Ignoring this point, and interpreting 'current assets' in 39.1 (a) as 'stocks and work-in-progress', it is quite clear that *no profit at all, whether réalisé ou non réalisé*, is allowed to be included in work-in-progress under Article 39.1.(a). The question of realization does not arise. The 1981 UK Companies Act included the identical requirement to Article 39.1.(a), now in paragraph 23 Schedule 4, 1985 Companies Act. Since 1981, therefore, SSAP9 as issued in 1975 was not compatible with legal requirements.

In September 1988 a revised SSAP9 was issued. The major change in this version is that the proportion of profits taken on uncompleted long-term contracts is now to be included in debtors. Work-in-progress is thus left at the true production cost (or lower, of course), i.e. fully consistent with Article 39.1.(a) and paragraph 23 of Schedule 4. Notice that the TFV issue has *not* been relevant to any part of the above discussion.

But so far we have considered only the debits, the balance sheet entries. We also need to consider the credits and the effect on the income statement. In this respect the question of whether the profits taken are realized or not is clearly crucial.

Article 31.1 (c) (aa) of the Directive reads:

> only profits made at the balance sheet date may be included.
> (NB Note 'made' in the English text, but 'realisierten' [realized] in the German and 'réalisés' [realized] in the French.)

This appears in the 1985 Companies Act, paragraph 12(a) of Schedule 4:

> only profits realized (sic) at the balance sheet shall be included in the profit and loss account.

There is no definition or explanation in the Fourth Directive of what is meant by 'profits made'. However the UK Companies Act does give a definition of realized profits – one of the classic examples of the lawyer at his work (Schedule 4, paragraph 91, Companies Act 1985).

> It is hereby declared for the avoidance of doubt that references in this schedule to realised profits, in relation to a company's accounts, are to such profits of the company as fall to be treated as realised profits for the purpose of those accounts in accordance with principles generally accepted with respect to the determination for accounting purposes of realised profits at the time when those accounts are prepared.

Are proportionate profits on partially completed long-term contracts realized? The UK answer in its fairy-tale simplicity mirrors the six-point logical sequence earlier about the application of TFV.

1. These profits are realized if it is a generally accepted principle that they are realized.
2. It *is* a generally accepted principle that they are realized.
3. Therefore they *are* realized.

The official version of this is in paragraph 44 of SSAP9 in its revised 1988 version.

> It is a 'generally accepted principle' that it is appropriate to recognise profit on long-term contracts when the outcome can be assessed with 'reasonable certainty'. The principle of recognising profit on long-term contracts under this standard, therefore, does not contravene (paragraph 91 of Schedule 4).

The essential conclusion from this discussion of SSAP9 and the treatment of long-term, contract work-in-progress has to be emphasized. The TFV argument has *not* been used *at any point* in this whole discussion of SSAP9. The argument is supported entirely by reference to one particular 'generally accepted principle'.

THE IMPORTANCE OF THE ISSUES

The issues raised in this paper are of fundamental importance. It is tempting to regard TFV as an undefinable and flexible construct (i.e. a will o' the wisp), which in a sense it is, and therefore as unimportant, which it certainly is not. First, it exists in law. Second, different perceptions of its meaning and significance are symptomatic of different cultural, legal and accounting attitudes and perceptions. If European accounting harmonization is going to progress sufficiently to be able to make its proper contribution to the 'level playing field' of the Single Market, then such differences must be fully exposed and discussed. Third, the issues are clearly recognized as both topical and important within the EC. See, for example, the November 1990 issue of *Accountancy*. The 'News' section contains the following item.

> UK accounting practice and requirements could well be in conflict with the Fourth Directive, according to a new report issued by the European Commission.
> The Accounting Harmonisation in the European Communities, which sum-

marises the views of the Contact Committee, concludes that the true and fair view override 'must be applied in relation to a given company and not in relation to all companies or a category of companies'. This conflicts with SSAP 19, Accounting for Investment Properties, which invokes the true and fair view override to excuse companies from depreciating investment properties.

The report also condemns the practice adopted by some UK companies of 'omitting to apply depreciation to certain buildings on the grounds that the actual value of those buildings was equal to or higher than the residual book value or that the estimated useful life was unlimited or at any rate so prolonged that annual depreciation would be insignificant'. . . .

The commission seems to be relaxed about the apparent conflict. 'The intention of the document is to bring some of the debates we had into the open,' Karel van Hulle said. 'At this stage we don't seek anything further than that.'

This suggestion, that the TFV override must be applied in relation to a given company and not in relation to all companies or a category of companies, seems obviously wrong, as the Fourth Directive explicitly states (Article 2 sub-paragraph 5) that Member States may define the exceptional cases in question and lay down the relevant special rules. It may be that the real underlying matter at issue concerns the mechanisms by which GAAP can be *changed*. GAAP stands for Generally Accepted Accounting *Principles*, or, according to some, for Generally Accepted Accounting *Practice*. It certainly does not stand for Generally Accepted Accounting *Regulation*. To put the point in American terms, TFV is related to the totality of GAAP, not merely to promulgated GAAP. TFV does not relate only to what people are *told* to do. It relates to what people, or at least the great majority of people, *do* do in attempting to communicate a proper impression into the mind of the user of the accounts.

This is where the trouble really starts. The possibility of controlled flexibility is certainly a major advantage. SSAP19 argued, in effect, that earlier GAAP were outdated and were now generally accepted as outdated, as regards Investment Properties. SSAP19 therefore proposed new regulation, explicitly using TFV as its justification. This new regulation has, as a matter of fact, been generally accepted in the UK. So SSAP19 *created* new GAAP. This in no way increases variability of treatment. It merely alters the treatment.

The trouble with the above is that SSAP19 is generally accepted (i.e. GAAP) by the majority *in the UK*. It is not accepted by the accounting majority in Europe or internationally. Can the SSAP19 treatment be properly regarded as giving a TFV in the UK, and at the same time as not giving a TFV in, say, Germany? Historically the answer is yes, in the same way as published accounts in Germany using tax-based figures, i.e. based on the *Massgeblichkeitsprinzip* (the principle of close connection between the tax accounts and the financial accounts), would not be regarded by UK accountants as giving a TFV. However, the answer could be expected to be no. Given the same broad framework (matching principle, fixed/current distinction, etc.) it would seem a priori that such a difference in treatment could occur only through illogicality by one party or the other.

However, accounting is not only about logic. It is about communicating difficult concepts between human beings. Such a process is inherently imperfect, but it will tend to be 'less imperfect' between human beings with similar outlooks, experiences and attitudes than between those with significant differences in outlook, experience and attitude.

Do the citizens of the EC represent a common culture – similar outlooks, experiences and attitudes? Demonstrably not. It is at least a viable proposition that the SSAP19 treatment of investment properties does give a TFV within UK accounting culture and does not in German accounting culture. Additionally, the EC is not Europe, and Europe is much the more important of the two. Common sense would suggest, and recent visits to Poland and Czechoslovakia have tended to confirm, that individual and accounting cultural characteristics are certainly no less different in the non EC countries of Europe than among the existing twelve. The present author has knowledge of accounting differences, but his experience of broader cultural issues tends to be more gastronomic than academic. Co-operation with other disciplines is needed to explore this whole area further.

THE FUTURE

Much of this paper is an explanation of TFV and national attitudes to it, using the UK, France and Germany as examples. It would be interesting to extend the discussion to other countries. Southern and Eastern Europe might produce interesting longitudinal studies of changing perceptions over the next decade or so. Suggestions for correspondence and co-operation are invited. It is not likely, however, that any new issues of principle would emerge. Rather perhaps it is in the implications of this TFV exploration that greater interest and uncertainty lies. There would seem in principle to be two idealistic ways forward:

1) to ensure that the preparer and the user of accounting information have a full understanding of the differences between each other's general and accounting culture;
2) to ensure that the preparer and the user of accounting information have identical general and accounting cultures, i.e. that there are no differences needing to be understood.

In the absolute sense neither of these is attainable. Given that the best we can do in each case is to move closer, rather than to reach, the two alternatives are not mutually exclusive. To what extent should we seek to move towards each of these two principles? Should the major target of

European accounting be commonality, or knowledge and understanding of differences? These are political questions – indeed Political questions. Current and recent federalist history outside the EC suggests very clearly what people tend to think of externally motivated moves towards commonality. This message cannot continue for ever to be lost on the regulationists within the current EC. We suggest that this attitude is just as relevant to the specifics of accounting as to the generalities of the political world. Exploration, understanding and education of differences, rather than attempted imposed commonality, is the way forward. A common Europe-wide view of TFV implies a common and homogeneous European culture. No thanks!

QUO VADIS?

We suggest that:

1. TFV is, and is necessarily, an overriding requirement. 'Il n'est pas possible qu'une règle puisse répondre à une multitude de situations possibles.'
2. TFV is always relevant, either directly or through influence on accounting regulation. 'L'image fidèle ne jouerait que lorsque . . .' is not an acceptable way of thinking.
3. In most situations TFV will work indirectly through influence on accounting and reporting regulations. This requires proper and sensible regulation prepared with rigour and intellectual honesty. The UK has failed in this respect in recent years and cannot be used as a model.
4. The way forward, with TFV as with financial reporting as a whole, is through increasing conceptually based understanding of what financial statements are trying to do and how they can best do it, coupled with exploration and education of actions and attitudes across Europe and beyond.
5. This is an never-ending process.

Comments are invited.

ACKNOWLEDGEMENTS

The author would like to thank former colleagues at Leeds Business School for advice from both accounting and linguistic perspectives, the participants at presentations of earlier drafts in Maastricht and Frankfurt during 1991 and, in particular, Anne Loft, John Flower and an anonymous reviewer. Errors and infelicities are entirely the author's responsibility.

The issues are complicated both philosophically and linguistically, and further debate would be welcome.

NOTES

1 The old Section 228 of the UK companies Act 1985 has in fact now been replaced by a new Section 226, via the Companies Act 1989. The original version has been retained here, to facilitate consistency of cross-quotation. The changes are purely semantic and have attracted little interest, or even notice, in the the UK. The main alteration is to remove the original Subsection (3) of the old Section 228. This was tautological with Subsections (4) and (5). As the original Subsections (4) and (5) are retained in the new Section 226, the dropping of the old Subsection (3) does not alter UK law.

2 *Memento Pratique Francis Lefebvre – Comptable* An authoritative annual guide to generally accepted accounting principles in France which groups together sources of regulations (statute, jurisprudence, stock exchange ruling, extracts from the Plan Comptable Général, rulings from the Conseil National de la Comptabilité, etc.) on an issue by issue basis and provides a commentary. Published in Paris by Editions Francis Lefebvre.

APPENDIX 1A: ARTICLE 2, 4TH DIRECTIVE, ENGLISH VERSIONS

1971 Draft
(Art. 2)

1. The annual accounts shall comprise the balance sheet, the profit and loss account and the notes on the accounts. These documents shall constitute a composite whole.
2. The annual accounts shall conform to the principles of regular and proper accounting.
3. They shall be drawn up clearly and, in the context of the provisons regarding the valuation of assets and liabilities and the layout of accounts, shall reflect as accurately as possible the company's assets, liabilities, financial position and results.

1974 Draft
(Art. 2)

1. (As 1971 Draft.)
2. The annual accounts shall give a true and fair view of the company's assets, liabilities, financial position and results.
3. They shall be drawn up clearly and in accordance with provisions of this Directive.

1978 Final
(Art. 2)

1. The annual accounts shall compromise the balance sheet, the profit and loss account and the notes on the accounts. These documents shall constitute a composite whole.
2. They shall be drawn up clearly and in accordance with the provisions of this Directive.
3. The annual accounts shall give a true and fair view of the company's assets, liabilities, financial position and profit or loss.
4. Where the application of the provisions of this Directive would not be sufficient to give a true and fair view within the meaning of paragraph 3, additional information must be given.
5. Where in exceptional cases the application of a provision of this Directive is incompatible with the obligation laid down in paragraph 3, that provision must be departed from in order to give a true and fair view within the meaning of paragraph 3. Any such departure must be disclosed in the notes on the accounts together with an explanation of the reasons for it and a statement of its effects on the assets, liabilities, financial position and profit or loss. The Member States may define the exceptional cases in question and lay down the relevant special rules.
6. The Member States may authorize or require the disclosure in the annual accounts of other information as well as that which must be disclosed in accordance with this Directive.

APPENDIX 1B: ARTICLE 2, 4TH DIRECTIVE, FRENCH AND GERMAN

1. Les comptes annuels comprennent le bilan, le compte de profits et pertes ainsi que l'annexe. Ces documents forment un tout.

2. Les comptes annuels doivent être établis avec clarté en conformité avec la présente directive.

3. Les comptes annuels doivent donner une image fidèle du patrimoine, de la situation financière ainsi que des résultats de la société.

4. Lorsque l'application de la présente directive ne suffit pas pour donner l'image fidèle visée au paragraphe 3, des informations complémentaires doivent être fournies.

5. Si, dans des cas exceptionnels, l'application d'une disposition de la présente directive se révèle contraire à l'obligation prévue au paragraphe 3, il y a lieu de déroger à la disposition en cause afin qu'une image fidèle au sens du paragraphe 3 soit donnée. Une telle dérogation doit être mentionnée dans l'annexe et dûment motivée, avec indication de son influence sur le patrimoine, la situation financière et les résultats. Les États membres peuvent préciser les cas exceptionnels et fixer le régime derogatoire correspondant.

6. Les États membres peuvent autoriser ou exiger la divulgation dans les comptes annuels d'autres informations en plus de celles dont la divulgation est exigée par la présente directive.

(1) Der Jahresabschluß besteht aus der Bilanz, der Gewinn- und Verlustrechnung und dem Anhang zum Jahresabschluß. Diese Unterlagen bilden eine Einheit.

(2) Der Jahresabschluß ist klar und übersichtlich aufzustellen; er muß dieser Richtlinie entsprechen.

(3) Der Jahresabschluß hat ein den tatsächlichen Verhältnissen entsprechendes Bild der Vermögens-Finanz- und Ertragslage der Gesellschaft zu vermitteln.

(4) Reicht die Anwendung dieser Richtlinie nicht aus, um ein den tatsächlichen Verhältnissen entsprechendes Bild im Sinne des Absatzes 3 zu vermitteln, so sind zusätzliche Angaben zu machen.

(5) Ist in Ausnahmefällen die Anwendung einer Vorschrift dieser Richtlinie mit der in Absatz 3 vorgesehenen Verpflichtung unvereinbar, so muß von der betreffenden Vorschrift abgewichen werden, um sicherzustellen, daß ein den tatsächlinen Verhältnissen entsprechendes Bild im Sinne des Absatzes 3 vermittelt wird. Die Abweichung ist im Anhang anzugeben und hinreichend zu begründen; ihr Einfluß aufdie Vermögens-, Finanz – und Ertragslage ist darzulegen. Die Mitgliedstaaten können die Ausnahmefälle bezeichnen und die entsprechende Ausnahmeregelung festlegen.

(6) Die Mitgliedstaaten können gestatten oder vorschreiben, daß in dem Jahresabschluß neben den Angaben, die aufgrund dieser Richtlinie erforderlich sind, weitere Angaben gemacht werden.

APPENDIX 2: UK COMPANIES ACT 1985, SECTION 228

(1)   A company's accounts prepared under section 227 shall comply with the requirements of Schedule 4 (so far as applicable) with respect to the form and content of the balance sheet and profit and loss account and any additional information to be provided by way of notes to the accounts.

(2) The balance sheets shall give a true and fair view of the state of affairs of the company as at the end of the financial year: and the profit and loss account shall give a true and fair view of the profit or loss of the company for the financial year.

(3) Subsection (2) overrides:

    (a) the requirements of Schedule 4, and

    (b) all other requirements of this Act as to the matters to be included in a company's accounts or in notes to those accounts: and accordingly the following two subsections have effect.

(4) If the balance sheet or profit and loss account drawn up in accordance with those requirements would not provide sufficient information to comply with subsection (2), any necessary additional information must be provided in that balance sheet or profit and loss account, or in a note to the accounts.

(5) If, owing to special circumstances in the case of any company compliance with any such requirement in relation to the balance sheet or profit and loss account would prevent compliance with subsection (2) even if additional information were provided in accordance with subsection (4), the directors shall depart from that requirement in preparing the balance sheet or profit and loss account (so far as necessary in order to comply with subsection (2)).

(6) If the directors depart from any such requirement, particulars of the departure, the reasons for it and its effect shall be given in a note to the accounts.

REFERENCES

Accountancy (1990) London: ICAEW, November.

Aktiengesetz (1965) Bonn.

Alexander, D. (1990) *Financial Reporting*. London: Chapman & Hall.

Chastney, J. G. (1975) *True and Fair View: History, Meaning and the Impact of the Fourth Directive*. London: ICAEW.

Code de Commerce (1983) Paris.

Committee on Company Law Amendment (1945). London: HMSO.

Companies Act 1900, London: HMSO.

Companies Act 1985, London: HMSO.

EC Commission (1978) *Fourth Directive*. Brussels (in English, French & German).

Handelsgesetzbuch (1986) Bonn.

Kaminski, H. (1979) 'New Regulations for the Preparation, Presentation, Audit and Publicity of Annual Accounts of Limited Liability Companies within the EEC according to the Fourth Council Directive', *UEC Journal*, April.

Mémento Pratique Lefevbre Comptable, Paris.

Ordelheide, D. (1990) 'Soft Transformations of Accounting Rules of the 4th Directive in Germany', *Les cahiers internationaux de la Comptabilité*, 3: 1–15.

Rutherford, B. A. (1985) 'The True and Fair View Doctrine: A Search for Explication', *Journal of Business Financing and Accounting*, Winter.

SSAP 9 (1975) *Stocks and Work-in-Progress*. London: ASC.

SSAP 19 (1981) *Accounting for Investment Properties*. London: ASC.
SSAP 20 (1983) *Foreign Currency Translation*. London: ASC.
Walton, P. (1990) 'Les Directives européennes et leurs incidences en Grande-Bretagne', *Les cahiers internationaux de la Comptabilité*, 1.

APPENDIX 1.B:
INCOME SMOOTHING

THE INCOME-SMOOTHING HYPOTHESIS

As early as 1953 it was argued that management's objectives may not necessarily be to report maximum profits but to smooth the firm's income over the years. Generally, management will choose accounting principles that smooth the net income series.

Income smoothing is the intentional dampening of fluctuations around some level of earnings that is currently considered to be normal for a firm. The various empirical studies assumed various smoothing objects (operating income or ordinary income), various smoothing instruments, and smoothing dimensions (accounting smoothing or real smoothing). Accounting smoothing affects income through accounting dimensions, namely, smoothing through the occurrence or recognition of events, smoothing through allocation of overtime, and smoothing through classification. In other words, accountants can manage earnings through three broad classes: changing accounting methods, fiddling with manager's estimates of costs, and changing the period when expenses and revenues are included in results. Real smoothing affects income through the intentional changing of the operating decisions and their timing.

In general, two main motivations for smoothing are speculated in the literature: (1) to enhance the reliability of prediction based on the observed smoothed series of accounting numbers along a trend considered best or normal by management; (2) to reduce the uncertainty resulting from the fluctuations of income numbers in general and the reduction of systematic market returns. Both reasons of motivation result from a need felt by management to neutralize environmental uncertainty and dampen the wide fluctuations in the operating performance of the firm subject to an intermittent cycle of good and bad times. To do so, management may resort to organizational slack behavior, budgeting slack behavior, or risk-avoiding behavior. Each of these behaviors necessitates decisions that affect the incurrence or allocation of discretionary expenses and results in income smoothing.

In addition to noting these behaviors intended to neutralize environmental uncertainty, it is also possible to identify organizational characterizations that differentiate along the extent of smoothing in different firms. One study examined the effects of the separation of ownership and control on income smoothing on the basis of the hypothesis that management-controlled firms are more likely to be engaged in smoothing as a manifestation of managerial discretion and budgetary slack. Their results confirm that a majority of firms examined behave as if they were smoothers; a particularly strong majority is included among management-controlled firms with high barriers to entry.

Other organizational characterizations may exist to differentiate among firms according to the dimension of the attempt to smooth. One such characterization, derived from the theories of economic dualism, divides the industrial sector into two distinct *core* and *periphery* sectors. The study hypothesized that a higher degree of smoothing of income numbers will be exhibited by firms in the periphery sector than by firms in the core sector because of a reaction to different opportunity structures and experiences. The results indicate that a majority of firms may be resorting to income smoothing and that a greater number of these income smoothers are firms in the periphery sector.

HOW IS IT REALLY DONE?

Managers do not really have to "cook the books" to manipulate earnings. The GAAP provides them with enough flexibility to be able to develop thousands of possible scenarios. That flexibility allows them to report earnings that follow a smooth, regular, upward path. That option suits most managers eager to avoid sharp fluctuations in their earnings. As a result, these managers give more attention to the accounting consequences of major decisions than to the economics. That is equivalent to letting the accounting tail wag the economic dog. It also shifts the objective function from the well-known maximization of shareholders' wealth to the maximization of management's wealth or welfare. To be more precise, most bonuses and other perquisites are tied to report earnings, providing managers with an excellent motivation to smooth earnings. A 1984 study by accounting professor Paul Healy of the Massachusetts Institute of Technology shows a relationship between bonus schemes and the accounting choices executives make. Healy found that executives whose bonus plans rewarded up to a ceiling tended to choose accounting options that minimized reported profits, and executives on bonus plans without upper limits chose profit-boosting options. To achieve any of their objectives toward maximizing their own welfare, managers have at their disposal various accepted accounting scenarios, including (a) changing accounting methods, (b) adjusting their cost estimates, and (c) allocating costs and revenues to whichever period is most beneficial, thus altering the timing of expenses and, to a much lesser degree, revenues. Most of this smoothing goes on in hard as well as good times. All of this "sugar bowling" is tolerated by auditors as long as it does not materially misrepresent earnings.

APPENDIX 1.C:
FRAUD CASES RESULTING FROM FAIRNESS IN
PRESENTATION

THE BANKS ARE SUING THE ACCOUNTANTS: THE DRYSDALE AFFAIR

It all started with bond prices sliding when Drysdale Government Securities, Inc., disclosed in the month of May 1982 that it was not able to pay about $160 million in interest as a result of its huge debts to various banks, including Chase Manhattan Bank, Inc., and about thirty securities firms. That prompted the Federal Reserve System to inject reserves into the banking system to allay the fear created in the market and to assist about thirty securities firms. Basically, Wall Street failed to follow its own adage: "know your customer." In this case Drysdale Government Securities, Inc., was able to fool bankers like Chase in the repurchase agreements arena. It worked like this: An investment banker agrees to sell government securities to a bank with the agreement that he or she will buy it back later on, getting thereby the equivalent of a loan from a bank. The bank, in this case Chase, pays for the security in cash and can use the security to enter into a repurchase agreement, this time with Drysdale. At the end of the agreement, the investment banker buys back the security at the arranged price and is entitled to the interest on the security. In this case Drysdale Government Securities, Inc., was not able to meet these interest payments because it lost too much money selling short the same securities it had bought.

The problem, in fact, started with Drysdale's aggressive trading, which led to large losses. One strategy used by Drysdale was to sell short government securities with substantial accrued interest built into their prices and buy other securities with little accrued interest, which involved borrowing securities with the hope of replacing them later at lower prices. The mechanics of the strategy went as follows: Drysdale bought government securities whose value was to increase as the interest payment dates approached and sold short those with bloated prices owing to the forthcoming interest payments. This implied that Drysdale was able to go to the market and replace the securities it sold short by buying them at the depressed prices after interest payments. The whole strategy failed, however, when the market unexpectedly rallied, raising the prices of those bonds that were to be bought to replace those sold short.

Another strategy supposed to have generated heavy losses for Drysdale Government Securities, Inc., called "bear spread," involved buying government bonds and bond futures while selling treasury bills.

Who is responsible for the payment of interest? Chase or Drysdale? In any case, Chase decided after all to take over Drysdale's government securities positions to be liquidated in an orderly manner and also to pay Drysdale's debts of more than $160 million.

Drysdale's default showed one more time the dangers of intricate financing agreements and put more pressure for a regulation of government securities trading. In fact, the Manhattan district attorney's office launched a criminal investigation of Drysdale Government Securities, Inc.,'s collapse, followed by another investigation by the Securities and Exchange Commission (SEC), which has only civil jurisdiction.

In addition, Chase Manhattan Bank and Manufacturers Hanover Trust Co. sued the principals, accountants, and agents of Drysdale Government Securities, Inc. Arthur Andersen & Co., as the accounting firm, was accused by the clients of Drysdale of being negligent in its review of the firm's financial statements, with Chase claiming $285 million in damages and Manufacturers the sum of $21 million of losses. Chase mentioned specifically the fact that Drysdale Government Securities, Inc., was insolvent of $135 million in February 1982, falsely stated its subordinated debt and equity amount as $20.8 million, and that Arthur Andersen & Co., was fully liable for the amount.

A few weeks later a county grand jury in New York indicted two officers of Drysdale Government Securities, Inc., on charges of stealing more than $270 million from Chase and more than $20 million from Manufacturers. In addition, it indicted a former partner of Arthur Andersen & Co. on charges of issuing false financial statements. Basically, it alleged that the day Drysdale Government Securities, Inc., opened for business in February 1981, its liabilities exceeded its assets by $150 million. *Naturally, as in all fraud cases, the accountant was accused of having done the magic trick, certifying that the false information about the Drysdale financial affair conformed with GAAP. In addition, the unqualified opinion given on February 22, 1981, was made without a second Arthur Andersen & Co. partner check of the final report, as the accounting firm's procedures required.*

The two officers of Drysdale agreed to the court orders that required their compliance with federal securities law to settle SEC charges of security fraud. The accounting partner from Arthur Andersen & Co. was, however, acquitted by a state court of charges that he issued false statements for the now defunct Drysdale Government Securities, Inc. The SEC also settled the civil charges against the partner from Arthur Andersen & Co. when he consented to be enjoined from any future violations of the antifraud provisions of the federal securities law.

A federal jury, however, issued a $17 million judgment against Arthur Andersen & Co. in the civil suit brought by Manufacturers. The judgment was upheld by a federal appeals court, contending that Arthur Andersen & Co. violated securities law and committed fraud and negligence in certifying financial statements for Drysdale and its Drysdale Government Securities, Inc., suit. It was in line with the accountants' liability for violations of federal securities laws, particularly section 10(b) and rule 10(b)-5 concerning fraud in connection with the purchase or sale of securities.

Arthur Andersen & Co. appealed higher. The Supreme Court refused to free the company from paying the $17 million, and it was ordered to pay the money to Manufacturers Hanover Trust Co.

All these events underscored one more time the need for the U.S. government securities industry to reexamine many of its informal practices and the need for more federal regulation of the market. It may have been too late, but the Public Securities Association released in October 1988 a nine-page report outlining "business-practice guidelines" for participants in the repurchase-agreement market. Specifically it recommended the use of formal written repurchase agreements with extensive details on terms and conditions and the adoption by each security firm of specific formal credit analysis procedures to examine the credit standing of customers and other dealers.

THE WEDTECH STORY: WELL CONNECTED IN POLITICS AND ACCOUNTING

Wedtech Corp., a Bronx-based defense contractor, collapsed in December 1987 amid a scandal involving political payoffs and the use of accounting gimmickry.

With regard to the political scandal, it seemed that Wedtech Corp. was receiving a favorable treatment as a government contractor, after it committed itself to hiring untrained and seemingly unemployable workers in the South Bronx, prompting President Reagan to call founder John Mariotta, a former tool and die maker, "a hero for the 80's." There was more truth in the characterization, as the $100 million-a-year military contractor was now listed on the New York Stock Exchange. Then the company was charged with and admitted forging more than $6 million in invoices submitted to the federal government. What emerged was a network of political payoffs used by the company to buy influence by paying off and/or hiring politically connected consultants, relatives of politicians, and former government officials. It had allowed itself to become one of the largest participants in a no-bid defense contract program of the Small Business Administration agency.

With regard to the accounting fraud, the question was how did Wedtech's books manage to receive clean bills of health from the time the company went public in 1983, in light of the scheme that inflated the company's earnings through false invoices and flagrant accounting gimmicks? *The answer is simple in all the cases examined in this book. As usual, we can find the accountant and/or auditor behind the fraud.* It seems in this case that Wedtech got a lot of help in normalizing its situation. In 1983 Main Hurdman, a former member of its previous outside auditor firm, KMG, become Wedtech's president. Before leaving KMG, Hurdman allegedly agreed to receive $1.5 million in Wedtech's stock and a $900,000 loan from Wedtech,

which casts a cloud on his *independence* while auditing the books of Wedtech. Added to that, it seems that Wedtech relied on "percentage of completion" accounting to boost its earnings. Basically, under the percentage of
completion method, revenue is recognized on the basis of its current costs,
the estimated costs of completing a project, and the certainty of receiving
the entire contract price. For example, say Wedtech has a contract with the
Defense Department at a cost of $200 million in material and labor and
charges $220 million for the job, making a $20 million or 18 percent profit.
If it incurred a $40 million cost the first year, it recognizes a $4 million
profit, 10 percent of its costs. Up to now everything conforms to generally
accepted accounting principles. However, it seems that Wedtech overstated
the amount of work done based on the spending already incurred. Wedtech
was able to appear profitable and sell more bonds and stocks to the "naive"
public. Where were Wedtech's auditors, KMG, in the face of these over-
statements? KMG claimed that it informed the company and its outside
attorneys of the fraud and was later satisfied that any irregularities had been
stopped. *Either KMG failed to accomplish its job, or Wedtech's management
did a good job of disguising the fraud.* The second version is more plausible,
as Touche Ross, replacing KMG, gave a clean opinion to Wedtech in 1985,
nine months before it filed for Chapter 11, failing to catch the pervasive
management fraud still going on in Wedtech.

The accounting firms did not carry the blame alone, as two major Wall
Street brokerage firms were sued by Wedtech holders over underwritings.
The suit charged that Bear, Stearns & Co. and Moseley Securities Corp.
failed to exercise "due diligence" in issuing the securities containing false
and misleading data about Wedtech's sales, earnings, and receivables.

The case includes a successful disguise of fraud by management, a failure
of two major accounting firms to detect and report the fraud, and a "naive"
client, the government of the United States. Wedtech was well connected to
two agents of society: political and accounting agents. *Did both of them
show enough greed and naivety to allow management to carry out its im-
mense and pervasive fraud?* How could false data be certified clean by two
major accounting firms? Were these firms victimized or plainly ineffective?
Why didn't either of the two auditors insist on the use of the *completed
contract method* rather than the percentage of completion method? Wedtech
was not certain it would get the entire amount of the government contracts.
If it was urged to use the completed contract method, it would not have
been able to record any profit until the completion of the contract.

BROKEN DREAMS HURT BY PENN SQUARE: WHERE
WERE THE AUDITORS?

When federal regulators closed Penn Square in July 1984, the once
small Oklahoma bank had caused losses for depositors and for five big
banks that had bought about $2 billion in loans. How can a small bank

fool the big banks, including Continental Illinois National Bank and Trust Co. for $1 billion, Chase Manhattan Corp. for $200 million to $300 million, Seafirst Corp. for $400 million, Michigan National Corp. for $200 million, and Northern Trust Corp. for $125 million? The reasons quickly emerging from the scandal included the gold rush euphoria about the energy business by banks at the time and their sudden rush to lend money, the less than adequate loan review procedures, and the aggressive salesmanship of Penn Square officers aggravated by an inbred relationship with other banks. Penn Square churned out billions of dollars to small oil and gas producers in risky loans made worse by being undercollateralized and overvalued.

Where were the auditors? Several months before its collapse, Penn Square got a qualified opinion of its 1980 financial statements by Arthur Young & Co. because of the lack of adequacy of reserves for possible loan losses. What else was there for Penn Square to do but fire the auditor who had questioned its lending practices and find another firm, in this case Peat, Marwick, Mitchell & Co., who naturally gave it a clean bill of health. The same judgment that found the adequacy of the reserve for possible loan losses unacceptable because of the lack of supporting documentation of collateral values of certain loans was altered later by Peat, Marwick, Mitchell & Co., arguing that the judgment by management on the allowance was adequate at both December 31, 1981 and 1980, and removing the qualification in the 1981 financial statements.

What happened may again be in the realm of creative accounting. It seems that management altered the bank's financial position, leading both Peat, Marwick, Mitchell & Co. and the U.S. comptroller of the currency to note Penn Square's efforts favorably. The irony is that Peat, Marwick, Mitchell & Co.'s report on March 19 preceded the bank's collapse by only three and a half months. Could anything drastic have happened in seven months to justify the removal of the qualifications? The answer lies again with Peat, Marwick, Mitchell & Co. In fact, Peat, Marwick, Mitchell & Co. knew about problems at the bank and warned directors in May that the bank's problems were on the rise. These problems included inadequate asset and liability management, poor liquidity, a large number of loan-documentation deficiencies, widening loan losses, several lending limit violations, and insufficient capital. But the irony again is that such damaging internal reports are not included with the audited financial statements because of the risk to depositor confidence. *Should Peat, Marwick, Mitchell & Co. have made public those reports to the U.S. comptroller of the currency, to the investors, to the depositors, or to the public?* That would have stopped some depositors at least from continuing to place millions of dollars of uninsured money with the bank, buoyed by the unqualified auditor's report. However, Peat, Marwick, Mitchell & Co. was prohibited by the accounting profession's standard of confidentiality from saying anything to other banks or to the public. The secrecy of the auditor as well as of the regulators allowed Penn Square to continue with its scheme of attracting deposits and loaning to borrowers already crippled by the energy slump.

Who would blame, for example, Professional Asset Management, a California-based broker, for filing a suit alleging that Penn Square's outside auditor, Peat, Marwick, Mitchell & Co., and two of the auditor's accountants were negligent in issuing a clean opinion of the bank's 1981 financial statements and that their behavior in light of their knowledge of Penn Square's problems amounted to fraud? *Was Peat, Marwick, Mitchell & Co.'s conclusion of an unqualified report when it knew about serious problems at the bank equivalent to fraud? Instead of sending a private letter to Penn Square's board recommending ways to correct fourteen problem areas, should they have qualified the 1981 statements?* That makes Peat, Marwick, Mitchell & Co. liable third parties for fraudulent information in audit reports.

What really went wrong with Peat, Marwick, Mitchell & Co.'s audit? Well, in 1984 the Federal Deposit Insurance Corp. (FDIC), when suing Peat, Marwick, Mitchell & Co. for the improper audit of Penn Square, added charges that the partners in Peat, Marwick, Mitchell & Co.'s Oklahoma City office compromised the firm's independence by accepting more than $1 million of loans, directly or indirectly, from Penn Square. This second allegation pointed to the fact that in 1981 all twelve partners in Peat, Marwick, Mitchell & Co. were members of an Oklahoma general partnership called Doral Associates, which borrowed $566,501 from Penn Square and guaranteed a Penn Square loan of $1,650,000 to a Doral joint venture. It seems that Peat, Marwick, Mitchell & Co. was aware of these loans and even advised Penn Square to sell those loans to other banks. *One more case of the accountant with his hand caught in the bank's cookie jar.*

The case did not stop there for Peat, Marwick, Mitchell & Co. In January 1985 a judgment required it to disclose completely an internal study of its 1981 audit of Penn Square. The case was a first test that will open all accounting firms to "self-incrimination" in cases in which firms have been sued for failing to spot financial troubles at client companies. The plaintiff suing Peat, Marwick, Mitchell & Co. for its audit failure of Penn Square had access to material that incriminated the accounting firm. In effect, the types of reviews a firm performs after an audit is over are candid and sometimes speculative. Can the accounting firms claim privilege for this type of material that should be protected as the work product of the accounting firm's attorney? By saying no the judge created a scary development.

Peat, Marwick, Mitchell & Co.'s problems were not over, as the Justice Department followed the example of the FDIC by suing the firm and the implicated partners, alleging fraud and conflict of interest in their auditing of Penn Square Bank before it failed.

In July 1986 Peat, Marwick, Mitchell & Co. settled the suit brought by the FDIC and agreed to a settlement.

2

Fairness in Distribution

Fairness judgments are taken for granted in accounting, although their clear meaning is not well specified. Two generally accepted meanings concern the idea of neutrality in preparation and presentation of financial reports and the idea of justice in outcome. While both notions play a useful role in accounting, the expansion of the notion of fairness to deal with distribution considerations links it to alternative philosophical concepts more compatible with moral concepts of justice. Basically, fairness may be viewed as a moral concept of justice subject to three different interpretations of the notions of distributive justice. Accordingly, this chapter expands the accounting discussion of fairness by introducing the main philosophical concepts of distributive justice in the accounting context. The end result is the possibility of viewing and comparing the concept of fairness through different distributive justice frameworks.

CONCERNS WITH DISTRIBUTION QUESTIONS

The problems of distribution have almost been ignored in the conventional view of fairness as neutrality in presentation. The concern here was merely the final production and disclosure of accounting results rather than their distribution. The view of fairness as neutrality in presentation is not without its critics. Paul Williams characterized it as an evaluation process with the following two attributes: (1) that the evaluator is aware of the conditions that any consequences of his or her actions will be judged as fair or unfair, and (2) that the evaluation attempts to adopt a perspective of impartiality.[1]

Williams presented two interesting arguments. The first argument is that decision usefulness, the principle of organizing accounting research and practice, is incomplete, while accountability, at least, possesses fairness as an inherent property. The second argument is that the concern of accounting with efficiency makes accounting's fairness judgment implicit, not absent. Explicit concern with fairness is warranted:

> If more explicit consideration of fairness is granted, certain implications emerge for the study and practice of accounting. One of the most obvious is that accounting has a moral dimension. Consequences of accounting activity have moral implications as well as "efficiency" ones. For a profession, becoming more scientific does not necessarily require abandoning moral decision making and the cultivation of modes for doing so. The two most notable professions, law and medicine, accommodate schools concerned only with legal or medical ethics. For unknown reasons, the ethics of accounting has virtually vanished as a subject worthy of scholarly concern.[2]

Williams' arguments were supported by June Pallot.[3] She agreed with the suggestion that fairness in accountability and fairness in distribution stem from different ethical frameworks and different, though complementary, assumptions about society. In addition, she made some preliminary suggestions as to how a community perspective might be added to the predominantly individualistic one in accounting as a step toward developing new approaches to the issues of accountability and distributive practice. The concept of "community assets"[4] fits well within R. Chen's model of social and financial stewardship, where management's performance is evaluated in terms of both profit and social objectives.[5] Pallot explains:

> This sort of accountability framework is fundamentally different from those where the starting assumption is one of private property and social responsibility accounting is seen as a matter of accounting for social costs and benefits viewed as externalities. In a world where a commitment to shared values, rather than the pursuit of self interest, was the norm, accountability might be seen as a voluntary obligation in the public interest rather than a mechanism for constraining self seeking behavior and protecting rights.[6]

There are three other notable exceptions in the accounting literature that have shown concern with distributive questions. The first exception emanates from the social accounting concern with accounting for externalities and reporting some forms of social report. A first example includes D. R. Scott's view of the social role of accounting in the revolution of conflicting social interest: "The compromise of conflicting interests is a process of valuation. It accomplishes social organization and results in a distribution of economic incomes. Value and distribution constitute a simple problem and accounting theory is especially and peculiarly a treatment of that problem."[7] A second example includes the various calls for the role of social accounting in some forms of the rectification of society's ills.[8] It is best stated by H. Schreuder and K. V. Ramanathan: "In the context of traditional economic analysis, the issue boils down to a distribution problem, namely the apportionment in a society of the costs and benefits of economic activity. Economists have long recognized that such distributional issues cannot be addressed without taking a normative position."[9]

Fairness in the social accounting literature becomes a matter of distribution of social responsibility in general, and social responsiveness as the capacity of corporations to respond to social pressures. Thus corporate social responsiveness, as an expression of fairness, goes beyond the moral and ethical connotation of social responsibility to the managerial process of response. The response to be fair involves the identification, measurement, and disclosure, where necessary, of the social costs and benefits created by the economic activities of the firm, as well as the adequate responses to these problems.

The second exception emanates from advocates of the political economy of accounting and the critical and Marxist approach to accounting.[10] They advocate a political economy approach that recognizes power and conflict in society and the effects of accounting reports on the distribution of income, wealth, and power in society.

The third exception emanates from the positive theory of accounting view that accounting can be used to optimally resolve conflicts over resource allocation to a limited set of participants.[11] Fairness in this context is ultimately in the shareholder's interest.[12]

FAIRNESS AS A MORAL CONCEPT OF JUSTICE

For fairness to be perceived as a moral concept of justice, parallels must be made to the main theories of distributive justice, those of J. A. Rawls, R. Nozick, and A. Gerwith.

Rawls' Contribution

Rawls' Theory of Justice

The goal of Rawls' theory of justice is to develop a theory about justice in the form of principles to apply to the development of the basic structure of society, and that presents a direct challenge to utilitarianism.[13] As an egalitarian theory, its main contention is the distribution of all economic goods and services equally except where an unequal distribution would actually work to everyone's advantage, or at least would benefit the worst-off society. Using what he calls the "Kantian concept of equality," Rawls starts by comparing life to a game of chance where nature bestows on each individual a generation, culture, a social system, a family, and set of personal attributes that determines his or her happiness. Accepting this random allocation is viewed as unjust, and a set of just institutions is required. To establish just institutions, Rawls suggests that individuals step behind a "veil of ignorance" that eliminates any knowledge about potential positions and benefits under a given set of principles. Then, to reach a social contract, they must choose from this original position principles of justice leading to the just society. From this original position and under the veil of ignorance, individuals will choose two principles of justice: "First: Each person is to have an equal right to the most extensive basic liberty compatible with a similar liberty for others. Second, social and economic inequalities are to be arranged so that they are both (a) reasonably expected to be to everyone's advantage, and (b) attached to positions and offices open to all."[14]

Rawls maintains that the two principles are lexicographically ordered, the first one over the second:

> Now it is possible, at least theoretically, that by giving up some of their fundamental liberties men are sufficiently compensated by the resulting social and economic gains. The general conception of justice implies no restrictions on what sort of inequalities; it only requires that everyone's position be improved . . . Imagine . . . that men forgo certain political rights when the economic returns are significant and their capacity to influence the course of policy by the exercise of these rights would be marginal in any case. It is this kind of exchange which the two principles as stated rule out; being arranged in serial order they do not permit exchanges between basic liberties and economic and social gains.[15]

The first principle shows the emphasis placed by Rawls on liberty and the precedence of liberty over the second principle of justice. Liberty can be restricted only when it is formulated as follows: "The principles of justice are to be ranked in lexical order and therefore, liberty can be restricted only for the sake of liberty. There are two cases: (a) a less restrictive liberty shared by all, and (b) a less than equal liberty must be acceptable to those citizens with the lesser liberty."[16]

The second principle of justice, which Rawls labeled the difference principle, contains a second lexicographic ordering of the welfare of the individuals from the lowest to the highest, where the welfare of the worst-off individual is to be maximized first before proceeding to higher levels. In its most general form, the difference principle states that "In a basic structure with no relevant representatives, first maximize the welfare of the worst-off representative, minimize the welfare of the second worst-off man, and so on until the last case which is, for equal welfare of all the preceding n-1 representatives, maximize the welfare of the best-off representative man. We think of this as the lexical difference principle."[17]

These two principles show a democratic conception that eliminates those aspects of the social world that seem arbitrary from a moral point of view. This does not necessarily eliminate economic inequality. Rawls justifies some difference in income first: as incentives to attract people into certain positions and motivate them to perform; and as a guarantee that certain public-interest positions will be filled. To implement Rawls' theory, the idea of "basic structure" may be "a constitutional democracy," which preserves equal basic liberties, with a government that promotes equality of opportunity and guarantees a social minimum and a market-based economic system. Rawls suggests that this social minimum be established before allowing the rest of the total income to be settled by the price system. It is to be settled by special payments for sickness and unemployment and monetary transfer systems such as negative income tax. Rawls, however, gives little attention to the identification of the worst-off representative. He offers only two alternatives: (1) to choose a particular social position, say that of the unskilled worker, and then to count as the least advantaged all those with the average income of this group, or less; or (2) to focus on the relative income and wealth with no reference to social position, that is, all persons with less than half of the median income and wealth may be taken as the least advantaged segment.[18] With regard to redistribution, Rawls finds large inequalities to be permissible if lowering them would make the working class even worse off. Basically, with the raising of expectations of the more advantaged, the situation of the worst-off is continuously improved. Inequalities will tend to be leveled down by the increasing availability of education and ever-widening expectations. However, Rawls calls for the establishment of social minimums through various transfers and redistributive mechanisms. But would Rawls' difference principle assure an adequate level of the necessary goods and services? There are a host of disagreements on this issue.[19]

Derek Phillips joins the opposite chorus:

> The major reason for this concerns Rawls' emphasis on incentives. With the difference principle . . . an unequal distribution of wealth and income is justified if and only if it will maximize benefits to the least advantaged segments within a society. But if, as Rawls assumes, these inequalities must be rather large, then it seems likely that the actual benefits—even if maximized—will not be sufficient to provide an adequate level for the least advantaged segment, they will fail to do so for those persons who require extra medical care, protection and other basic goods. This is a consequence of the fact . . . that the difference

principle makes no allowances for the particular needs of especially disadvantaged individuals.[20]

While better criteria still need to be developed to resolve these issues, Gerwith asserts that what is needed is a drastic redistribution of wealth and an effective exercise of the fundamental rights to freedom and well-being.[21] Basically, Rawls and Gerwith disagree on how the needs of the disadvantaged are to be met. While Rawls is willing to accept an unequal distribution of economic rewards, if it benefits the least advantaged, Gerwith maintains that the wealthy have an obligation to assist the disadvantaged.

Fairness in Accounting According to Rawls

Rawls' contract theory—a theory of just social institutions—may be offered as a concept of fairness in accounting. Applied to accounting, it suggests first the potential reliance on the veil of ignorance in all the situations calling for an accounting choice eventually to yield solutions that are neutral, fair, and socially just. Second, it also suggests the expanded role of accounting in the creation of just institutions and the definition of the social minimum advocated by Rawls. This role, as also espoused by advocates of accounting, will lead to the elimination of those aspects of the social world in general, and the accounting world in particular, that seem arbitrary from a moral point of view. This view of fairness would be most welcome to advocates of social accounting. As stated by Williams:

> Rawlsian principles also may prove to be a useful set of premises for speculation about alternative accounting systems. For example, one plausible reason for the slow theoretical development of social accounting, at least in the United States, could be the constraining effect of conventional accounting premises about character and legitimacy of institutions, both public and private. Accounting scholars with interests in social accounting are certainly free to generate and test hypotheses about measuring and reporting, in Rawlsian, or any other, institutional setting.[22]

Nozick's Contribution

Nozick's Theory of Justice

While Rawls is interested in the justice of one or another pattern of distribution, Nozick is interested in the process through which distribution comes about.[23] He first argued that Rawls' theory of justice violates people's rights, and consequently cannot be morally justified; that it ignores people's entitlement and is, like most other theories of justice, patterned. Patterned theories of justice imply that a distribution is to vary along some natural dimension, weighted sum of natural dimensions, or lexicographic ordering of natural dimensions.[24] Examples of such distributions include those based on need, merit, or work. Nozick maintains: "To think that the task of a theory of justice is to fill in the blank in each according to his _____ is to be predisposed to search for a pattern; and separate treatment from each according to his _____ treats production and distribution as two separate and independent issues.[25]

Nozick argues that such theories of justice, based on the patterned and end-state principles, violate people's rights and exclude recognition of an entitlement principle of distributive justice, whereby individuals are entitled to their possessions as long as they acquired them by legitimate means, including voluntary transfers, exchanges, and cooperative productive activity. Nozick's theory focuses on the importance of historical principles, in the sense that a distribution is just or not depending on how it came about. He justifies his theory as follows:

1. A person who acquires a holding in accordance with the principle of justice in acquisition is entitled to that holding.
2. A person who acquires a holding in accordance with the principle of justice in transfer, from someone else entitled to that holding, is entitled to the holding.
3. No one is entitled to a holding except by (repeated) applications of 1. and 2.[26]

The principles involve, respectively, the question of original acquisition of holdings and the rectification of injustices in holdings. Nozick introduced a proviso, however, to ensure that an individual's entitlement does not result in a net loss in what remains for other persons to use. Nozick's theory is, then, a theory of justice in holdings. It is a very special kind of theory of distributive justice, as Nozick emphasizes:

The term "distributive justice" is not a neutral one. Hearing the term "distribution," most people presume that some thing or mechanism uses some principle or criterion to give out a supply of things . . . However, we are not in the position of children who have been given portions of pie by someone who now makes last-minute adjustments to rectify careless cutting. There is no central distribution, no person or group entitled to control all the resources, jointly deciding how they are to be doled out. What each person gets, he gets from others who give it to him in exchange for something, or as a gift. In a free society, diverse persons control different resources, and new holdings arise out of the voluntary exchanges and action of persons. There is no more a distribution of shares than there is a distribution of mates in a society in which persons choose whom they shall marry. The total result is the product of many individuals' decisions which the different individuals involved are entitled to make.[27]

Although some criteria remain to be used, Nozick's theory has been criticized for its failure to recognize the right to well-being. The question generally asked is: Is it just to tie the socioeconomic standing of other family members entirely to the moral acceptability of historical process through which the breadwinner has acquired his or her holdings? Those answering "no" argue that it may appear to anyone involved with a sense of justice and concerned about some family members reducing their standard of living radically, when, in other cases, correction is required because of someone else's unjust acquisition; and feeling something morally unsatisfactory about some people being very well compared to others.[28]

Fairness in Accounting According to Nozick

The use of economic man theory in accounting and the decision usefulness criterion used in empirical accounting research link fairness and distributive justice to a free market mechanism. Accounting is viewed as essential to the efficient running of an organization, and the mere reaching of efficiency is presumed to make everybody better off in possession of their just share.[29] Fairness to the positivists and the rationality theorists is linked to an efficient market that allows a just transfer to shareholders.

It is essentially a libertarian theory of distribution à la Nozick, based on a principle of justice in acquisition and in transfer. This concept of distributive justice with its reliance on a free market mechanism does not allow for dealing adequately with fairness as a distributive function, because it is assumed to fail in the discussion of the social obligations of humans to each other, perpetuate past violations of principles of acquisition and transition, and distort the meaning of well-offness in a world of scarcity. The reliance on the market mechanism, the absence of a moral language to discuss social obligations, as well as the absence of a concept of redistributive justice are some of the cited failures of the libertarian theory of justice. In addition, the growing importance of meritocracy in the context of a basically market system has created problems for a Nozickean theory of justice. The conflicting rules of distribution are not well accepted in contemporary culture. Most often, members of the organization demand to receive what they justly deserve.

Under the tutoring of the school system, and reinforced by other meritocratic organizations, a person has been socialized to feel that he or she ought to get what has been earned and to be protected from the vagaries and irrationalities of the market. Basically, stakeholders and other shareholders may not be satisfied by the conventional reporting emphasis on returns to shareholders. For example, labor may feel that the profit generated dictates a different distribution than the one dictated by justice in holding and transfer, and a reporting system emphasizing the "mere" just distribution is warranted.

A good evaluation of the Nozickean libertarian view of accounting follows:

In summary, a Libertarian interpretation of accounting's deference to a market mechanism for making its fairness judgments leaves accounting inadequately equipped to deal with the distributive aspects of the accounting process. Without a moral language to discuss the social obligations of humans to each other, the principles of justice in acquisition and transition have no substance. Without a concept of redistributive justice, past violations of principles of acquisition and transition are perpetuated. And in a world of scarcity well-offness acquires a meaning beyond the capabilities of the language of property rights to define. Markets do distribute society's prizes, but a Libertarian interpretation of that mechanism certainly provides no assurance that it is fair or even that fairness is a mediating process.[30]

Gerwith's Contribution

Gerwith's Theory of Justice

The goal of Gerwith's theory of justice was to provide a rational justification for moral principles to objectively distinguish morally right actions and institutions from morally wrong ones.[31] The necessary content of morality is in actions and their generic features. The actions are distinguished in terms of two categorical features: voluntariness and purposiveness. Given the importance of action as the necessary and universal matter of all moral and other practical precepts, Gerwith presents his doctrine of the structure of actions in three main steps:

First, every agent implicitly makes evaluative judgments about the goodness of his purposes and hence about the necessary goodness of the freedom and well-being that are necessary conditions of his acting to achieve his purposes. Second, because of this necessary goodness, every agent implicitly makes a deontic judgment in which he claims that he has to freedom and well-being. Third, every agent must claim these rights for the sufficient reason that he is a prospective agent who has purposes he wants to fulfill, so that he logically must accept the generalization that all prospective agents have rights to freedom and well-being.[32]

The rights to freedom and well-being are seen as generic, fundamental, and universal. As a result, Gerwith asserts that every agent logically must acknowledge certain generic obligations:

> Negatively, he ought to refrain from coercing and from harming his recipients; positively, he ought to assist them to have freedom and well-being whenever they cannot otherwise have the necessary goods and he can help them at no comparable loss to himself. The general principle of these obligations and rights may be expressed as the following precepts addressed to every agent; Act in accord with the generic rights of your recipients as well as yourself. I call this the Principle of Generic Consistency (PGC) since it combines the formal consideration of rights to generic features or goods of action.[33]

Gerwith calls the PGC the supreme moral principle, as it requires the agents not to interfere with the freedom and well-being of others. It remains that the PGC has both direct and indirect application. The direct application concerns the requirement for agents to act in accord with the right to freedom and well-being of all other persons. The indirect application concerns the requirement that institutional arrangements must express or serve the freedom and well-being of all other persons.

The indirect application involves specifically social rules and arrangements to be implemented in a static and dynamic phase. The static phase generates rules to protect an existing equality of generic rights, while the dynamic phase calls for redistributive justice to eliminate inequalities through a "supportive state." The social rules between the two extremes are as follows: (1) a certain libertarian extreme that would defend the existing distribution of wealth, arising presumably from just acquisition, and (2) an egalitarian extreme that calls for a drastic redistribution to be guided solely by the aim of maximally benefiting those who are the least advantaged. Both extremes appear deficient.[34]

Fairness in Accounting According to Gerwith

Gerwith's theory of justice may be offered as a concept of fairness in accounting. Applied to accounting, it suggests the primacy of the concerns for the rights of freedom and well-being of all persons affected by the activities of the firm and for the creation of institutional and accounting arrangements to guarantee these rights. These arrangements call for some form of rectification through the creation of a "supportive system" and specific social rules to be followed by organizations and members within the organization. Accounting may be called on to facilitate a drastic redistribution of wealth and an effective exercise of the fundamental rights to freedom and well-being of the stakeholders in organizations. Gerwithian principles may prove to be a useful set of premises for speculation about the merit of value-added reporting. This supports the emphasis in value-added reporting to report the total return of all members of the "production team": shareholders, bondholders, suppliers, labor, government, and society. Not one of these members is relegated to the position of "disadvantaged" as in other concepts of distributive justice, as they are all given a place of importance in the measurement, reporting, and allocation of the total return of the firm. Basically, the Gerwithian principles applied to fairness in accounting include a recognition of the rights of all those affected by the activities of the organization,[35] and, as stated by Gerwith himself.

It calls for action that is voluntary and purposive to affirm an egalitarian universalist moral principle. As Marx's "man makes its own history," the role of action toward making moral judgments applies to accounting making efficiency and distribution judgments that protect the generic rights of all the recipients of accounting information. Accounting will create its own history of a moral agent in the marketplace, an agent concerned with the rights of the recipients of accounting information. The merits of applying the principle of generic consistency to the concept of fairness in accounting derives from its capacity of presenting the accountant with rationally grounded answers to each of the three questions of moral philosophy:

1. The distributive question of which persons' interests ought to be favorably considered is answered by calling for the respect of the generic rights of all recipients and for the equality of the rights of all prospective agents.

2. The substantive question of which interests ought to be favorably considered is answered by focusing on the primacy of freedom and well-being.

3. The authoritative question of why should anyone be moral in the sense of taking favorable account of other people's interests is justified by the reason of avoiding self-contradiction. Basically, an action that violates the PGC principle cannot be rationally justified.[36]

CONCLUSIONS

While fairness has been generally associated in accounting and auditing with a connotation of either neutrality in presentation or justice in outcome, it may, borrowing from theories of distributive justice and its expansion to considerations of distribution, play a moral role in accounting. That moral dimension of fairness in matters of distribution may easily be associated with the market for entitlement of Nozick, or the reliance on a veil of ignorance concept and the creation of just institutions of Rawls, or as a guarantor and implementer of the rights to freedom and well-being of all persons affected by the activities of the firm and a basis for the creating of institutional and accounting arrangements to guarantee these rights of Gerwith.

NOTES

1. Williams, Paul F., "The Legitimate Concern with Fairness," *Accounting, Organizations and Society* 12 (1987): 169–192.

2. Ibid., 185.

3. Pallot, June, "The Legitimate Concern with Fairness: A Comment," *Accounting, Organizations and Society* 16 (1991): 201–208.

4. Pallot, June, "The Nature of Public Assets: A Response to Rawls," *Accounting Horizons* (June 1990): 79–85.

5. Chen, R., "Social and Financial Stewardship," *The Accounting Review* (July 1975): 533–543.

6. Pallot, "The Legitimate Concern with Fairness," 206.

7. Scott, D. R., "The Basic Accounting Principles," *The Accounting Review* (December 1941): 248.

8. Belkaoui, Ahmed, *Socio-Economic Accounting* (Westport, Conn.: Greenwood Press, 1973).

9. Schreuder, H., and K. V. Ramanathan, "Accounting and Corporate Accountability: An Extended Comment," *Accounting, Organizations and Society* (Fall 1984): 407.

10. Cooper, D. J., and M. J. Sherer, "The Value of Corporate Accounting Reports: Arguments for a Political Economy of Accounting," *Accounting, Organizations and Society* (Fall 1984): 207–232.

11. Jensen, N. C., and W. H. Heckling, "Theory of the Firm: Managerial and Ownership Structure," *Journal of Financial Economics* (October 1976): 305–362.

12. Watts, A. L., and J. L. Zimmerman, "Towards a Positive Theory of the Determination of Accounting Standards," *The Accounting Review* (January 1978): 112–134.

13. Rawls, J. A., *A Theory of Justice* (Cambridge, Mass.: Harvard University Press, 1971).

14. Ibid., 67.

15. Ibid., 62–63.

16. Ibid., 250.

17. Ibid., 83.

18. Ibid., 64.

19. Barry, Brian, *The Liberal Theory of Justice* (Oxford: Oxford University Press, 1973).

20. Phillips, Derek L., *Toward a Just Social Order* (Princeton, N.J.: Princeton University Press, 1986), 354.

21. Gerwith, A., *Reason and Morality* (Chicago: University of Chicago Press, 1978), 313.

22. Williams, "The Legitimate Concern with Fairness," 184.

23. Nozick, R., *Anarchy, State, and Utopia* (New York: Basic Books, 1974).

24. Ibid., 156.

25. Ibid., 159–160.

26. Ibid., 160.
27. Ibid., 149–150.
28. Phillips, *Toward a Just Social Order,* 348.
29. Williams, *The Legitimate Concern with Fairness,* 184.
30. Ibid., 181.
31. Gerwith, *Reason and Morality.*
32. Ibid., 48.
33. Ibid., 153.
34. Ibid., 313–314.
35. Ibid., 137–148.
36. Ibid., 150.

REFERENCES

Arnett, H. E. "The Concept of Fairness." *The Accounting Review* (April 1967): 251–297.

Barry, Brian. *The Liberal Theory of Justice.* Oxford: Oxford University Press, 1973.

Belkaoui, Ahmed. *Socio-Economic Accounting.* Westport, Conn.: Greenwood Press, 1973.

Blau, Peter M., and Otis Dudley Duncan. *The American Occupational Structure.* New York: John Wiley, 1976.

Chambers, R. C. *Securities and Obscurities: A Case for Reform of the Law of Company Accounts.* Sydney, Australia: Gower Press, 1973.

Chen, R. "Social and Financial Stewardship." *The Accounting Review* (July 1975): 533–543.

Cooper, D. J., and M. J. Sherer. "The Value of Corporate Accounting Reports: Arguments for a Political Economy of Accounting." *Accounting, Organizations and Society* (Fall 1984): 207–232.

Deutsche, Morton. "Equity, Equality and Need: What Determines Which Value Be Used as a Basis of Distributive Justice?" *Journal of Social Issues* 31, no. 3 (1975).

Devine, C. T. "Research Methodology and Accounting Theory Formation." *The Accounting Review* (July 1960): 387–399.

Financial Accounting Standards Board. *Statement of Financial Accounting Concepts No. 1: Objective of Financial Reporting by Business Enterprises.* Stamford, Conn.: FASB, 1978.

———. *Statement of Financial Accounting Concepts No. 2: Objective of Financial Reporting by Business Enterprises.* Stamford, Conn.: FASB, 1980.

Gambling, T. *Societal Accounting.* Chicago: University of Chicago Press, 1978.

Gerwith, A. *Reason and Morality.* Chicago: University of Chicago Press, 1978.

Homans, Georges C. *Social Behavior: Its Elementary Forms.* New York: Harcourt Brace Jovanovich, 1965.

Iijri, Y. "On the Accountability-Based Conceptual Framework of Accounting." *Journal of Accounting and Public Policy* (Summer 1983): 16–26.

Jasso, G., and P. H. Rossi. "Distributive Justice and Earned Income." *Journal of Accountancy* (December 1967): 13–25.

Jensen, N. C., and W. H. Heckling. "Theory of the Firm: Managerial and Ownership Structure." *Journal of Financial Economics* (October 1976): 305–362.

Joseph, K., and J. Sumptions. *Equality*. London: Rowman, 1979.

Kohler, E. L. "Fairness." *Journal of Accountancy* (December 1967): 58–60.

Lee, T. A. *Contemporary Financial Reporting: Issues and Analysis*. London: Thomas Nelson and Sons, 1976.

Lev, Baruch. "Toward a Theory of Equitable and Efficient Accounting Policy." *The Accounting Review* (January 1988): 1–92.

Miller, David. *Social Justice*. Oxford: Clarendon Press, 1976.

Moonitz, M. *The Basic Postulates of Accounting*, Accounting Research Study No. 1. New York: AICPA, 1961.

Nozick, Robert. *Anarchy, State, and Utopia*. New York: Basic Books, 1974.

Okum, A. M. *Equality and Efficiency: The Big Tradeoff*. Washington, D.C.: Littlefield, 1975.

Pallot, June. "The Legitimate Concern with Fairness: A Comment." *Accounting, Organizations and Society* 16 (1991): 201–208.

———. "The Nature of Public Assets: A Response to Rawls." *Accounting Horizons* (June 1990): 79–85.

Patillo, James W. *The Foundation of Financial Accounting*. Baton Rouge: Louisiana State University Press, 1965.

Phillips, Derek L. *Toward a Just Social Order*. Princeton, N.J.: Princeton University Press, 1986.

Rawls, J. A. *A Theory of Justice*. Cambridge, Mass.: Harvard University Press, 1971.

Rubinstein, David. "The Concept of Justice in Sociology." *Theory and Society* 17 (1988–89).

Schreuder, H., and K. V. Ramanathan. "Accounting and Corporate Accountability: An Extended Comment." *Accounting, Organizations and Society* (Fall 1984).

Scott, D. R. "The Basic Accounting Principles." *The Accounting Review* (December 1941).

Tinker, A. M., B. D. Merino, and M. D. Neimark. "The Normative Origins of Positive Theories: Ideology and Accounting Thought." *Accounting, Organizations and Society* (Spring 1982): 167–200.

Watts, A. L., and J. L. Zimmerman. "Towards a Positive Theory of the Determination of Accounting Standards." *The Accounting Review* (January 1978): 112–134.

Williams, Paul F. "The Legitimate Concern with Fairness." *Accounting, Organizations and Society* 12 (1987): 169–192.

Wolff, Robert Paul. *Understanding Rawls*. Princeton, N.J.: Princeton University Press, 1977.

3

Fairness in Disclosure

The previous two chapters examined the principle of fairness in presentation and the principle of fairness in distribution. This chapter extends the discussion of improving the concept of fairness by examining the principle of fairness in disclosure. Basically, as a result of the more equitable concept of fairness in distribution, the principle of fairness in disclosure calls for an expansion of the conventional accounting disclosures to accommodate all the other interest groups, in addition to investors and creditors, that have a vested interest in the affairs of the firm.

CALLS FOR EXPANDED DISCLOSURES

The reliance on conventional fairness in presentation in conformity with generally accepted accounting principles has created some limitations and unfairness in reporting and disclosure. Three proposals for reducing and/or eliminating this unfairness in reporting and disclosure are examined next.

Bedford's Disclosure Proposals

Bedford proposed extensions in accounting disclosure to alleviate the problems created by the fairness doctrine in accounting.[1] Rather than merely relying on generally accepted accounting principles as the only measurement method, Bedford called for the development of new tools to provide management and decision makers with useful information. These tools are described as follows:

These new tools have been gathered together under diverse new disciplines, such as Administrative Science, Management Science, Operations Research, and Organizational Theory—*competitors* of traditional accounting in the sense that the information they provide may be more useful to management than traditional accounting information—which are typically interdisciplinary arrangements of traditional disciplines. They are made up of parts of such basic disciplines as Economics, Sociology, Psychology, Mathematics, Statistics, Political Science, Neurology, Servomechanism Engineering, Anthropology and Advanced Computer Design.[2]

With the expansion of accounting measurements comes the expansion of accounting disclosures for covering wealth-structures to socioeconomic structures, and from being limited to the measurement and communication of economic data to the measurement and communication of data revealing socioeconomic activities that use economic resources.[3] The expansion of accounting disclosures dictates the expansion of the following characteristics of disclosure (see Exhibit 3.1):

1. An expansion of the scope of users from shareholders, creditors, managers, and the general public to public groups.

2. An expansion of the scope of users from evaluating economic progress, enabling base assessments and aiding investment decisions to providing for intercompany coordination, meeting specific user information needs, and developing public confidence in firm activities.

3. An expansion of the type of information from transaction-based monetary valuations of internal activities of the firm to internal and external data to reveal both internal activities and the environmental setting of the internal activities of a socioeconomic nature.

4. An expansion of measurement techniques from arithmetic and the bookkeeping system to the total management science area.

5. An expansion of the quality of disclosure from excellent in terms of past needs to improved relevance for specific decisions.

6. An expansion of disclosure devices from conventional financial statements to multimedia disclosures based on the psychology of human communications.[4]

These expansions are influenced and motivated by a series of attitudes of "theorists" influencing accounting. The following theories are representative:

Exhibit 3.1
Scope of Disclosures

Disclosure Characteristic	Current Situation	Current Trends	Future Possibilities
1. Users	Shareholders, creditors, managers, and general public	Interest groups of shareholders, creditors, managers, and general public	Greatly expanded; general public groups
2. Uses	To evaluate economic progress, enable tax assessments, and aid investment decisions	To plan company activities, motivate control activities, and improve investment decisions	To provide for intercompany coordination, meet specific user information needs, and develop public confidence in firm activities
3. Types of Information	Transaction-based monetary valuations of internal activities of the firm	Accruals and motivational valuations of internal activities	Internal and external data to reveal both internal activities and the environmental setting of the internal activities of a socioeconomic nature
4. Measurement Techniques	Arithmetic and the bookkeeping system	Expanding into computer-based storage, probability measures, and limited mathematical analyses	Further expansion into the total management-science area
5. Quality of Disclosures	Excellent in terms of past needs, although the reliability of different items varies	Attempts to narrow the use of alternative principles and define the materiality concept	Improved relevance for specific decisions without reducing reliability of accounting disclosures
6. Disclosure Devices	Numerical reports such as balance sheet, income statement, and various managerial-structured reports	Charts, information rooms, and computer printouts as supplements to structured numerical reports	Multimedia disclosures based on the psychology of human communications

Source: Bedford, Norton M., *Extensions in Accounting Disclosure,* © 1973, p. 73. Reprinted by permission of Prentice-Hall, Inc., Upper Saddle River, N.J.

1. The theory of the "right to know" identifies both the general public and the owners as having a "right" to information which should concern accountants in the performance of the disclosure function.

2. The theory of "information overload" suggests limitations in human information processing of expanded accounting disclosures

and considerations for contracting the amount of information disclosed and compressing the disclosed information itself.

3. The theory of "retrieved systems" leaves to the accountant the function of production and storage of data, and presenting the users
with either an information self-retrieval system or an information
project retrieval system.

4. The theory of "relevance" is used to determine the relevant disclosure requirements, and supports the disclosure of additional information having a high relevance evaluation, such as human assets,
market value, and nonfinancial measures.

5. The theory of "preciseness" dictates a rigor of analysis and unam-
biguous concepts.[5]

The clear implication of Bedford's proposals is an expanded disclosure-based
notion of fairness.

Lev's Theory of Equitable and Efficient Accounting Policy

Lev proposed a theory of equitable and efficient accounting policy.[6] Lev
argued that progress in addressing the fundamental accounting policy issues
can be achieved by including the explicit concern of policy makers—equity
in the capital markets. This equity is defined as equality of opportunity or
symmetric information when all investors would be equally endowed with
information and risk-adjusted expected returns would be identical across
investors. This is important since both theoretical analysis and empirical
evidence show that the existing increased information asymmetry, or inequity, is associated with a lower number of investors, higher transaction costs,
lower liquidity of securities, thinner volumes of trade, and in general decreased social gains from trade. The equity concept will eliminate the major
source of inequity, which is the informational advantage held by informed
investors, lessen the generally harmful effects of the defensive measures that
are naturally taken by the uninformed, and as a result improve overall welfare. The standard for the equity concept is stated as follows: *"The interests
of the less informed investors should, in general, be favored in favor of those
of the more informed investors."*[7] This standard entails the systematic decrease of information asymmetries and offers accounting policy makers an
operational and rather simple "public interest" criterion for disclosure
choices. It is in fact based on a well-known principle in public policy:

It is possible in our society to argue for a government program to help
the poor. But, the argument is not that the poor, being part of the
winning coalition, should benefit at the expense of others. The argument is that by helping the poor we can make everyone better off, that

helping the poor is not merely a means to make the poor happier but a means to reduce crime, make us all feel less guilty, make the cities livable, etc. What may, from the standpoint of wealth, be (small) redistribution is defended as, from the standpoint of utility, a Pareto improvement.[8]

Gaa's User Primacy

Corporate financial reporting policy faces collective device problems that affect the allocation of resources to the production and consumption of information.[9] The following dilemma faces any standard-setting body set to resolve the allocation problems:

> Every policy choice represents a trade-off among different individual preferences, and possibly among alternative consequences, regardless of whether the policy-makers see it that way or not. In this sense, accounting policy choice can never be neutral. There is someone who is granted his preference, and someone who is not. The ethical question is what morality should guide the policy-making process.[10]

Two alternatives are available. A first alternative is that the interests of all individuals will be connected equally by the standard setter. It is a principle of neutrality that dictates the selection of standards that maximize social welfare. A second alternative is that the interests of one group of users would be given preferential treatment. One such group is the user group. This second alternative is therefore the user primacy guide to accounting reporting policy. Two versions of the user primacy principle have been advocated in the literature. The version known as the basic user primacy principle focuses on needs of users with limited abilities. As stated in *Objectives of Financial Statements,* published by the American Institute of Certified Public Accountants: "An objective of financial statements is to serve primarily those who have limited authority, ability, or resources to obtain information and who rely on financial statements as their principal source of information about an enterprise's economic activities."[11] Another version, known as extended user primacy, focuses on the information needs of sophisticated users. As stated in the Empirical Framework of the Financial Accounting Standards Board:

> Financial Reporting should provide information that is useful to present and potential investors and creditors and other users in making rational investment, credit, and similar decisions. The information should be comprehensible to those who have a reasonable understanding of business and economic activities and are willing to study the information with reasonable diligence.[12]

Gaa investigated the logical formulations of the user primacy principle, based on contemporary work in ethics and social and political philosophy, in which humans are regarded as decision makers, and in which principles governing individual and group behavior are the result of rational decisions. Basically:

> A standard setter would be established to enforce user primacy, thereby redressing an imbalance between investors (users) and managers. By acting in accordance with this principle, the standard setter aids all securities market agents in exploiting the potential trading gains provided by such a market. At the same time, investors are protected from possible losses arising from the basic relationship between them and managers of widely held corporations.[13]

The Jenkins Committee Findings

In order to improve external reporting, the AICPA established in 1991 the Special Committee on Financial Reporting, or Jenkins Committee (Edmond L. Jenkins was the chairman). The committee was charged with the determination of (a) the nature and extent of information that should be made available to others by management, and (b) the extent to which the auditors should report on the various elements of that information. After two years of research into the needs of external reporting users (investors, creditors, and their advisers), the committee issued in November 1993 its report titled *The Information Needs of Investors and Creditors.* The report identified the following areas in financial statements that should be enhanced to meet users' need for information.

1. Improve disclosure of business segment information.
2. Address the disclosures and accounting for innovative financial instruments.
3. Improve disclosures about the identity, opportunities, and risks of off-balance-sheet financing arrangements and reconsider the accounting for those arrangements.
4. Report separately the effects of core and noncore activities and events, and measure at fair value noncore assets and liabilities.
5. Improve disclosures about the uncertainty of measurements of certain assets and liabilities.
6. Improve quarterly reporting by reporting in the fourth quarter separately and including business segment data.

The report also proposed a comprehensive model including ten elements within five broad categories of information that are designed to fit the decision process users employ to make projections, value companies, or assess the prospect of loan repayment. These elements are as follows:

Financial and nonfinancial data

Financial statements and related disclosures

High-level operating data and performance measurements that management uses to manage the business

Management's analysis of the financial and nonfinancial data

Reasons for changes in the financial, operating, and performance-related data, and the identity and past effect of key trends

Forward-looking information

Opportunities and risks, including those resulting from key trends

Management's plans, including critical success factors

Comparison of actual business performance to previously disclosed opportunities, risks, and management's plans

Information about management and shareholders

Directors, management, compensation, major shareholders, and transactions and relationships among related parties

Background about the company

Broad objectives and strategies

Scope and description of business and properties

Impact of industry structure on the company.[14]

An illustration of the Special Committee's recommendations is presented in Appendix 3.A.

EXPANDED ACCOUNTING DISCLOSURES

The principle of fairness in presentation restricts recognition and disclosures to the situations governed by existing generally accepted accounting principles. The distinction between recognition and disclosure is emphasized by the Financial Accounting Standards Board (FASB). According to the FASB Concepts Statement no. 5, *Recognition and Measurement in Financial Statements of Business Enterprises,* "Recognition is the process of formally recording or incorporating an item into the financial statements of an entity as an asset, liability, revenue, expense, or the like. Recognition includes depiction of an item in both words and numbers, with the amount included in the totals of the financial statements."[15] The same statement states that "since recognition means depiction of an item in both words and numbers, with the amount included in the totals of the financial statements, disclosure by other means is not recognition. Disclosure of information about the items in financial statements and their measures that may be provided by notes or parenthetically on the face of financial statements, by supplementary information, or by other means of financial reporting is not a substitute for recognition in financial statements for items that meet recognition criteria."[16] The purposes of disclosure were stated as follows:

1. To describe recognized items and to provide relevant measures of those items other than the measures in the financial statements.
2. To describe unrecognized items and to provide a useful measure of those items.
3. To provide information to help investors and creditors assess risks and potentials of both recognized and unrecognized items.
4. To provide important information that allows financial statement users to compare within and between years.
5. To provide information in future case inflows or outflows.
6. To help investors assess return on their investment.[17,18]

Examples are provided in Exhibit 3.2. An analysis of required financial statement disclosures led to the following five conclusions:

1. The most frequently required disclosures relate to amounts recognized in the financial statements, particularly to desegregating them and providing relevant measures other than the measure in the financial statements—disaggregation of recognized amounts represents 26 percent of all required disclosures.
2. Six subjects—stockholders' equity, leases, pensions, income taxes, other postretirement employee benefits, and commitments and contingencies—account for 43 percent of all required disclosures; five standards—SFAS nos. 13, 87, 88, 106, and 109—account for 28 percent.
3. Few disclosures explicitly provide information on future cash inflows or outflows.
4. Few provide measures of unrecognized items.
5. Disclosure requirements have increased over time; few have been eliminated.[19]

All the previous calls for expanded disclosures are motivated by the principle of fairness in disclosure. The principle would advocate expanding the

Exhibit 3.2
Purposes of Required Financial Statement Disclosures

Purpose	Example
1. Describe recognized items and provide relevant measures of those items other than the measure in the financial statements.	
1a. Describe item.	General character, including interest rate, of recorded obligation.
1b. Disaggregate item.	Components of net periodic pension cost.
1c. Provide alternative measure.	Estimated fair value of on balance sheet financial instruments.
1d. Disclose critical assumption used in determining amounts.	Weighted-average expected long-term rates of return on pension plan assets.
2. Describe unrecognized items and provide a useful measure of those items.	
2a. Describe item.	Description of direct and indirect guarantees of indebtedness of others.
2b. Disaggregate item.	Amount of unrecognized deferred tax liability for temporary differences related to essentially permanent investments in foreign subsidiaries.
2c. Provide alternative measure.	Estimates of fair values of off balance sheet financial instruments.
2d. Disclose critical assumption used in determining amounts.	Significant assumptions used to estimate fair values of off balance sheet financial instruments.
3. Provide information to help investors and creditors assess risks and potentials of both recognized and unrecognized items.	
3a. Provide description of underlying economic situations.	Description of substantive defined benefit postretirement plan(s).[1]
3b. Provide description to assess risks and potentials.	Company's collateral policy for each significant concentration of credit risk.
3c. Provide maximum amount involved.	Number and option price for shares under options.
3d. Provide information necessary for user to make independent calculation of an amount.	Number of shares exercisable under stock options.
4. Provide information that allows financial statement users to compare numbers to other companies and between years.	
4a. Describe company's accounting policies and practices.	Method of inventory cost determination.
4b. Describe effects of unusual transactions.	Portion of income tax expense relating to extraordinary items, cumulative effect of an accounting change, and prior period adjustments.[2]
4c. Describe effect of unusual transaction on a prior year, or portion of a period.	In purchase business combinations, results of operations for immediately preceding period as though the companies had combined at the beginning of that period.
5. Provide information on future cash inflows or outflows.	Combined aggregate amount of maturities and sinking fund requirements for all long-term borrowings for each of the next five years.
6. Help investors assess return on their investment.	Preferred stock dividend rate.

---

[1] (3a) is similar to describe a recognized or unrecognized item (1a or 2a) except that (3a) descriptions typically provide general background information whereas items (1a) or (2a) provide specific information directly relating to the recognized or unrecognized item. To avoid unnecessary duplication we classify a disclosure as (3a) if it could be classified as either (3a) or (1a) or (2a).

[2] (4b) is similar to disaggregating a recognized amount (1b). However, (4b) disclosures go beyond disaggregation to enable financial statement users to adjust for unusual items, permitting comparability between years. We classify disclosures as (4b) that could be classified as (1b).

Source: Barth, Mary E., and Christine M. Murphy, "Required Financial Statement Disclosures: Purposes, Subject, Number, and Trends," *Accounting Horizons* (December 1994), p. 5. Reprinted with permission.

scope of accounting information beyond conventional accounting information. Examples of new accounting disclosures under this principle of fairness in disclosure include:

1. Value Added Reporting
2. Employee Reporting
3. Human Resource Accounting
4. Social Accounting and Reporting
5. Budgetary Information Disclosures
6. Cash Flow Accounting and Reporting

These are examined next. An analysis of the benefits and costs of additional disclosures is provided in Appendix 3.B.

VALUE ADDED REPORTING

Conventional reporting in most countries does not include value added reporting. Instead, it measures and discloses the financial position (through the balance sheet), the financial performance of the firm (through the income statement), and the financial conduct of the firm (through the statement of changes in the financial position). Although the usefulness of these statements has been established by their sheer use over time, they fail to give important information on the total productivity of the firm and the share of each team of members involved in the management of resources—shareholders, bondholders, employees, and the government. The value added statement can fill that crucial role. Value added is the increase in wealth generated by the productive use of the firm's resources before its allocation among shareholders, bondholders, workers, and the government. It can be easily computed by a modification of the income statement as follows:

Step 1: The income statement computes retained earnings as a difference between sales revenue, on one hand, and costs, taxes, and dividends, on the other:

$$R = S - B - DP - W - I - DD - T \qquad (1)$$

where

    R = retained earnings
    S = sales revenue
    B = bought-in materials and services
    DP = depreciation
    W = wages

I = interest
DD = dividends
T = taxes.

Step 2: The value added equation can be obtained by rearranging the profit equation as

$$S - B = W + I + DP + DD + T + R \qquad (2)$$

or

$$S - B - DP = W + I + DD + T + R \qquad (3)$$

Equation 2 expresses the gross value added method. Equation 3 expresses the net value added method. In both cases, the left part of the equation shows the value added among the groups involved in the managerial production team (the workers, the shareholders, the bondholders, and the government). The right-hand side is also known as the additive method and the left-hand side the subtractive method.

Exhibit 3.3 shows the value added statement can be derived from a regular income statement. The company in this example deducted bought-in materials, services, and depreciation from sales, to arrive at a value added of $2,240,000. The $2,240,000 was divided among the team of workers ($800,000), shareholders ($200,000), bondholders and creditors ($240,000), and the government ($600,000), leaving $400,000 for retained earnings.

The value added statement can be presented in either the gross or net format. The value added statement has some very good benefits:

1. With the disclosure of value added, employees get the satisfaction of knowing the value of their contribution to the total wealth of the firm.

2. Value added represents a better base for the computation of worker bonuses.

3. Value added information has been proven to be a good predictor of economic events and market reaction.[20,21,22,23]

4. Value added is a better measurement of size than sales.

5. Value added may be useful to employee groups because it can affect the aspirations and thoughts of its negotiating representatives.

6. Value added may be extremely useful in financial analysis by relating various crucial events to value added variables.

Exhibit 3.3
Deriving the Value Added Statement

A. The conventional income statement of a company for 19x8 was:

Sales		$4,000,000
Less: Materials used	$400,000	
Wages	$800,000	
Services Purchased	$1200,000	
Interest Paid	$240,000	
Depreciation	$160,000	
Profit Before Tax		$1200,000
Income Tax (assume 50% tax rate)		$600,000
Profit After Tax		$600,000
Less Dividend Payable		$200,000
Retained Earnings for the Year		$400,000

B. A value added statement for the same year would be:

Sales		$4000,000
Less: Bought-in Materials and Services and Depreciation		$1760,000
Value Added Available for Distribution or Retention		$2240,000
Applied as Follows		
To Employees		$800,000
To Providers of Capital		
Interest	$240,000	
Dividends	$200,000	$440,000
To Government		$600,000
Retained Earnings		$400,000
Value Added		$2240,000

EMPLOYEE REPORTING

With the emergence of employees and unions as potential users of accounting information, it also appears, and for a good many reasons, that the annual report to shareholders is not the all-inclusive document suitable for all unions. The solution lies in the production of a special report to employees and unions. This solution has been accepted in many country members of the Organization of Economic Cooperation and Development, including the United States, West Germany, Canada, France, Denmark, Norway, Sweden, and the United Kingdom. The idea has been accepted not only operationally but conceptually. For example, in the United Kingdom, the *Corporate Report* identifies *employees as a user group of published company annual reports.*[24]

Because different factors apply for employees and unions, each will be reviewed separately. In fact, a sample employment report, included as an appendix to the *Corporate Report,* showed quantitative data under the following headings:

1. Number employed (analyzed in various ways)
2. Location of employment
3. Age distribution of permanent work force
4. Hours worked during the year (analyzed)
5. Employee costs
6. Pension information
7. Education and Training (including costs)
8. Recognized trade unions
9. Additional information (race relations, health and safety statistics, etc.)
10. Employment ratios.[25]

Similarly, in Canada, the Canadian Institute of Chartered Accountants published a research study in June 1980 entitled *Corporate Reporting: Its Future Evolution.*[26] The report explicitly identified employees (past, present, and future) as users of corporate reports.

Firms do have a continuous communications process with employees through various media including plant-level discussions, quality circles, audiovisual presentations, and in-house journals and notices. The purpose of the formal employees' annual report is to provide an integrative and exhaustive report rather than a piecemeal approach. The same point is argued as follows:

It must be a report, capable of satisfying additional information needs of employees, rather than simply supply information already provided through alternative internal channels, or providing unwanted information. Unless the preparers of an annual report to employees can identify a genuine information void left by other internal communication media, and can justifiably believe that such a report can fill this void, then the report has no real justification.[27]

The literature has identified various aims and reasons for reporting to employees. A survey of the literature on financial reporting to employees between 1919 and 1979 identified the following reasons: (a) heralding changes, (b) presenting management propaganda, (c) promoting interest in understanding of company affairs and performance, (d) explaining management decisions, (e) explaining the relationship between employees, management, and shareholders, (f) explaining the objectives of the company, (g) facilitating greater employee participation, (h) responding to legislative or union pressure, (i) building company image, (j) meeting information requirements peculiar to employees, (k) responding to management fear of wage demands, strikes, and competitive disadvantages, and (l) promoting a higher degree of employee interest.[28] The same survey shows that the level of interest in reporting to employees reached a higher level when the following four socioeconomic factors were also present: (a) the use of new technology in the workplace, (b) increased mergers in the corporate sector, (c) the emergence of antiunion sentiment, and (d) fears of economic recessions.[29] It seems that management may have increased the level of employee reporting in reaction to the potential consequence of each of these factors or a combination of these factors. N. R. Lewis, L. D. Parker, and P. Sutcliffe, the authors of the survey, speculated that management may have hoped to:

1. allay fears of lost rank, skill, or employment through technological advances

2. counter fears of "bigness," monopoly power, employee relocation, and loss of identity through corporate mergers

3. take advantage of community antiunion sentiments by bypassing union communication channels (reporting directly to employees), emphasizing management prerogatives and the need to control wages and associated costs, and generally weakening the unions' potential to disrupt operations

4. prepare employees for hard times, confirm or dispel rumors of imminent company failure, allay fears of unemployment, and urge employees to greater efforts in difficult economic times.[30]

Dennis Taylor, Laurie Webb, and Les McGinley identified the following personal benefits which management might attempt to seek for itself by providing an annual report to employees in addition to using the conventional management-employee communication media: (a) building a favorable employee impression of the management group, (b) reducing the resistance of employees to changes initiated by management, and (c) providing a useful response to union pressure for more corporate financial information from management.[31] They also identified the following personal benefits which might accrue to employees with employee reporting: (a) having the basis for deciding whether to continue employment with the company or an organization section of the company; (b) having the basis for assisting the relative position of the employees within the corporate structure, particularly in terms of getting a "fair go"; and (c) understanding the image of the company, as a basis for deciding at a personal level whether to identify with this image.[32]

Finally, B. J. Foley and K. T. Maunders identified arguments supporting disclosure directly to employees: (a) feedback of information to employees will improve job performance via learning effects and also serve to increase motivation; (b) the role of employee reporting is crucial to effective worker participation which will contribute to the efficiency of the company; (c) the fundamental change in the nature of the firm and its "social responsibility" legitimizes employee reporting; (d) employee reporting may be seen by some employers as a possible way of resurrecting the concept of joint consultation as a means of avoiding unionization; (e) finally, the socialist tradition, with its ultimate objective of changing the basis of ownership and the control of resources, sees employee reporting as a step to increase "workers' control" and develop "workers' self confidence."[33] The case for employee reporting using the socialist argument rests on two fundamental principles:

1. That it is a technique which helps employees establish greater democratization of decision making in industry
2. That it may usefully act as a check on those aspects of the market system which result in adverse external effects in the form of pollution and environmental degradation.

HUMAN RESOURCE ACCOUNTING

Investors should be provided with all the information necessary to make efficient decisions. They need to have adequate information about one "neglected" asset of the firm—the human asset. At the same time, they can benefit from a knowledge of the extent to which the human assets of the firm have increased or decreased during a given period. The conventional accounting treatment of human resource outlays consist of expensing all human capital formation expenditures, while similar outlays on physical assets are *capitalized*. More valid treatments of human assets are needed rather than the mere expensing approach. That is the objective of human resource accounting (HRA). HRA focuses on the provision of adequate information on human assets. Like physical assets, individuals or groups may be attributed a value because of their ability to render future services to the firm. Various models have been proposed in the literature for accounting for the cost and value of human resources:

1. The historical, acquisition, or cost method consists of capitalizing all the costs associated with recruiting, selecting, hiring, and training, and then amortizing these costs over the useful life of the human asset, recognizing losses in cases of departure and recognizing any increase in the potential value of the asset.[34]

2. The replacement cost method consists of estimating the cost of replacing a firm's existing human resources. Such costs may include all the costs of recruiting, selecting, hiring, training, placing, and developing new employees to reach the level of competence of existing employees.[35]

3. The opportunity cost method suggests a competitive bidding process where investment center managers bid for the scarce employees they need to recruit.[36]

4. The discounted cash flow method computes the value of human capital of a person as the present value of his or her remaining future earnings from employment.[37]

5. The adjusted discounted future wages method suggests that the discounted future wages are adjusted by an "efficiency factor" intended to measure the relative effectiveness of the human capital of a given firm. The efficiency factor is measured by the ratio of the return on investment of the given firm to all other firms in the economy for a given period.[38]

6. The discounted future value method suggests forecasting a firm's present value of earnings at a normal rate of return and allocating a portion of this economic value of the firm to human resources based on their relative contribution.[39]

7. Many nonmonetary measures of human assets may be used, such as a simple inventory of skills and capabilities of people, the assignment of ratings or rankings to individual performance, and measurement of attitudes.

SOCIAL ACCOUNTING AND REPORTING

The measurement of social performance falls in the general area of social accounting.[40] Under this area there are four various activities that may be

Exhibit 3.4
The Characteristics of the Various Component Parts of Social Accounting

Division	Purpose	Area of Main Use	Time Scale	Measurements Used	Associated Areas
1. Social responsibility accounting (SRA)	Disclosure of individual items having a social impact	Private sector	Short term*	Levels I, II, mainly nonfinancial and qualitative	Employee reports, human resource accounting, industrial democracy
2. Total impact accounting (TIA)	Measures the total cost (both public and private) of running an organization	Private sector	Medium and long term	Financial AAA Level III	Strategic planning, cost-benefit analysis
3. Socioeconomic accounting (SEA)	Evaluation of publicly funded projects involving both financial and nonfinancial measures	Public sector	Short and medium term	Financial, nonfinancial, Levels II and III	Cost-benefit analysis, planned programmed budgeting systems, zero-based budgeting, institutional performance indicators
4. Social indicators accounting (SLA)	Long-term nonfinancial quantification of societal statistics	Public sector	Long term	Nonfinancial quantitative AAA Level II	National income accounts, census statistics

*Normally short term to fit annual reporting patterns.
Source: Reprinted by permission of the publisher from "A Suggested Classification for Social Accounting Research," by M. R. Mathews, *Journal of Accounting and Public Policy* 3 no. 3, p. 202. Copyright 1984 by Elsevier Science Inc.

delineated: social responsibility accounting (SRA), total impact accounting (TIA), socioeconomic accounting, and social indicators accounting.[41] Exhibit 3.4 shows the characteristics of the various component parts of social accounting. One can see that the general concept and disclosure of social performance are products of SRA and TIA, and social accounting is appropriately defined as "the process of selecting firm-level social performance variables, measures and measurements procedures; systematically developing information useful for evaluating the firm's social performance, and communication of such information to concerned social groups, both within and outside the firm."[42] This is a good conceptual framework for social accounting, proposed by K. V. Ramanathan, and comprises three objectives and six concepts. This framework applies equally to SRA and TIA.

A question arises about who is "pushing" for corporate social reporting. Are they to the right or to the left of the political spectrum? R. Gray et al. presented corporate social reporting (CSR) as a dialectic between four positions: "(1) The extreme left-wing of politics ('left-wing radicals'); (2) the acceptance of the *status quo*; (3) the pursuit of subject/intellectual property rights; (4) the extreme right-wing of politics (the 'pristine capitalists' or 'right-wing radicals.' "[43] The second group appears to represent those true advocates of corporate social reporting. They are represented by people

1. who assume that the purpose of CSR is to enhance the corporate image and hold the, usually implicit, assumption that corporate behavior is fundamentally benign;
2. who assume that the purpose of CSR is to discharge an organization's accountability under the assumption that a social contract exists between the organization and society. The existence of this social contract demands the discharge of social accountability;
3. who *appear* to assume that CSR is effectively an extension of traditional financial reporting and its purpose is to inform investors.[44]

Various arguments are used for the measurement and disclosure of social performance.

1. The first argument is that of *social contract.* Implicitly, it is assumed that organizations ought to act in a manner that maximizes social welfare, as if a social contract existed between the organization and society. By doing so, organizations gain a kind of organizational legitimacy vis-à-vis society. While the social contract may be assumed to be implicit, various societal laws may render certain covenants of the contract more explicit. These laws that constitute the rules of the game in which organizations choose to play become the terms of the social contract.[45] Through these implicit and explicit laws, society defines the rules of accountability for organizations.

The state, however, plays a primary role in the formulation of these laws and the specification of the rules of the game. In the U.S. contract, these laws and the general concern with social performance created a need for tracking environmental risk. With the 1989 SEC requirement that companies disclose any potential environmental cleanup liabilities they may face under the federal Superfund law, the 1990 annual reports of companies started the disclosure process. The 10k disclosures, added to the host of required filings with state and federal environment agencies, led to the creation of data banks that provided information on companies specializing in the tracking of environmental risk. Examples of these companies include Ersite, based in Denver; Environmental Audits, in Lyonville, Pennsylvania; the Environmental Risk Information Center in Alexandria, Virginia; the Petroleum Information Corporation, Littleton, Colorado; Toxicheck, in Birmingham, Michigan; Vista Environmental Information in San Diego; Environmental Data Resources in Southport, Connecticut.[46] This new industry gives a glimpse of a future characterized by concerned shareholders regarding the social performance of firms and more accurate and reliable information on the environmental risks of U.S. corporations.

2. A second argument is that of *social justice.* Three theories of justice— John Rawls' theory of justice, as presented in his book *A Theory of Justice,*[47]

Robert Nozick's "entitlement theory" as presented in his book *Anarchy, State, and Utopia*,[48] and A. Gerwith's theory of justice as presented in *Reason and Morality*[49]—contain principles for evaluating laws and institutions from a moral standpoint. Both Rawls' and Gerwith's models argue for a concept of fairness favorable to social accounting (see Chapter 2).

3. The third argument is that of *users' needs*. Basically, users of financial statements need social information for their revenue allocation decisions. An argument may be made by some that shareholders are conservative and care only about dividends. In fact, according to a recent survey of shareholders, they want corporations to direct resources toward cleaning up plants, stopping environmental pollution, and making safer products.[50] As a result, Marc Epstein advises corporations to do the following in order to manage expenditures on social concerns:

- Integrate corporate awareness of social, ethical and environmental issues into corporate decisions at all levels, and make sure such concerns have representation on the board of directors;
- Develop methods to evaluate and report on the social and environmental impacts of corporate activities;
- Modify the corporate structure to set up a mechanism to deal with social, environmental and ethical crisis. Then a company can be a crisis-prepared organization rather than a crisis-prone organization. Companies that do not prepare themselves for crises simply flounder;
- Create incentives for ethical, environmental and socially responsible behavior on the part of employees and integrate those incentives into the performance evaluation system and corporate culture. Unless this is institutionalized it never enters the corporate culture and significant, permanent change cannot occur;
- Recognize that if the environment is to be cleaned up, business must take a leadership role in the reduction of pollutants and the wise use of natural resources.[51]

There is, however, a lack of normative and/or descriptive models on the users' needs in terms of social information.

4. The fourth argument is that of *social investment*. Basically, it is assumed that an *ethical investor* group is now relying on social information provided in annual reports for making investment decisions. The disclosure of social information becomes, therefore, essential if investors are going to consider properly the negative effects of social awareness expenditures on earnings per share, along with any compensating positive effects that reduce risk or create greater interest from a particular investment clientele. Some argue

that the risk-reducing effects will more than compensate for social awareness expenditures: "Between firms competing in the capital markets those perceived to have the highest expected future earnings in combination with the lowest expected risk from environmental and other factors will be most successful at attracting long term funds."[52]

Others believe that "ethical investors" form a clientele that responds to demonstrations of corporate social concern.[53] Investors of this type would like to avoid particular investments entirely for ethical reasons and would prefer to favor socially responsible corporations in their portfolios.[54] A survey by J. Rockness and P. F. Williams identifies an emerging consensus on the primary characteristics of social performance among fund managers.[55] The performance factors—environmental protection, treatment of employees, business relations with repressive regimes, product quality and innovation, and defense criteria—are considered investment criteria by most of the managers.

An emerging theory of social investment is provided by S. T. Bruyn who suggests that "social and economic values can be maximized together, and this creative synergism is the practical direction taken by social investors today.[56] Bruyn's investor is assumed to contribute to the development of a social economy design to promote human values and institutions, as well as self-interests. The social investor bases investment decisions not only on economic and financial considerations, but also on sociologically grounded considerations. Both "social inventions" and technological inventions hold an expectation of profit and economic development. With regard to accountability, social investors, while concerned with the management of profits and scarce resources, are also interested in the corporations' accountability to other stakeholders in the environment besides stockholders.

BUDGETARY INFORMATION DISCLOSURES

Faced with the challenge from diverse users to develop more relevant financial reporting techniques, accountants and nonaccountants alike have recommended that forecasted information can be incorporated into financial statements. Proposals vary from the suggestion that budgetary data be disclosed to the suggestion that public companies provide earnings forecasts in their annual or interim reports and prospectuses. One objective of financial reporting set forth in the "Trueblood Report" supports this type of disclosure: "An objective of financial statements is to provide information useful for the predictive process. Financial forecasts should be provided when they will enhance the reliability of users' prediction."[57]

Although the objective does not constitute a strong recommendation for corporate financial forecasts, steps have been taken to ensure that forecasts are included in accounting reports. In Great Britain, the revised version of the English *City Code on Takeovers and Mergers* requires profit forecasts to be included in takeover-bid circulars and prospectuses.[58] In the English case, the interest of the accounting profession was created by the requirement that not only must "the assumptions, including the commercial assumptions," be stated but the "accounting bases and calculation must be examined and reported on by the auditors or consultant accountants."[59] In the United States, in February 1973, the SEC first announced its intention to require companies disclosing the forecasts to conform with certain rules to be laid down by the Commission. In April 1976, in reaction to public criticism, the SEC called for voluntary filings of forecasts. The SEC's amended position presents some problems in terms of (1) the definition of earnings forecasts, (2) whether disclosure should be mandatory or optional, and (3) the possible advantages of such disclosures.

The first problem concerns determining which forecasted items are to be disclosed. The two possible solutions are disclosing budgets or disclosing probable results (forecasts). This distinction may be made because budgets are prepared for internal use and, for motivational reasons, may be stated in a way that differs from expected results. Y. Ijiri makes the distinction as follows: "Forecasts are estimates of what the corporation considers to be the most likely to occur, whereas budgets may be inflated from what the corporation considers to be most likely to occur in order to take advantage of the motivational function of the budget."[60] From the point of view of the user, therefore, the disclosure of forecasts, rather than budgets, may be more relevant to his or her decision-making needs. In fact, the trend seems to be in favor of the disclosure of forecasts of specific accounts in general and earnings in particular.

The second problem is whether the disclosure of earnings forecasts should be mandatory or optional. Each position may be easily justified. The principal argument in favor of mandatory disclosure is that it creates a similar and uniform situation for all companies. However, mandatory disclosure could create an unnecessary burden in terms of competitive advantage, and certain firms would have to be viewed as exceptions (for example, private companies, companies in volatile industries, companies in the process of major changes, and companies in developmental stages).[61] Another argument against mandatory disclosure is that some firms lack adequate technology, experience, and competence to disclose forecasts adequately and that the outlays to correct this situation may create an unnecessary burden on these firms. Such a firm may doubt the benefits of a forecasts-disclosure procedure that justifies the cost of installing a new reporting system.

The third problem concerns the desirability of forecast publication. Several arguments have been advanced against the reporting of corporate financial forecasts. One argument is that both companies and analysts have been unsuccessful in accurately forecasting earnings. R. A. Daily points out that budgeted "information must be reasonably accurate to be relevant; otherwise the investors will have no confidence in the information and consequently not utilize it."[62] Both his study and D. L. McDonald's study[63] support the contention that, on average, management earnings forecasts are likely to be materially inaccurate. A number of factors may affect the accuracy of forecasts, for example, the length of time covered by the forecasts, the nature of the industry in which the company operates, the external environment, and the degree of sophistication and experience of the company making the forecast. Ijiri classifies the primary issues involved in corporate financial forecasts as (1) reliability, (2) responsibility, and (3) reticency.[64] *Reliability* is related to the relative accuracy of the forecasts; *responsibility,* to the possible large liabilities of firms making forecasts and accountants auditing these forecasts; and *reticency,* to the degree of silence and inaction of firms that are at a competitive disadvantage due to forecast disclosure. Similarly, R. K. Mautz suggests that three kinds of differences must be considered in evaluating the overall usefulness of published forecasts:

- Differences in the forecasting abilities of publicly owned firms
- Differences in the attitudes with which managements in publicly owned companies might be expected to approach the forecasting task
- Differences in the capacities of investors to use forecasts.[65]

Finally, given the difficulties associated with identifying and estimating forecasts, to what is an accountant expected to attest? Mautz suggests the following range of possibilities: (1) arithmetic accuracy, (2) internal integrity of the forecast data, (3) consistency in the application of accounting principles, (4) adequacy of disclosure, (5) reasonableness of assumptions, and (6) reasonableness of projections.[66]

CASH FLOW ACCOUNTING AND REPORTING

A dominant characteristic in early views of the purpose of financial statements is the *stewardship function.* According to this view, management is entrusted with control of the financial resources provided by capital suppliers. Accordingly, the purpose of financial statements is to report to concerned parties to facilitate the evaluation of management's stewardship. To accomplish this objective, the reporting system favored and deemed essential and superior to others is the *accrual system.* Simply stated, the *accrual basis of accounting* refers to a form of record keeping that records not only transactions that result from the receipt and disbursement of cash but also the amounts that the entity owes others and that others owe the entity.[67] At the core of this system is the *matching* of revenues and expenses. Interest in the accrual method has generated a search for the "best" accrual method in general and the "ideal income" in particular. For a long time, this accounting paradigm governed the evaluation of accounting alternatives and the asset-valuation and income-determination proposals. However, this approach was constantly challenged by proponents of *cash flow accounting.* The *cash flow basis of accounting* has been correctly defined as the recording not only of cash receipts and disbursements of the period (the *cash* basis of accounting) but also of the *future cash flows* owed to or by the firm as a result of selling and transferring the title to certain goods (the *accrual* basis of accounting).[68] The advocacy of cash flow accounting is more evident in a questioning of the importance and efficacy of accrual accounting and a shift toward the cash flow approach in security analysis.[69]

The question of the superiority of accrual accounting over cash flow accounting is central to the determination of the objectives and the nature of financial reporting. Accrual accounting facilitates the evaluation of management's stewardship and is essential to the matching of revenues and expenses, which is required to properly align efforts and accomplishments. The efficiency of the accrual system has been questioned, however. Thomas states that all allocations are arbitrary and incorrigible and recommends the minimization of such allocations.[70] D. Hawkins and W. Campbell report a shift in security analysis from earnings-oriented valuation approaches to cash flow-oriented valuation approaches.[71] Many decision-usefulness theorists advocate a cash flow accounting system based on the investor's desires to predict cash flows.[72,73] Most advocates of cash flow accounting feel that the problems of asset valuation and income determination are so formidable that they warrant the derivation of a separate accounting system and propose the inclusion of a comprehensive cash flow statement in company reports. For instance, T. A. Lee describes how cash flow accounting and net-realizable-value accounting can be combined in a series of articulating statements that provide more relevant information about cash and cash management than either system can provide individually.[74]

Cash flow accounting is viewed by supporters as superior to conventional accrual accounting because:

1. A system of cash flow accounting might provide an analytic framework for linking past, present, and future financial performance.[75]

2. From the perspective of investors, the projected cash flow would reflect both the company's ability to pay its way in the future and its planned financial policy.[76]

3. A price-discounted flow ratio would be a more reliable investment indicator than the present price-earnings ratio, due to the numerous arbitrary allocations used to compute earnings per share.[77]

4. Cash flow accounting may be used to correct the gap in practice between the way in which an investment is made (generally based on cash flows) and the way in which the results are evaluated (generally based on earnings).[78]

The important question remaining is whether or not cash flow accounting will be restored to its predominant position as an important and relevant source of financial information. All trends seem to indicate that the answer is in the affirmative. Witness the following eloquent and optimistic statement:

Of all the available systems of financial reporting, cash-flow accounting is one of the most objective and understandable. It attempts to state facts in financial-accounting terms, without the accountant having to become involved in making subjective judgements as to which period the data relate. And it is expressed in terms that should be familiar to all nonaccountants—cash resources and flows are things that anyone in a developed economy has to administer from day to day. Thus, cash-flow reports are potentially comprehensible, a matter that is of increasing concern to accountants as the number of report users and groups increases year by year.[79]

How would users react to cash flow information? Evidence to date seems to indicate that security analysts use earnings information more often than they use cash flow information in their professional reports.

CONCLUSIONS

The principle of fairness in disclosure calls for an expansion of the conventional disclosures to include new information that may be very relevant to decision making by both managers and external users of accounting information. These new forms of reporting will include (a) value added reporting, (b) employee reporting, (c) human resource accounting, (d) social accounting, (e) budgetary information disclosures, and (f) cash flow accounting and reporting.

NOTES

1. Bedford, N. M., *Extensions in Accounting Disclosure* (Englewood Cliffs, N.J.: Prentice-Hall, 1973).

2. Ibid., 19.

3. Ibid., 40.

4. Ibid., 23.

5. Ibid., 144.

6. Lev, Baruch, "Toward a Theory of Equitable and Efficient Accounting Policy," *The Accounting Review* (January 1988): 1–22.

7. Ibid., 13.

8. Friedman, D., "Many, Few, One: Social Harmony and the Shrunken Choice Set," *American Economic Review* (March 1980): 231.

9. Gaa, James C., "User Primacy in Corporate Financial Reporting: A Social Contract Approach," *The Accounting Review* (July 1986): 435.

10. American Accounting Association, *Report of the Committee on the Social Consequences of Accounting Information* (Sarasota, Fla.: AAA, 1977), 248.

11. American Institute of Certified Public Accountants, *Objectives of Financial Statements* (New York: AICPA, 1973), 17.

12. Financial Accounting Standards Board, *Statement of Financial Accounting Concepts No. 1: Objectives of Financial Reporting of Business Enterprises* (Stamford, Conn.: FASB, 1978), vii.

13. Gaa, "User Primacy in Corporate Financial Reporting," 435.

14. AICPA, Special Committee on Financial Reporting, *Improving Business Reporting—A Customer Focus* (New York: AICPA, 1994), 9.

15. Financial Accounting Standards Board Concepts Statement No. 5, *Recognition and Measurement in Financial Statements of Business Enterprises* (Stamford, Conn.: FASB), par. 6.

16. Ibid., par 9.

17. Johnson, L. Todd, "Research on Disclosure," *Accounting Horizons* (March 1992): 102.

18. Barth, Mary E., and C. M. Murphy, "Required Financial Statement Disclosures: Purposes, Subject, Number and Trends," *Accounting Horizons* (December 1994): 4.

19. Ibid., 1.

20. Riahi-Belkaoui, Ahmed, "Earnings-Returns Relation Versus Net Value Added-Returns Relation: The Case for Nonlinear Specification," *Advances in Quantitative Analysis of Finance and Accounting* (Forthcoming).

21. Riahi-Belkaoui, Ahmed, and Ali Fekrat, "The Magic in Value Added: Merits of Derived Accounting Indicator Numbers," *Managerial Finance* 20, no. 9 (1994): 16–26.

22. Riahi-Belkaoui, Ahmed, and Ronald D. Picur, "Explaining Market Relations: Earnings Versus Value Added Data," *Managerial Finance* 20, no. 9 (1994): 44–55.

23. Riahi-Belkaoui, Ahmed, "The Information Content of Value-Added, Earnings and Cash Flows: U.S. Evidence," *The International Journal of Accounting* 28, no. 2 (1993): 140–146.

24. Accounting Standards Steering Committee, *The Corporate Report* (London: Accounting Standards Steering Committee, 1975), 200.

25. Ibid., 88–91.

26. Stamp, Edward, *Corporate Reporting: Its Future Evolution* (Toronto: Canadian Institute of Chartered Accountants, 1980).

27. Taylor, Dennis, Laurie Webb, and Les McGinley, "Annual Reports to Em-

ployees: The Challenge to the Corporate Accountant," *Chartered Accountant in Australia* (May 1979): 33.

28. Lewis, N. R., L. D. Parker, and P. Sutcliffe, "Financial Reporting to Employees: The Pattern of Development 1919 to 1979," *Accounting, Organizations and Society* (June 1984): 278.

29. Ibid., 281.

30. Ibid.

31. Taylor, Webb, and McGinley, "Annual Reports to Employees," 35.

32. Ibid., 36.

33. Foley, B. J., and K. T. Maunders, *Accounting Information Disclosure and Collective Bargaining* (London: Macmillan, 1977), 27–34.

34. Jaggi, B. L., "The Valuation of Human Resources in a Firm," *The Chartered Accountant* (India) (March 1974): 467–470.

35. Flamholtz, E. G., "Human Resource Accounting: Measuring Potential Replacement Costs," *Human Resource Management* (Spring 1973): 8–16.

36. Hekimian, J. S., and J. G. Jones, "Put People on Your Balance Sheet," *Harvard Business Review* (January–February 1967): 108.

37. Lev, B., and A. Schwartz, "On the Use of the Economic Concept of Human Capital," *The Accounting Review* (January 1971): 105.

38. Hermanson, R. H., "Accounting for Human Assets," Occasional Paper No. 14 (East Lansing, Mich.: Bureau of Business, Graduate School of Business, Michigan State University, 1964).

39. Ibid.

40. See Belkaoui, A., *Socio-Economic Accounting* (Westport, Conn.: Quorum Books, 1984).

41. Mathews, M. R., "A Suggested Classification for Social Accounting Research," *Journal of Accounting and Public Policy* 3 (1984): 199–222.

42. Ramanathan, K. V., "Toward a Theory of Corporate Social Accounting," *The Accounting Review* (July 1976): 518.

43. Gray, R., D. Owen, and K. Maunders, "Corporate Social Reporting: Emerging Trends in Accountability and the Social Contract," *Accounting, Auditing and Accountability* 1, no. 1 (1988): 8.

44. Ibid., 5.

45. Ibid., 13.

46. See Henriques, D. B., "Tracking Environmental Risk," *New York Times* (April 28, 1991): 13.

47. Rawls, J. A., *A Theory of Justice* (Cambridge, Mass.: Harvard University Press, 1971).

48. Nozick, R., *Anarchy, State, and Utopia* (New York: Basic Books, 1974).

49. Gerwith, A., *Reason and Morality* (Chicago: University of Chicago Press, 1978).

50. Epstein, Marc J., "What Shareholders Really Want," *New York Times* (April 28, 1991): 11.

51. Ibid.

52. See "Pollution Price Tag: 71 Billion Dollars," *U.S. News and World Report* (August 17, 1970): 41.

53. American Accounting Association, "Report of the Committee on External Reporting," *The Accounting Review* 44, Supplement (1969): 41.

54. American Accounting Association, "Report of the Committee on Environmental Effects of Organization Behavior," *The Accounting Review* 44, Supplement (1969): 88.

55. Rockness, J., and P. F. Williams, "A Descriptive Study of Social Responsibility Mutual Funds," *Accounting, Organizations and Society* (1988): 397–411.

56. Bruyn, S. T., *The Field of Social Investment* (Cambridge: Cambridge University Press, 1987), 12.

57. *Objectives of Financial Statements,* Report of the Study Group on the Objectives of Financial Statements (New York: AICPA, 1973), 13.

58. *The City Code on Takeovers and Mergers* (Great Britain), revised February, 1972.

59. Ibid., Rule 16.

60. Ijiri, Yuji, "Improving Reliability of Publicly Reported Corporate Financial Forecasts," in *Public Reporting of Corporate Financial Forecasts,* ed. P. Prakash and A. Rappaport (Chicago: Commerce Clearing House, 1974), 169.

61. Sycamore, R. J., "Public Disclosure of Earnings Forecasts by Companies," *The Chartered Accountant Magazine* (May 1974): 72–75.

62. Daily, R. A., "The Feasibility of Reporting Forecasted Information," *The Accounting Review* (October 1971): 686–692.

63. McDonald, Daniel L., "An Empirical Examination of the Reliability of Published Predictions of Future Earnings," *The Accounting Review* (July 1973): 502–559.

64. Ijiri, "Improving Reliability of Publicly Reported Corporate Financial Forecasts," 163.

65. Mautz, Robert K., "A View from the Public Accounting Profession," in *Public Reporting of Corporate Financial Forecasts,* ed. Prakash and Rappaport, 102.

66. Ibid., 110.

67. Gross, M. J., Jr., *Financial and Accounting Guide for Nonprofit Organizations* (New York: The Ronald Press, 1972).

68. Hicks, B. E., *The Cash-Flow Basis of Accounting,* Working Paper No. 13 (Sudbury, Ontario: Laurentian University, 1980).

69. Hawkins, D., and W. Campbell, *Equity Valuation: Models, Analysis, and Implications* (New York: Financial Executives Institute, 1978).

70. Thomas, A. L., *The Allocation Problem in Financial Accounting Theory,* Accounting Research Study No. 3, (Sarasota, Fla.: American Accounting Association, 1969); *The Allocation Problem: Part Two,* Accounting Research Study No. 9, (Sarasota, Fla.: American Accounting Association, 1974).

71. Hawkins and Campbell, *Equity Valuation,* 5.

72. Staubus, G. J., *A Theory of Accounting to Investors* (Berkeley, Calif.: University of California Press, 1961).

73. Revsine, L., *Replacement-Cost Accounting* (Englewood Cliffs, N.J.: Prentice-Hall, 1973).

74. Lee, T. A., "Reporting Cash Flows and Net Realizable Values," *Accounting and Business Research* (Spring 1981): 163–170.

75. Lawson, G. H., "Cash-Flow Accounting I & II," *The Accountant* (October 28–November 4, 1971): 586–589.

76. Lee, T. A., "A Case for Cash-Flow Accounting," *Journal of Business Finance* (1972): 27–36.

77. Ashton, R. H., "Cash-Flow Accounting: A Review and a Critique," *Journal of Business Finance and Accounting* (Winter 1976): 63–81.

78. Lee, T. A., "Cash-Flow Accounting and Reporting," in *Developments in Financial Reporting*, ed. T. A. Lee (Oxford: Philip Allan, 1981), 148–170.

79. Govindarajan, V., "The Objectives of Financial Statements: An Empirical Study of the Use of Cash Flow and Earnings by Security Analysts," *Accounting, Organizations and Society* (December 1980): 392.

REFERENCES

Calls for Expanded Disclosures

American Institute of Certified Public Accountants. Special Committee on Financial Reporting. *Improving Business Reporting—A Customer Focus*. New York: AICPA, 1994.

Barth, Mary E., and Christine M. Murphy. "Required Financial Statement Disclosures: Purposes, Subject, Number and Trends." *Accounting Horizons* (December 1994): 1–22.

Bedford, N. M. *Extensions in Accounting Disclosures*. Englewood Cliffs, N.J.: Prentice-Hall, 1973.

Elliott, Robert K., and Peter D. Jacobson. "Costs and Benefits of Business Information Disclosure." *Accounting Horizons* (December 1994): 80–96.

Gaa, James. "User Primacy in Corporate Financial Reporting: A Social Contract Approach." *The Accounting Review* (July 1986): 435–456.

Johnson, L. Todd. "Research on Disclosure." *Accounting Horizons* (March 1992): 101–103.

Lev, Baruch. "Toward a Theory of Equitable and Efficient Accounting Policy." *The Accounting Review* (January 1988): 1–22.

Value Added Reporting

Accounting Standards Steering Committee. *The Corporate Report*. London: Accounting Standards Steering Committee, 1975.

Ball, R. J. "The Use of Value Added in Measuring Managerial Efficiency." *Business Ratios* (Summer 1968): 5–11.

Burchell, Stuart, Colin Clubb, and Anthony G. Hopwood. "Accounting and Its Social Context: Towards a History of Value Added in the United Kingdom." *Accounting, Organizations and Society* 10, no. 4 (1985): 381–413.

Cameron, S. "Added Value Plan for Distributing ICI's Wealth." *Financial Times* (January 7, 1977).

Copeman, George. "Wages of Added Value." *Management Today* (June 1977): 84–88, 138.

Cox, Bernard. *Value Added: An Application for the Accountant Concerned with Industry.* London: Heinemann, 1978.

DaCosta, Vickers. "Testing for Success," mimeo. London, 1979.

Department of Trade. *The Future of Company Reports.* London: HMSO, 1977.

Engineering Employers Federation. *Business Performance and Industrial Relations.* London: Kogan Page, 1977.

Gilchrist, R. R. *Managing for Profit: The Value Added Concept.* London: Allen and Unwin, 1971.

Gray, Sidney J., and K. T. Maunders. *Value Added Reporting Uses and Measurement.* London: Association of Certified Accountants, 1980.

Jones, F. C. *The Economic Ingredients of Industrial Success.* London: James Clayton Lecture, Institution of Mechanical Engineers, 1976.

Lev, B., and J. A. Ohlson. "Market Bank Empirical Research: A Review, Interpretation and Extensions." *Journal of Accounting Research* (Supplement, 1982): 239–322.

Maunders, K. T. "The Decision Relevance of Value Added Reports." In *Frontiers of International Accounting: An Anthology,* ed. Frederick D. Choi and Gerhard G. Mueller. Ann Arbor, Mich. UMI Research Press, 1985, pp. 230–251.

Meek, Gary K., and Sidney J. Gray. "The Value Added Statement: An Innovation for U.S. Companies?" *Accounting Horizons* (June 1988): 73–81.

Morley, Michael F. "Value Added Reporting." In *Development in Financial Reporting,* ed. Thomas A. Lee. London: Philip Allan, 1981, pp. 251–269.

———. *The Value Added Statement.* London: Gee and Co., for the Institute of Chartered Accountants of Scotland, 1978.

———. "The Value Added Statement: A British Innovation." *Chartered Accountant Magazine* (May 1978): 31–34.

———. "The Value Added Statement in Britain." *Accounting Review* (July 1979): 618–689.

New, C. "Factors in Productivity That Should Not Be Overlooked." *Times* (February 1, 1978).

"Our Manufacturing Industry: The Missing $100,000 Million." *National Westminster Bank Quarterly Review* (May 1978): 8–17.

Rahman, M. Zubaidur. "The Local Value Added Statement: A Reporting Requirement for Multinationals in Developing Host Countries." *International Journal of Accounting* (February 2, 1990): 87–98.

Renshall, Michael, Richard Allan, and Keith Nicholson. *Added Value in External Financial Reporting.* London: Institute of Chartered Accountants in England and Wales, 1979.

Riahi-Belkaoui, Ahmed. "Earnings-Returns Relation Versus Net Value Added-Returns Relation: The Case for Nonlinear Specification." *Advances in Quantitative Analysis of Finance and Accounting* (Forthcoming).

———. "The Information Content of Value Added, Earnings, and Cash Flows: U.S. Evidence." *The International Journal of Accounting* 28 no. 2 (1993): 140–146.

———. "Net Value Added as an Explanatory Variable for Returns." *Managerial Finance* 20, no. 9 (1994): 55–64.

Riahi-Belkaoui, Ahmed, and James Bannister. "Value Added and Corporate Control." *Journal of International Financial Management and Accounting* (Autumn 1991): 241–252.

Riahi-Belkaoui, Ahmed, and Ali Fekrat. "The Magic in Value Added: Merits of Derived Accounting Indicator Numbers." *Managerial Finance* 20, no. 9 (1994): 3–15.

Riahi-Belkaoui, Ahmed, and Philip Karpik. "The Relative Relationship between Systematic Risk and Value Added Variables." *Journal of International Financial Management and Accounting* (Autumn 1989): 259–276.

Riahi-Belkaoui, Ahmed, and Ellen Pavlik. "The Effects of Ownership Structure on Value Added Based Performance." *Managerial Finance* 20, no. 9 (1994): 16–26.

Riahi-Belkaoui, Ahmed, and Ronald D. Picur. "Explaining Market Returns: Earnings Versus Value Added Data." *Managerial Finance* 20, no. 9 (1994): 44–55.

Ruggles, R., and N. D. Ruggles. *National Income Accounts and Income Analysis,* 2nd edition. New York: McGraw-Hill, 1965.

Rutherford, B. A. "Five Fallacies about Value Added." *Management Accounting* (September 1981): 31–33.

Sinha, Gokul. *Value Added Income.* Calcutta: Book World, 1983.

Suojanen, W. W. "Accounting Theory and the Large Corporation." *Accounting Review* (July 1954): 391–398.

Woodmansay, M. *Added Value: An Introduction of Productivity Schemes.* London: British Institute of Management, 1978.

Human Resource Accounting

Acland, D. "The Effects of Behavioral Indicators on Investor Decisions: An Exploratory Study." *Accounting, Organizations and Society* 1, no. 8 (1976): 133–142.

Alexander, M. O. "An Accountant's View of the Human Resource." *The Personnel Administrator* (November–December 1971): 9–13.

American Accounting Association. *Report of the Committee on Accounting for Human Resources. Committee Reports,* Supplement to *The Accounting Review* 48 (1973): 169–185.

———. *Report of the Committee on Accounting for Human Resources. Committee Reports,* Supplement to *The Accounting Review* 49 (1974): 115–126.

Ansari, S. L., and D. T. Flamholtz. "Management Science and the Development of Human Resource Accounting." *The Accounting Historian's Journal* (Fall 1978): 11–35.

Becker, S. *Human Capital.* New York: National Bureau of Economic Research, 1962.

Biagioni, L. F., and P. Ogan. "Human Resource Accounting for Professional Sports Teams." *Management Accounting* (November 1977): 25–29.

Brummet, R. L., E. G. Flamholtz, and W. C. Pyle. "Human Resource Measurement: A Challenge for Accountants." *The Accounting Review* (April 1968): 217–224.

Cannon, J. A. "Applying the Human Resource Accounting Framework to an International Airline." *Accounting, Organizations and Society* 1, no. 8 (1976): 253–263.

Caplan, E. H., and S. Landekick. *Human Resource Accounting: Past, Present, and Future.* New York: National Association of Accountants, 1974.

Carper, W. B., and J. M. Posey. "The Validity of Selected Surrogate Measures of Human Resource Value: A Field Study." *Accounting, Organizations and Society* 1, no. 8 (1976): 143–152.

Conger, Jay A., and Rabindra N. Kanungo. "The Empowerment Process: Integrating Theory and Practice." *Academy of Management Review* 13 (1988): 471–482.

Dermer, J., and J. P. Siegel. "The Role of Behavioral Measures in Accounting for Human Resources." *The Accounting Review* (January 1974): 88–97.

Dittman, D. A., H. A. Juris, and L. Revsine. "On the Existence of Unrecorded Human Assets: An Economic Perspective." *Journal of Accounting Research* (Spring 1976): 49–65.

———. "Unrecorded Human Assets: A Survey of Accounting Firms' Training Programs." *The Accounting Review* (April 1980): 640–648.

Elias, N. "The Effects of Human Assets Statements on the Investment Decision: An Experiment." *Empirical Research in Accounting: Selected Studies* (1972): 215–233.

Elliott, Robert K. "The Third Wave Breaks on the Shores of Accounting." *Accounting Horizons* (December 1991): 61–81.

Flamholtz, E. "Assessing the Validity of a Theory of Human Resource Value: A Field Study." *Empirical Research in Accounting: Selected Studies* (1972): 241–266.

———. *Human Resource Accounting.* Encino, Calif.: Dickenson, 1974.

———. *Human Resource Accounting.* San Francisco.: Jossey-Bass, 1985.

———. "Human Resource Accounting: Measuring Potential Replacement Costs." *Human Resource Management* (Spring 1973): 8–16.

———. "A Model for Human Resource Valuation: A Stochastic Process with Service Rewards." *The Accounting Review* (April 1971): 253–267.

———. "The Impact of Human Resource Valuation on Management Decisions: A Laboratory Experiment." *Accounting, Organizations and Society* 1 no. 8 (1976): 153–165.

———. "The Process of Measurement in Managerial Accounting: A Psycho-technical Systems Perspective." *Accounting, Organizations and Society* 5, no. 8 (1980): 31–42.

———. "The Theory and Measurement of an Individual's Value to an Organization." Ph.D. dissertation, University of Michigan, 1969.

———. "Towards a Psycho-technical Systems Paradigm of Organizational Measurement." *Decision Sciences* (January 1979): 71–84.

———. "Valuation of Human Assets in a Securities Brokerage Firm: An Empirical Study." *Accounting, Organizations and Society* 12, no. 7 (1987): 309–318.

Flamholtz, E., and R. Coff. "Valuing Human Resources in Buying Service Companies." *Mergers and Acquisitions* (January–February 1989): 40–44.

Flamholtz, E., and G. Geis. "The Development and Implementation of a Replacement Cost Model for Measuring Human Capital: A Field Study." *Personnel Review* (UK) 13, no. 2 (1984): 25–35.

Flamholtz, E., G. Geis, and R. J. Perle. "A Markovian Model for the Valuation of

Human Assets Acquired by an Organizational Purchase." *Interfaces* (November–December 1984): 11–15.

Flamholtz, E., and R. A. Kaumeyer, Jr. "Human Resource Replacement Cost Information and Personnel Decisions: A Field Study." *Human Resource Planning* (Fall 1980): 111–138.

Flamholtz, E., and T. Lundy. "Human Resource Accounting for CPA Firms." *CPA Journal* 45 (October 1975): 45–51.

Flamholtz, E., J. Bell Oliver, and R. Teague. "Subjective Information Valuation and Decision-Making." Paper presented at the American Accounting Association Annual Meeting, Atlanta, Georgia, 1976.

Flamholtz, E., and D. G. Searfoss. "Developing an Integrated System." In *Human Resource Accounting.* San Francisco: Jossey-Bass, 1985, pp. 336–355.

Flamholtz, E., and J. B. Wollman. "The Development and Implementation of the Stochastic Rewards Model for Human Resource Valuation in a Human Capital Intensive Firm." Paper presented at the XXIII International Meeting of the Institute of Management Sciences, Athens, Greece, 1977.

Frantzreb, R. B., L.L.T. Landau, and D. P. Lundberg. "The Valuation of Human Resources." *Business Horizons* (June 1974): 73–80.

Friedman, A., and B. Lev. "A Surrogate Measure for the Firm's Investment in Human Resources." *Journal of Accounting Research* (Autumn 1974): 235–250.

Gambling, T. E. "A System Dynamic Approach to HRA." *The Accounting Review* (July 1974): 538–546.

Harrell, A. M., and H. D. Klick. "Comparing the Impact of Monetary and Nonmonetary Human Asset Measures on Executive Decision-Making." *Accounting, Organizations and Society* 5, no. 12 (1980): 393–400.

Jaggi, B., and S. Lau. "Toward a Model for Human Resource Valuation." *The Accounting Review* (April 1974): 321–329.

Lau, A. H., and H. Lau. "Some Proposed Approaches for Writing Off Capitalized Human Resource Assets." *Journal of Accounting Research* (Spring 1978): 80–102.

Ogan, P. "Application of a Human Resource Value Model: A Field Study." *Accounting, Organizations and Society* 1, no. 8 (1976): 195–218.

Schwan, E. S. "The Effects of Human Resource Accounting Data on Financial Decisions: An Empirical Test." *Accounting, Organizations and Society* 1, no. 8 (1976): 219–237.

Tsaklanganos, A. A. "Human Resource Accounting: The Measure of a Person." *CA Magazine* (May 1980): 44–48.

Woodruff, R. L., Jr. "Human Resource Accounting." *Canadian Chartered Accountant* (September 1970): 2–7.

Employee Reporting

Bougen, P., and S. Odgen. "Power in Organizations: Some Implications for the Use of Accounting in Industrial Relations." *Managerial Finance* (1981): 22–26.

Burchell, S., Clubb, C., Hopwood, A. G., Hughes, J., and Nahapiet, J. "The Roles of Accounting in Organizations and Society." *Accounting, Organizations and Society* 5 (1980): 5–28.

Cooper, D., and S. Essex. "Accounting Information and Employee Decision Making." *Accounting, Organizations and Society* (1977): 201–217.

Craft, J. A. "Information Disclosure and the Role of the Accountant in Collective Bargaining." *Accounting, Organizations and Society* (1981): 97–107.

Craig, R., and R. Hussey. *Employee Reports: An Australian Study.* Sydney, Australia: Enterprise Australia, 1981.

Foley, B. J., and K. T. Maunders. *Accounting Information Disclosure and Collective Bargaining.* London: Macmillan, 1977.

Gogarty, J. P. "What Employees Expect to Be Told." *Management Accounting* (U.K.) (November 1975): 359–360.

Gospel, H. "The Disclosure of Information to Trade Unions: Approaches and Problems." *Industrial Relations Journal* (1978): 18–26.

Granof, M. F. "Financial Evaluation of Labor Contracts." *Management Accounting* (July 1973): 42.

Holmes, G. "How UK Companies Report." *Accountancy* (November 1977): 66.

Hussey, R. "Developments in Employee Reporting." *Managerial Finance* 7 (1981): 12–16.

———. *Employees and the Employee Report.* London: Touche Ross, 1978.

———. *Who Reads Employee Reports?* Oxford: Touche Ross, 1974.

Hussey, R. and R. J. Craig. *Keeping Employees Informed.* Sydney, Australia: Butterworth, 1982.

Institute of Chartered Accountants in England and Wales. *The Reporting of Company Financial Results to Employees.* London, 1976.

Jack, H. H. "The Accountant's Role in Labor Relations." *Management Accounting* (October 1973): 60.

Jackson-Cox, J., J. E. Thirkell, and J. McQueeney. "The Disclosure of Company Information to Trade Unions: The Relevance of the ACAS Code of Practice on Disclosure." *Accounting, Organizations and Society* (June 1984): 253–273.

Jenkins, C. "A Trade Unionist's Viewpoint on Financial Information Requirement." *Management Accounting* (November 1975): 359.

Jones, D.M.C. "Designing Accounts to Inform More Effectively." *Management Accounting* (November 1975): 359.

Lau, C. T., and M. Nelson. *Accounting Implications of Collective Bargaining.* Ontario: The Society of Management Accountants in Canada, 1981.

Lewis, N. R., L. D. Parker, and P. Sutcliffe. "Financial Reporting to Employees: The Pattern of Development 1919 to 1979." *Accounting, Organizations and Society* (June 1984): 275–285.

———. "Financial Reporting to Employees: Towards a Research Framework." *Accounting and Business Research* (Summer 1984): 229–239.

Martin, R. "Providing an Employee Report." *Management Accounting* (September 1977): 341–348.

Maunders, K. T. "Employee Reporting." In *Development in Financial Reporting,* ed. Thomas A. Lee. London: Philip Allan, 1981, pp. 171–195.

Maunders, K. T., and B. J. Foley. "Accounting Information, Employees and Collective Bargaining." *Journal of Business Finance and Accounting* (Spring 1974): 109–127.

———. "How Much Should We Tell Trade Unions?" *Accounting Age* (February 22, 1974): 340–346.

Miller, J. "Financial Information for Employees." *Accounting* (May 29, 1975): 690.
Ogden, S., and P. Bougen. "A Radical Perspective on the Disclosure of Information to Trade Unions." *Accounting, Organizations and Society* 10, no. 2 (1985): 211–224.
Owen, D. L., and A. J. Lloyd. "The Use of Financial Information by Trade Union Negotiators in Plant Level Collective Bargaining." *Accounting, Organizations and Society* 10 (1985): 329–350.
Palmer, J. R. *The Use of Accounting Information in Labor Negotiations.* New York: National Association of Accountants, 1977.
Parker, L. D. "Financial Reporting to Corporate Employees: A Growing Practice in Australia." *Chartered Accountant in Australia* (March 1977): 5–9.
Pfeffer, J. "Power and Resource Allocation in Organizations." In B. Staw and G. Salancik, eds., *New Directions in Organizational Behavior.* Chicago: St. Clair Press, 1977, pp. 12–32.

Social Accounting

Belkaoui, A. *Socio-Economic Accounting.* Westport, Conn.: Quorum Books, 1984.
Belkaoui, A., and P. Karpik. "Determinants of the Corporate Decision to Disclose Social Information." *Accounting, Auditing and Accountability Journal* 2 (1989): 36–41.
Boal, K. B., and N. Peery. "The Cognitive Structure of Corporate Social Responsibility." *Journal of Management* 11 no. 3 (1985): 71–82.
Bruyn, S. T. *The Field of Social Investment.* Cambridge: Cambridge University Press, 1987.
Carroll, A. B. "A Three-Dimensional Conceptual Model of Corporate Social Performance." *Academy of Management Review* 4 (1979): 479–505.
Davis, K. "The Case For and Against Business Assumptions of Social Responsibilities." *Academy of Management Journal* 16 (1973): 312–322.
Post, J. E. *Corporate Behavior and Social Change.* Reston, Va.: Reston Publishing, 1978.
Preston, C. E., and J. E. Post. *Private Management and Public Policy: The Principle of Public Responsibility.* Englewood Cliffs, N.J.: Prentice-Hall, 1975.

Public Reporting of Corporate Financial Forecasts

Abdel-Khalik, A. R., and R. Thompson. "Research on Earnings Forecasts: The State of the Art." *Accounting Journal* (Winter 1977–78): 180–217.
Abdelsamad, M. H., and G. H. Gilbreath. "Publication of Earnings Forecasts: A Report of Financial Executives Opinions." *Managerial Planning* (January–February 1978): 26–30.
American Institute of Certified Public Accountants. *Presentation and Disclosure of Financial Forecasts.* New York: AICPA, 1975.
Asebrook, R., and D. Carmichael. "Reporting on Forecasts: A Survey of Attitudes." *Journal of Accounting* (August 1973): 38–48.
Backer, A. "Reporting Profit Expectations." *Management Accounting* (February 1972): 33–37.

Barefield, R. M., and E. Comiskey. "The Accuracy of Analysts' Forecasts of Earnings Per Share." *Journal of Business Research* (July 1975): 241–252.

Barnes, A., S. Sadan, and M. Schiff. "Afraid of Publishing Forecasts." *Financial Executive* (November 1977): 52–58.

Cash Flow Accounting

American Accounting Association, Committee on External Reporting. "An Evaluation of External Reporting Practices," a Report of the 1966–1968 Committee on External Reporting, *The Accounting Review* (Supplement, 1969): 79–123.

Ashton, R. H. "Cash-Flow Accounting: A Review and a Critique." *Journal of Business Finance and Accounting* (Winter 1976): 63–81.

Barlev, B., and H. Levy. "On the Variability of Accounting Income Numbers." *Journal of Accounting Research* (Autumn 1979): 305–315.

Belkaoui, A. "Accrual Accounting and Cash Accounting: Relative Merits of Derived Accounting Indicator Numbers." *Accounting and Business Research* (Summer 1983): 299–312.

Climo, T. "Cash-Flow Statements for Investors." *Journal of Business Finance and Accounting* (Autumn 1976): 3–16.

APPENDIX 3.A:
FAUXCOM INC.

Current Year Review

In the information technology industry, change is the name of the game. As a result, success is dependent on a company's ability to anticipate change and having the flexibility to manage it.

Over the years, change has been both a friend and a foe to FauxCom. In 1987, the Company was a leading manufacturer of dedicated word processing systems; by 1989 it was completely out of the business. In 1986, FauxCom acquired a personal computer manufacturer and enjoyed several years of growth in a high-margin business; by 1992 the industry had shifted to a high volume, low margin business where annual unit sales must increase substantially in order to maintain operating profits at prior year levels. In 1989, the Company entered the emerging system design and installation business; by 1993 competition had increased to where differentiation is now based primarily on price.

By any measure, 1993 was a successful year for FauxCom. Revenue grew to $2.5 billion, a 55% increase over 1992 while core earnings increased from $59 million to $122 million. Core earnings per share totalled $2.38 in 1993 compared with $1.19 in 1992. Cash flows from operating activities, both core and noncore, totalled $155 million.

These results reflect Company's ability to both anticipate and manage change.

The PC Segment maintained its reputation for innovation and quality through the introduction of several low price products which gained immediate market acceptance as well as its decision to quickly recall and discontinue a high-end product line when reliability concerns surfaced. Distribution channels were expanded with the successful launch of a direct marketing program as well as increased sales efforts in markets outside of the U.S. Cost controls and productivity improvements allowed the Company to increase unit sales by over 80% while the average number of employees decreased. The Integration Segment continued to develop with growth coming from both internal efforts as well as from the acquisition of the Chicago-based InfoSource Consulting Group.

In the accompanying report, we have summarized our view of the information technology industry, what changes lie ahead as well as our plans to deal with those changes.

February 15, 1994

Financial and Nonfinancial Data

Five Year Summary of Business Data

(dollars in millions except share data)	1993	1992	1991	1990	1989[1]
FauxCom, Inc. and Subsidiaries					
Revenue	$2,484	$1,605	$1,288	$1,231	$ 941
Core earnings	122	59	57	90	74
Net income (loss)	96	74	52	89	(139)
Long-term debt	146	168	113	41	—
Stockholders' equity	862	753	677	629	768
Current ratio	2.32	2.72	2.86	2.67	3.61
Ratio of debt to total capitalization	0.14	0.18	0.17	0.09	0.00
Ratio of revenue to average assets	1.91	1.47	1.38	1.61	1.44
Cash flows provided by core operating activities	$ 125	$ 174	$ 98	$ 138	$ 72
Capital expenditures	124	148	125	96	200
Weighted average shares outstanding (thousands)	51,200	49,700	48,300	47,100	46,200
Per share data					
Core earnings	$ 2.38	$ 1.19	$ 1.18	$ 1.91	$ 1.60
Net income (loss)	1.88	1.49	1.07	1.89	(3.01)
Cash flows from core operating activities	2.44	3.50	2.03	2.93	1.56

[1] Non-core expense in 1989 includes a $212 million after-tax charge relating to the Company's word-processing segment which was classified as a discontinued operation.

Revenue *($ millions)*

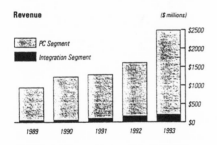

Return on Equity *(%)*

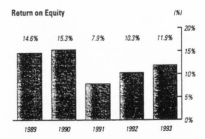

Assets *($ millions)*

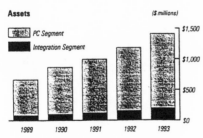

Five Year Summary of Business Data

(dollars in millions)	1993	1992	1991	1990	1989
PC Segment Data					
Revenue	$2,277	$1,441	$1,181	$1,169	$ 890
Core earnings	118	60	63	95	79
Gross margin (%)	28.1	33.9	41.2	44.0	44.2
Working capital	$ 393	$ 331	$ 269	$ 218	$ 187
Property, plant and equipment	373	355	320	277	251
Cash flows provided by core operating activities	122	167	103	139	68
PC Units sold (thousands)	1,085	588	347	308	238
Server Units sold (thousands)	27	15	8	4	1
Average number of employees	3,439	3,741	4,725	4,910	4,480
Revenue per employee (thousands)	$ 662	$ 385	$ 250	$ 238	$ 199

Results per Employee

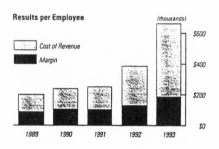

PC Segment Gross Margin

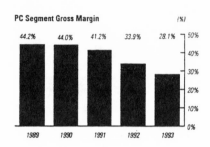

Five Year Summary of Business Data

(dollars in millions)	1993	1992	1991	1990	1989
Integration Segment Data					
Revenue	$ 207	$ 164	$ 107	$ 62	$ 51
Core earnings	13	7	2	2	2
Gross margin (%)	25.6	23.2	22.4	27.4	27.4
Working capital	$ 44	$ 32	$ 27	$ 12	$ 10
Cash flows provided by core operating activities	18	11	(1)	5	4
Number of design and installation contracts	3,060	2,667	2,046	1,359	1,438
Number of system maintenance contracts	7,714	5,538	3,016	1,551	943
Average number of employees	1,518	1,400	1,170	760	735
Revenue per employee (thousands)	$ 136	$ 117	$ 91	$ 82	$ 69
Design and installation contract backlog	24	31	19	11	7

Offices at Year-End

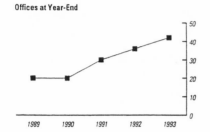

Results per Employee *(thousands)*

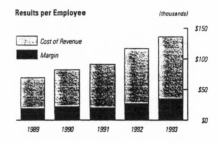

Consolidated Financial Statements

Consolidated Balance Sheet

For the years ended December 31, 1993 and 1992
(dollars in millions)

	1993	1992
Assets		
Current assets		
Cash and equivalents	$ 44	$ 46
Accounts receivable, net	427	285
Inventories, net	361	244
Deferred tax assets	19	16
Other core current assets	18	15
Non-core current assets	—	53
	869	659
Property, plant and equipment	396	381
Other long-term assets	137	135
Non-core assets	10	9
Total assets	$1,412	$1,184
Liabilities		
Current liabilities		
Accounts payable and accrued expenses	$ 363	$ 238
Income tax payable	9	2
Current portion of long-term debt	3	2
	375	242
Long-term debt	143	166
Deferred tax liabilities	32	23
Total liabilities	550	431
Stockholders' Equity		
Common stock, $1 par value; shares authorized 80 million; shares issued		
and outstanding 48,520,000 and 47,100,000, respectively	49	47
Additional paid-in capital	419	401
Retained earnings	411	315
Cumulative comprehensive income excluded from net income	(17)	(10)
Total stockholders' equity	862	753
Total liabilities and stockholders' equity	$1,412	$1,184

The accompanying notes to consolidated financial statements are an integral part of these statements.

Consolidated Statement of Core Earnings and Net Income

For the years ended December 31, 1993 and 1992

(dollars in millions except share data)	1993	1992
Revenue	$2,484	$1,605
Cost of revenue	1,792	1,079
Gross margin	692	526
Operating expenses		
Selling and marketing	193	156
Depreciation and amortization	130	133
Research and development	88	75
General and administrative	77	64
	488	428
Pretax core earnings	204	98
Income taxes related to core earnings	82	39
Core earnings	122	59
Non-core items and interest expense	(45)	25
Income tax expense (benefit) related to non-core items and interest expense	(19)	10
	(26)	15
Net income	$ 96	$ 74
Per share		
Core earnings	$ 2.38	$ 1.19
Net income	1.88	1.49
Weighted average shares outstanding (thousands)	51,200	49,700

The accompanying notes to consolidated financial statements are an integral part of these statements.

Consolidated Statement of Cash Flows		
For the years ended December 31, 1993 and 1992		
(dollars in millions)	1993	1992
Cash flows from operating activities		
Core		
Core earnings	$ 122	$ 59
Depreciation and amortization	130	133
Deferred tax provision	(3)	(2)
(Increase) decrease in accounts receivable, net	(141)	(54)
(Increase) decrease in inventories, net	(110)	(18)
(Increase) decrease in other current assets	(2)	5
Increase (decrease) in accounts payable and accrued expenses	122	54
Increase (decrease) in income tax payable	7	(3)
Cash flows provided by core activities	125	174
Non-core		
Non-core items and interest expense	(26)	15
Deferred tax provision	9	3
Realized gain on sale of land held for investment, net of income taxes	(6)	—
(Increase) decrease in accounts receivable from U.S. Department of Justice	53	(53)
Cash flows provided by (used in) non-core activities	30	(35)
Cash flows from investing activities		
Purchases of property, plant and equipment	(124)	(148)
Investment in joint venture	—	(15)
Loan to supplier	(15)	—
Acquisition of subsidiaries	(8)	(10)
Proceeds from sale of land held for investment, net of income taxes	7	—
Cash flows used in investing activities	(140)	(173)
Cash flows from financing activities		
Proceeds from long-term debt borrowings	147	173
Repayments of long-term debt	(170)	(143)
Proceeds from exercise of stock options	6	6
Cash flows provided by (used in) financing activities	(17)	36
Net increase (decrease) in cash	(2)	2
Cash and equivalents at beginning of year	46	44
Cash and equivalents at end of year	$ 44	$ 46
Cash flows from core activities per share	$ 2.44	$ 3.50

The accompanying notes to consolidated financial statements are an integral part of these statements.

Consolidated Statement of Stockholders' Equity

(in millions)	Shares	Common stock	Paid-in capital	Retained earnings	Cumulative comprehensive income excluded from net income	Total
Balances at December 31, 1991	46	$ 46	$387	$241	$ 3	$677
Net income	–	–	–	74	–	74
Tax benefit realized from stock purchase plans	–	–	8	–	–	8
Currency translation adjustment, net of income taxes	–	–	–	–	(13)	(13)
Exercise of stock options	1	1	6	–	–	7
Balances at December 31, 1992	47	47	401	315	(10)	753
Net income	–	–	–	96	–	96
Tax benefit realized from stock purchase plans	–	–	14	–	–	14
Currency translation adjustment, net of income taxes	–	–	–	–	(8)	(8)
Changes in unrealized appreciation of land held for investment, net of income taxes	–	–	–	–	1	1
Exercise of stock options	2	2	4	–	–	6
Balances at December 31, 1993	49	$ 49	$419	$411	$ (17)	$862

The accompanying notes to consolidated financial statements are an integegral part of these statements.

Notes to Consolidated Financial Statements

Note 1. Significant Accounting Policies

The following paragraphs summarize the significant accounting policies used in the preparation of the consolidated financial statements that the Company has selected from acceptable alternative accounting principles.

Cash equivalents

Marketable securities with original maturities of three months or less are carried at cost plus accrued interest which approximates market value.

Inventories

Inventories are stated at the lower of cost or market, cost being determined on a first-in, first-out basis.

Long-lived assets

Depreciation and amortization of property, plant, equipment and intangibles are computed by applying the straight-line method over the following estimated useful lives.

Asset Category	Estimated Useful Lives
Buildings	10 years
Machinery and equipment	5 years
Furniture and fixtures	5 years
Goodwill	5 years
Intangible assets	Life of asset

Core and Non-Core Assets, Liabilities, Revenues, Expenses, and Cash Flows

The financial statements distinguish between core and non-core assets, liabilities, revenues, expenses and cash flows. Core items are used in or result from continuing, recurring and usual operating activities. In contrast, items in the non-core category are used in or result from nonrecurring, unusual, and infrequent transactions or events and discontinued operations. Non-core earnings and cash flows also include the effects of interest income and expense. Non-core assets and liabilities are recorded at fair value with changes in unrealized appreciation or depreciation charged or credited directly to stockholders' equity. Land held for investment is the Company's only non-core asset. The accompanying balance sheet includes no non-core liabilities.

Revenue recognition

The Company recognizes revenue at the time products are shipped or services are provided. Provision is made currently for estimated product returns that may occur under programs that the Company has with certain third-party resellers as well as for the estimated cost of product warranties.

Foreign currency

The Company's foreign subsidiaries utilize the local currency as the functional currency for financial reporting purposes. Accordingly, local currency financial statements are translated into dollars at current rates of exchange with gains or losses resulting from translation included in the determination of comprehensive income. Cumulative translation adjustments are reflected in a separate component of stockholders' equity.

The Company periodically enters into forward and option contracts as one means of hedging its exposure to changes in foreign currency exchange rates. Gains and losses on these contracts are deferred and recognized as offsets to the foreign exchange gains and losses resulting from the designated transactions.

Loss contingencies

The Company recognizes contingent losses which are both probable and estimable. In this context, the Company defines probability as those events which are more likely than not to occur.

Note 2. Acquisitions

The Company acquired InfoSource, Inc. in January 1993 for $8 million and WestNet, Inc. in January 1992 for $10 million. These transactions were accounted for as purchase business combinations and, as a result, the amount by which the respective purchase prices exceeded the fair value of identifiable assets acquired and liabilities assumed was recorded as goodwill. Goodwill resulting from these acquisitions totaled $4.8 million and $5.3 million, respectively. Pro forma information reflecting the InfoSource acquisition as of January 1, 1992 has not been provided as the impact of that acquisition on 1992 pro forma core earnings is not significant.

Note 3. Inventories

Inventories consisted of the following at December 31.

(In millions)	1993	1992
Purchased components and materials	$214	$137
Work-in-process	72	47
Finished goods	90	75
	376	259
Less: valuation allowance	(15)	(15)
	$361	$244

Note 4. Property, Plant and Equipment

Property, plant and equipment consisted of the following at December 31.

(In millions)	1993	1992
Land	$ 10	$ 10
Buildings	345	254
Equipment	350	332
Furniture and fixtures	73	55
	778	651
Less: Accumulated depreciation	(382)	(270)
	$ 396	$ 381

Note 5. Other Long-Term Assets

Other long-term assets consisted of the following at December 31.

(In millions)	1993	1992
Investment in Predicta	$ 80	$ 80
Goodwill and other intangibles	42	53
Loan to supplier	15	—
Prepaid pension cost	—	2
	$137	$135

In 1989, the Company joined with nine of its primary component suppliers to form Predicta, a research and development partnership whose primary objective is to develop advanced PC technology. Under terms of the partnership agreement, each participant was required to fund its share of the permanent capital needed to develop a research and development facility in North Carolina. The Company's share of such capital contributions totaled $80 million and is recorded as its investment in Predicta. The Company is also required to fund its pro-rata share of Predicta's annual operating costs. The Company's share of these costs, which totaled $40 million in 1993 and $25 million in 1992, is classified within core earnings as research and development expense.

Selected financial data for Predicta as of and for the years ended December 31 is as follows.

(In millions)	1993	1992
Research contract revenue	$400	$250
Core earnings (loss)	3	(4)
Net income (loss)	3	(4)
Working capital	$210	$193
Total assets	580	607
Partner capital	800	800

In December 1993, the Company loaned $15 million to its primary disk drive supplier to finance the expansion of the supplier's primary manufacturing facility to support the Company's increasing requirements for disk drives.

The loan, which bears interest at prime plus 1% and is secured by the related facility expansion, is due in full in December 1998. Based upon the supplier's financial condition and the fact that the interest rate varies with market conditions, the Company believes that the fair value of the loan approximates its carrying value.

Note 6. Long-Term Debt

The Company maintains a line of credit with a group of banks which permits borrowings of up to $250 million. The line of credit expires in June 1995 at which time amounts outstanding become due and payable. Interest is payable at either the agent bank's prime rate or the short-term Eurodollar interbank offered rate (6% and 7.5% at December 31, 1993 and 1992, respectively). The agreement provides for a commitment fee at an annual rate of one quarter of one percent on the unused portion of the bank's commitment and a facility fee of one quarter of one percent on the entire commitment. Borrowings outstanding under this agreement totaled $139 million and $160 million at December 31, 1993 and 1992, respectively.

The line of credit agreement requires the Company to maintain compliance with certain financial covenants. The Company's compliance with these covenants at December 31 is summarized below.

Financial Covenants

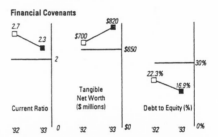

The Company leases equipment under the terms of non-cancellable lease agreements which generally do not exceed five years. The present value of future minimum lease payments, which totaled $7 million and $8 million in 1993 and 1992, respectively, is recorded as long-term debt in the accompanying consolidated balance sheet. As of December 31, 1993, these leases, which are secured by the related equipment, require future minimum payments of $4 million in 1994, $4 million in 1995 and $2 million in 1996.

The fair value of borrowings outstanding under the line of credit as well as the Company's lease obligations approximate the related carrying values.

Note 7. Income Taxes

Geographic sources of pre-tax core earnings for the years ended December 31 consisted of the following.

(In millions)	1993	1992
United States	$155	$ 68
Foreign	49	30
	$204	$ 98

Income tax expense for the years ended December 31 consisted of the following.

(In millions)	1993	1992
Currently payable		
Federal	$ 27	$ 23
State and local	11	12
Foreign	19	13
	57	48
Deferred		
Federal	7	(1)
State and local	4	(1)
	11	(2)
	$ 68	$ 46

A reconciliation of the U.S. statutory tax rate to the Company's effective tax rate on pre-tax core earnings for the years ended December 31 is as follows.

	1993	1992
Statutory tax rate	35.0%	34.0%
Taxes attributable to foreign, state and local taxes	6.0	6.0
Research and development credits	(3.0)	(2.0)
Other, net	2.0	2.0
Effective tax rate	40.0%	40.0%

Deferred income tax assets (liabilities) consisted of the following at December 31.

(In millions)	1993	1992
Liability for product warranties	$ 6	$ 4
Allowance for doubtful accounts	6	4
Inventory valuation allowance	6	6
Other	1	2
	19	19
Valuation allowance	—	—
	19	16
Depreciation	(26)	(18)
Other	(6)	(5)
	(32)	(23)
	$ (13)	$ (7)

Income tax payments totalled $50 million in 1993 and $47 million in 1992.

Note 8. Non-Core Items and Interest Expense

Non-core items and interest expense consisted of the following for the years ended December 31.

(In millions)	1993	1992
Discontinuation of product line	$ (43)	$ —
U.S. Department of Justice Sale	—	38
Interest expense	(12)	(14)
Realized gain on land held for investment	9	—
Interest income	2	2
Interest component of pension expense	(1)	(1)
	$ (45)	$ 25

In December 1992, the Company introduced a high-end PC product for sophisticated engineering applications. Product reliability concerns surfaced shortly after introduction as a result of the failure of certain key component parts and, as a result, the Company elected to recall the product in February 1993. After a thorough evaluation, the Company determined that the reliability concerns could not be overcome in a cost effective manner and, in March 1993, the decision was made to discontinue the product. In connection with this decision, the Company recorded a pre-tax charge of $43 million to write-off the product inventory and to provide for other related costs. The Company classified this charge as a non-core item in 1993 as this was the first time in the Company's history that a product was discontinued as a result of product reliability concerns.

During the fourth quarter of 1992, the Company negotiated the sale of approximately 115,000 PCs to the U.S. Department of Justice. This sale, which generated approximately $153 million of revenue and $38 million of gross profit, was classified as a non-core item due to the infrequent nature of a transaction this size.

In 1989, the Company identified approximately 100 acres of land adjacent to its domestic manufacturing facility as a non-operating asset held for investment or sale. At December 31, 1992, the carrying amount of the land approximated $9 million while the related unrealized appreciation totaled $7 million on a pre-tax basis. In March 1993, the U.S. Department of Transportation announced that a new regional airport would be developed within five miles of the property. This announcement had a positive impact on land values in the area including the value of the Company's land. The Company obtained an independent appraisal of the land in June 1993 which indicated a value of $20 million assuming that the property could be sold for the development of light industrial property. Based on the results of this appraisal, the land was written-up to its appraisal value. In late 1993, the Company sold 50 acres of the property for $10 million realizing a pre-tax gain of $9 million which is included as a non-core item. The following table summarizes 1993 activity relating to the Company's land held for investment or sale.

(in millions)	Historical Cost	Unrealized Appreciation	Carrying Amount
Balance, December 31, 1992	$ 2	$ 7	$ 9
Increase in value resulting from airport announcement	—	11	11
Sale of 50 acres	(1)	(9)	(10)
Balance, December 31, 1993	$ 1	$ 9	$ 10

Unrealized appreciation, which approximated $5 million on an after tax basis at December 31, 1993, is included in cumulative comprehensive income excluded from net income in the accompanying consolidated balance sheet.

Interest payments totalled $11 million in 1993 and $12 million in 1992.

Note 9. Employee Stock Option Plan

At December 31, 1993, there were 15 million shares of the Company's common stock reserved for issuance under an employee stock option plan which was approved by the stockholders in 1984. Options are granted at the fair market value of the Company's common stock on the date of grant and, as a result, no compensation expense has been recorded. Options granted under the plan vest after five years and must be exercised within ten years. At December 31, 1993, 230,000 options were exercisable at an average price of $3 per share. Option activity for the years ended December 31, 1992 and 1993 is as follows.

	Option Shares (in thousands)	Exercise Price Range Per Share	Weighted Average Exercise Price
Outstanding, December 31, 1991	7,330	$ 3-28	$ 7.45
1992 Activity			
Grants	1,500	$18-20	19.00
Exercises	(1,550)	$ 3-17	4.23
Cancellations	(110)	$ 3-28	12.05
Outstanding, December 31, 1992	7,170	$ 3-28	10.65
1993 Activity			
Grants	1,500	$28-32	30.00
Exercises	(1,420)	$ 3-28	3.79
Cancellations	(20)	$ 3-28	3.00
Outstanding, December 31, 1993	7,230	$ 3-32	16.04

Option shares outstanding under the plan at December 31, 1993 were held by 225 individuals. If all such shares were exercised as of that date, the number of common shares outstanding would increase by approximately 13%.

Note 10. Employee Benefits

The Company sponsors a defined benefit pension plant that covers substantially all of its U.S. employees. Benefits are based on years of service or the employee's compensation during the last five years of employment. Participants become fully vested upon attaining five years of service. The Company's policy is to contribute annually the maximum amount that can be deducted for federal income tax purposes. The Company also provides substantially all of its employees who retire with ten or more years of service with health insurance benefits. Benefits under this plan are based on years of service and in some cases require employee contributions. Benefits under this plan are generally paid as covered expenses are incurred.

Actuarial assumptions utilized in the determination of pension and retiree health costs and the related benefit obligations were as follows.

	1993	1992
Plan cost for the year		
Discount rate	8.5%	9.0%
Compensation increases	5.5	6.0
Return on assets	9.5	9.5
Health care cost trend (a)	12.0	12.5
Benefit obligations at year-end		
Discount rate	7.25	9.0
Compensation increases	4.25	6.0
Health care cost trend (a)	9.5	12.0

(a) Gradually declining to 6.6% after 2005.

Employer costs and funding for the pension and retiree health plans are as follows.

(in millions)	1993	1992
Plan cost		
Pension plan	$6	$5
Retiree health plan	3	2
Plan funding		
Pension plan	6	5
Retiree health plan	1	1

The following table compares the market value of assets with the present value of the related benefit obligations.

(in millions)	1993	1992
Pension plan		
Market value of assets	$48	$44
Projected benefit obligation	46	46
Retiree health plan		
Market value of assets	—	—
Accumulated benefit obligation	25	22

The actual return on pension plan assets was 12% in 1993 and 11.5% in 1992.

In February 1992, the Company instituted a defined contribution retirement plan that complies with Section 401(k) of the U.S. Internal Revenue Code. All U.S. employees who have completed one year of service are eligible to participate in the plan. The plan provides for Company matching contributions of 25% of employees' voluntary contributions up to 10% of their income. Company matching contributions approximated $2 million and $1.5 million in 1993 and 1992, respectively, while employee contributions totaled $8 million and $6 million, respectively.

Note 11. Measurement Uncertainties — Litigation

Product Liability — As of December 31, 1993, the Company had been named in a total of 28 lawsuits by individuals who claim that the keyboards on several of the Company's personal computer products caused them to suffer repetitive stress related injuries. Aggregate damages claimed in these suits approximate $20 million. These suits are all in the relatively early stages and trial dates have not been set.

The Company has previously been involved in three lawsuits of a similar nature. The first such case went to trial in 1990 with the jury finding in favor of the plaintiff and awarding damages of $200,000. The Company appealed this decision; however, the appellate court affirmed the trial court's ruling. The two remaining cases went to trial in 1992 with verdicts reached in favor of the Company.

The Company believes that its keyboards are not responsible for the alleged injuries and intends to defend itself vigorously in these matters. Although its experience in this type of suit has been favorable to date, should the pending cases go to trial, it is reasonably possible that decisions will be reached which are adverse to the Company.

Patent Infringement — In October 1993, Mortan Electronics, Inc. (MEI) filed a patent infringement suit against the Company in U.S. District Court seeking unspecified damages and an injunction prohibiting the Company from selling personal computers which allegedly infringe on certain of MEI's patents. The Company denies MEI's allegations and is vigorously defending itself in this matter.

The Company has been successful in previous patent infringement matters, however, the related defense costs have been substantial. In 1993, the Company accrued $2.5 million in costs, primarily legal fees, which it estimates will be incurred in defense of this matter.

Environmental — In September 1992, the Company received notification from the U.S. Environmental Protection Agency (EPA) that it may be a potentially responsible party (PRP) at the Middlesex Township Landfill Superfund Site (the Site) as a result of its waste disposal practices during years 1985-1987. The Company utilized an independent waste disposal company to dispose of certain manufacturing solvents during this period. The Company's records indicate that its involvement in the Site is insignificant. The Company provided the EPA with the information requested in its notification in January 1993. Additionally, the Company has joined with other PRP's to fund costs relating to a preliminary investigation of the Site. The Company's share of such costs to date has been insignificant.

Based upon information currently available as well as the opinion of counsel, the ultimate resolution of legal matters affecting the Company is not expected to materially impact it's financial position. Litigation and defense costs, however, could have a significant impact on core earnings in one or more future years.

Note 12. Measurement Uncertainties — Valuation Allowances

Allowance for Doubtful Accounts — The Company records a valuation allowance for accounts receivable which ultimately may not be collected. The Company regularly evaluates the allowance based on historical loss experience, specific problem accounts and general economic conditions in its geographic markets and adjustments are charged or credited to income. Although the Company believes that the allowance is adequate to provide for losses that are inherent in the year-end accounts receivable balance, there is a possibility that actual losses will differ from the amount estimated. An analysis of activity in the allowance for doubtful accounts during 1993 along with other data relating to accounts receivable is as follows.

(dollars in millions)	PC Segment	Integration Segment	Total
Allowance for doubtful accounts			
Beginning of year	$ 8.0	$ 1.5	$ 9.5
Provision for doubtful accounts	9.1	2.1	11.2
Charge-offs of bad debts	(3.9)	(1.2)	(5.1)
End of year	$13.2	$ 2.4	$ 15.6
Accounts receivable (before allowance)			
Beginning of year	$ 256	$ 39	$ 295
End of year	388	54	443
Days sales outstanding			
Beginning of year	62	82	65
End of year	60	92	64

On a consolidated basis, the provision for doubtful accounts increased by 51% from $7.4 million in 1992 to $11.2 million in 1993 because of increased sales activity and the resulting growth in the year-end accounts receivable balance. Charge-offs during 1993 totalled $5.1 million compared with $3.2 million in 1992 with the increase primarily resulting from the bankruptcy in early 1993 of one of the PC Segment's regional distributors.

Days sales outstanding for the PC Segment improved during the year in spite of increased sales as accounts less then 60 days represented 95% of the receivable balance at the end of the year compared with 89% at the beginning of the year. The increase in days sales outstanding for the Integration Segment is primarily attributable to competitive pressures which have required the Segment to offer extended payment terms on design and installation contracts. Accounts less than 60 days for the Integration Segment represented 71% of the receivable balance at the end of the year compared with 77% at the beginning of the year.

Inventory Valuation Allowance — With the rapid rate of technological change in the computer industry, the risk of excess or obsolete inventory is relatively high. Additionally, substantial decreases in unit selling prices increase the risk that product costs may exceed such prices. The Company closely monitors the market to anticipate product introductions that could adversely impact sales of its existing product line. Also, per unit margins are analyzed to determine if product costs exceed the related net realizable values.

The Company maintains a valuation allowance to ensure that the inventories of its PC Segment are stated at the lower of cost or market. On a regular basis, agings of inventories by product type, both on hand and at key points within the Company's distribution channels, are prepared and compared to expected customer demand. If sales for certain products are not expected to materialize or if the Company has knowledge of impending product introductions or reductions in unit selling prices, the aggregate exposure is determined and, if appropriate, the valuation allowance is increased with a charge to income. Although the Company believes that its inventories are stated at the lower of cost or market, it is possible that presently unforeseen events could occur that would impair the Company's ability to fully recover the net inventory carrying amount. An analysis of activity in the inventory valuation allowance during 1993 along with other data relating to inventories is as follows.

(in millions)

Inventory valuation allowance	
Beginning of year	$15.0
Provision to reduce inventory carrying values	8.5
Amounts charged against the allowance	(8.5)
End of year	$15.0
Inventory (before allowance)	
Beginning of year	$ 259
End of year	$ 376
Days of supply on-hand	
Beginning of year	82
End of year	73

Amounts charged against the allowance, which increased by $4.0 million to $8.5 million in 1993, related to products in the lower-end of the PC product line which were replaced by products released during the fourth quarter featuring a more powerful microprocessor. The decrease in days of supply on hand is attributable to increased sales as well as programs designed to reduce average inventory levels. Inventories pertaining to the Company's Integration Segment are insignificant.

Note 13. Measurement Uncertainties — Liability for Product Warranties

In 1991, the Company began providing its PC customers with a three-year unconditional warranty for parts and service. The Company accrues the cost of future warranty repairs at the time of sale using the ratio of warranty repair expense to revenue for the preceding 24 months. On a quarterly basis, warranty claim frequency and severity are analyzed to determine if adjustments to the liability for product warranties are required. Although the Company believes that the liability for product warranties at December 31, 1993 is adequate to provide for the cost of future warranty services pertaining to 1991-1993 sales, there is a possibility that the frequency and severity of such claims will differ from amounts assumed and that the cost of such services will be more or less than the amount currently provided. The liability for product warranties approximated $15 million and $9 million at December 31, 1993 and 1992, respectively while warranty expense approximated $10 million in 1993 and $7 million in 1992. The following table provides information on actual and expected warranty claims for 1991-1993 sales.

	1991	1992	1993
Estimated warranty claims	10,650	17,950	24,464
Warranty claims processed			
1991	533	—	—
1992	2,662	898	—
1993	4,793	4,488	1,223
	7,988	5,386	1,223
Estimated warranty claims to be processed after December 31, 1993	2,662	12,564	23,241

The weighted average cost per warranty claim assumed on sales in 1991-1993 was $382 while the actual average cost of warranty claims processed was $228 in 1993 and $597 in 1992. The unusually high cost per claim in 1992 was attributable to the failure of certain components in one of the Company's server products which has been rectified.

Note 14. Measurement Uncertainties — Concentration of Credit Risk

Concentration of credit risk with regard to short-term investments is not considered to be significant due to the Company's cash management policies. These policies restrict investments to low risk, highly liquid securities (i.e., commercial paper, money market instruments, etc.), outline issuer credit requirements and limit the amount which may be invested in any one issuer.

The Company's accounts receivable are spread among a large number of customers who operate in many different industries and geographic regions. Accordingly, concentration of credit risk is not significant. In 1992, the U.S. Department of Justice accounted for 15% of the year-end accounts receivable balance. This amount was collected in February 1993.

At December 31, 1993 and 1992, the Company had entered into forward exchange contracts with several large financial institutions to sell $13 million and $11 million of foreign currencies, respectively. Those contracts, which are valued in U.S. dollars based on year-end spot rates, had maturity dates ranging from three to six months. In the unlikely event that the financial institutions fail to honor one or more of the contracts involved in these transactions, losses would be limited to the difference in exchange rates from the time the contract was entered into and the time it was closed out. At December 31, 1993 the Company's aggregate exposure under these contracts was not significant.

Note 15. Segment Financial Data

The Company's operations are primarily conducted through its two industry segments, Personal Computer (PC) and Integration, while certain business functions such as treasury, income taxes, and legal affairs are conducted at the corporate level. The following schedules present disaggregated income and cash flow information for the PC Segment and the Integration Segment. Intersegment transactions are insignificant.

(in millions)	PC Segment 1993	PC Segment 1992	Integration Segment 1993	Integration Segment 1992
Revenue				
Computer sales	$2,277	$1,441	$ —	$ —
Design and installation services	—	—	153	128
System maintenance services	—	—	54	36
	2,277	1,441	207	164
Cost of revenue				
Purchased components, materials	1,477	848	24	18
Compensation and benefits	84	67	119	100
Other	77	38	11	8
	1,638	953	154	126
Gross margin	639	488	53	38
Selling and marketing				
Compensation and benefits	93	109	6	5
Advertising	81	33	2	1
Other	8	4	2	3
	182	146	10	9
Depreciation and amortization	117	120	11	11
Research and development	88	75	—	—
General and administrative				
Compensation and benefits	31	27	6	5
Other	25	20	3	2
	56	47	9	7
Pretax core earnings	196	100	23	11
Income taxes related to core earnings	(78)	(40)	(10)	(4)
Core earnings	$ 118	$ 60	$ 13	$ 7
Non-core items and interest expense	$ (45)	$ 38	$ —	$ —
Cash flows provided by (used in) operating activities				
Core	$ 122	$ 167	$ 18	$11
Non-core	$ 26	$ (30)	—	—

A reconciliation of the segment data to the consolidated financial statements is as follows (intersegment transactions are insignificant).

(in millions)	1993	1992
Pretax core earnings (loss)		
PC Segment	$196	$100
Integration Segment	23	11
Corporate	(15)	(13)
	204	98
Income tax expense	82	39
Core earnings	122	59
Non-core items and interest expense		
PC Segment	(45)	38
Corporate	—	(13)
	(45)	25
Income tax expense (benefit)	(19)	10
	(26)	15
Net income	$ 96	$ 74

The PC Segment manufacturers personal computers and network servers at plants in Boston, Massachusetts and Dublin, Ireland for sale primarily in the United States and Western Europe. The following tables summarize revenue and gross margin data by manufacturing plant and by country for the years ended December 31, 1993 and 1992.

	1993		1992	
(dollars in millions)	$	%	$	%
By Plant				
Revenue				
Boston	$ 1,593	70.0	$ 981	68.1
Dublin	684	30.0	460	31.9
	$ 2,277	100.0	$ 1,441	100.0
Gross margin:				
Boston	$ 444	69.5	$ 330	67.6
Dublin	195	30.5	158	32.4
	$ 639	100.0	$ 488	100.0
By Country				
Revenue				
United States	$ 1,020	44.8	$ 617	42.8
United Kingdom	301	13.2	201	13.9
Canada	254	11.2	158	11.0
France	243	10.7	184	12.8
Germany	197	8.6	128	8.9
All Other	262	11.5	153	10.6
	$ 2,277	100.0	$ 1,441	100.0
Gross margin				
United States	$ 284	27.8	$ 209	33.9
United Kingdom	86	28.6	69	34.3
Canada	71	28.0	53	33.6
France	69	28.4	63	34.2
Germany	56	28.4	43	33.6
All Other	73	27.9	51	33.3
	$ 639		$ 488	

The Company believes that the opportunities and risks of its Integration Segment do not vary on the basis of geographic locations.

Note 16. Leases

The Company leases office space under agreements which expire over the next 7 years. Minimum payments for operating leases having initial or remaining noncancelable terms in excess of one year are as follows.

(in millions)	
1994	$ 7
1995	6
1996	6
1997	5
1998	4
Remainder	7
	$ 35

Total net expense for all operating leases amounted to approximately $8 million and $7 million for 1993 and 1992, respectively.

Management's Analysis of Financial and Nonfinancial Data

PC Segment

The information summarized below relates to the PC Segment and is the basis for management's analysis which follows

(dollars in millions)	1993 $	1993 %	1992 $	1992 %
Revenue	$ 2,277	100.0	$ 1,441	100.0
Cost of revenue	1,638	71.9	953	66.1
Gross margin	639	28.1	488	33.9
Selling and marketing	182	8.0	146	10.1
Depreciation and amortization	117	5.1	120	8.3
Research and development	88	3.9	75	5.2
General and administrative	56	2.5	47	3.4
Pretax core earnings	196	8.6	100	6.9
Income taxes	78	3.4	40	2.8
Core earnings	$ 118	5.2%	$ 60	4.1%

Revenue

PC Segment revenue increased by $836 million or 58% over 1992 revenue of $1,441 million. The following table summarizes the reasons for that increase:

(in millions)	PCs	Servers	Total
1992 Revenue	$ 1,323	$ 118	$ 1,441
Revenue changes attributable to			
Increase in units sold	1,125	95	1,220
Decrease in average unit prices	(374)	(10)	(384)
1993 Revenue	$ 2,074	$ 203	$ 2,277

The composition of the Segment's product line has shifted significantly from 1990 when it focused on the high-price end of the market. Intense price competition forced the Segment to develop low price products to remain competitive. The Segment's introduction of low price PCs occurred in late 1991. Although fierce price cutting has continued, as demonstrated by 28% drop in unit prices in 1992 and an additional 15% drop experienced in 1993, the Segment competes effectively in the low-price portion of the market as evidenced by the 85% increase in PC units sold in 1993. Low price products accounted for approximately 30% of 1993 unit sales and are expected to be 35-40% of total unit sales in 1994.

The Segment introduced its network server products in late 1989 and sales have increased to approximately 9% of total revenue. Average unit prices decreased slightly in 1993; a significant change from the 34% drop experienced in 1992. Although pricing pressure is expected to continue, it should be less significant than noted in prior years as a number of manufacturers have dropped this product because of the significant research and development require-

ments. Server unit sales increased by 80% over 1992 primarily as a result of the Segment's introduction of its F-Net server line in the fourth quarter of 1992. F-Net unit sales accounted for 55% of total server unit sales in 1993.

During the fourth quarter of 1992, the Segment sold approximately 115,000 PCs to the U.S. Department of Justice. As described in Note 8 to the consolidated financial statements, this transaction was treated as a non-core item and, therefore, its impact is not included in the foregoing statistics.

Gross Margin

The Segment's gross margin increased by $151 million or 31% over 1992 levels; however, gross margin as a percentage of revenue declined. Substantially higher unit volumes could not offset the lower per unit contributions caused by continuing price reductions as well as the shift in the sales mix to a higher percentage of lower price, lower margin products. These factors are illustrated in the following table.

(in millions)	
1992 Gross Margin	$ 488
Contribution from additional units sold in 1993	
PCs	262
Servers	31
	293
Decreased contribution caused by price reductions and shift in product mix	
PCs	(134)
Servers	(8)
	(142)
1993 Gross Margin	$ 639

Gross margin per employee increased by $56,000 or 43% from $130,000 in 1992 to $186,000 in 1993. This increase is attributable to customer demand for the Segment's lower price products as well as manufacturing process improvements made in mid-1992 which allowed the Segment to attain higher production levels without a substantial increase in manufacturing employees. Unit sales per employee doubled from 161 units in 1992 to 323 units in 1993.

PC Units Sold Per Employee

Cost of Revenue

Cost of revenue increased by $685 million or 72% over 1992 levels. Purchased components and materials continue to be the most significant portion of cost of revenue accounting for 90.2% of such costs in 1993 and 89.0% in 1992. The average per unit cost of purchased components and materials decreased by 7.2% as a result of the shifting product sales mix as well as discounts resulting from significantly higher volumes of components purchased.

Cost of Revenue

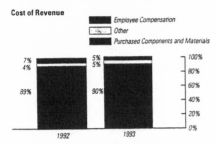

Employee compensation and related expenses increased by $17 million or 25% over 1992 as a result of a slight increase in manufacturing employees, normal wage increases and higher health care and worker's compensation costs. Employee costs as a percentage of revenue decreased from 1992 levels as a result of productivity improvements from the manufacturing process realignments previously described.

Average Number of Employees

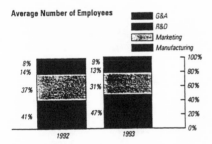

Other costs of revenue consist of several items which generally vary with production and sales levels. Increases in these costs as a percentage of revenue are primarily attributable to the impact of inflation.

Operating Expenses

Selling and marketing expenses increased by $36 million or 25% over 1992. This increase resulted from increased advertising expenses and from approximately $23 million in costs associated with the direct marketing program implemented during the first half of the year. Those increases were partially offset by a $16 million decrease in employees' compensation due to staffing cuts resulting from the shift in the Segment's distribution strategy towards direct marketing programs.

Research and development costs increased by $13 million or 17% over 1992. This increase is primarily due to a $15 million increase in the Segment's pro rata share of costs incurred by Predicta, the research and development partnership in which the Segment is a 10% participant. (The Segment funded $40 million of such costs in 1993 compared with $25 million in 1992.) This increase was offset by a $3 million decrease in employee compensation resulting from a 14% drop in the number of individuals devoted to internal efforts given the higher level of research and development performed through Predicta.

General and administrative expenses increased by $9 million or 19% over 1992. This increase resulted from a $5 million increase in employee compensation caused by an 8% increase in employees required to support significantly increased sales volumes and normal salary increases. Other costs increased by $4 million primarily due to increased data processing charges.

Changes in Financial Position

The Segment invested $120 million and $140 million in property, plant and equipment in 1993 and 1992, respectively. 1993 expenditures related primarily to manufacturing equipment and were evenly split between domestic and Irish manufacturing facilities. Approximately 85% of 1992 additions related to the initial expansion of the Irish manufacturing facility which was required to meet increasing customer demand in European markets. The Segment anticipates that property and equipment additions will approximate $125 million in 1994.

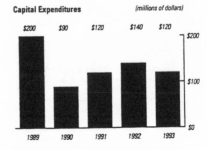

The Segment's accounts payable balance increased from $137 million at December 31, 1992 to $229 million at year-end 1993; an increase of 67% which corresponds to the 74% increase in purchased components and materials in 1993. The Segment's policy is to pay its suppliers within the terms of the related purchase agreements which generally range from 15-45 days. The Segment also attempts to take advantage of all meaningful purchase discounts. Approximately 92% of the Segment's accounts payable balance was current at December 31, 1993 and 1992, respectively, with the remaining balance attributable to disputed billings which are generally resolved within sixty days.

An average net working capital investment of 16¢ was required for each dollar of revenue in 1993 compared with 19¢ in 1992. This decrease was attributable to sales volumes increasing at a greater rate than the net working capital investment required to support such increase.

Integration Segment

The information summarized below relates to the Integration Segment and is the basis for management's analysis which follows.

(dollars in millions)	1993		1992	
	$	%	$	%
Revenue	$ 207	100.0	$ 164	100.0
Cost of revenue	154	74.4	126	76.8
Gross margin	53	25.6	38	23.2
General and administrative	9	4.4	7	4.3
Selling and marketing	10	4.8	9	5.5
Depreciation and amoritzation	11	5.3	11	6.7
Pretax core earnings	23	11.1	11	6.7
Income taxes	10	4.8	4	2.4
Core earnings	$ 13	6.3%	$ 7	4.3%

Revenue

Integration Segment revenue increased by $43 million or 26% over 1992 revenue of $164 million. The following table summarizes the reasons for that increase:

(in millions)	DI	SM	Total
1992 Revenue	$128	$36	$164
Revenue increases from			
InfoSource acquisition	12	—	12
Increase in contracts	9	15	24
Increase in average contract value	4	3	7
1993 Revenue	$153	$54	$207

The January acquisition of the four-office InfoSource consulting group accounted for 53% of the increase in Design and Installation (DI) contracts. The increase in the average value of DI contracts is primarily due to the increasing complexities brought about by rapid changes in network technology. The increase in System Maintenance (SM) contracts is due to the Segment's ability to generate such contracts from DI clients as well as to retain existing

SM clients at the time of annual renewal. The InfoSource acquisition did not significantly impact SM revenues as such services were not offered by those offices until late in the year. The increase in average revenue per SM contract is due to price increases which went into effect in early 1993 to compensate for the increasing level of services provided.

In 1993, the Segment obtained 2,853 DI contracts through competitive proposal compared to 12,480 proposals submitted for a success rate of approximately 23%. This success rate represents a 15% improvement on the 1992 rate of 20%.

The Segment provided services to 7,714 clients in 1993 pursuant to annual system maintenance contracts. Of this amount, 2,125 contracts were obtained from current year DI clients (69% of 1993 DI contracts compared with 78% in 1992) while 5,156 contracts resulted from renewals of prior year contracts (93% of prior year contracts were renewed in 1993 compared with 94% in 1992). The ratio of contracts generated from current year DI clients declined because InfoSource did not offer system maintenance services prior to its acquisition in January 1993. These services were introduced by these offices in late 1993 and the Segment believes that its target level of 75% will be obtained in 1994.

Number of Contracts

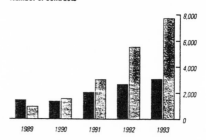

Backlog represents the contractual amount of revenue to be earned in the following year under DI contracts in process or in place at year-end. Backlog decreased from $31 million or 24% of 1992 DI revenue at December 31, 1992 to $24 million or 15% of 1993 DI revenue at December 31, 1993. The $7 million decline in backlog is primarily due to the timing and size of contracts in process at year-end. The Segment does not anticipate a reduction in DI business in 1994 as evidenced by the significant increase in proposal requests received in the first two months of 1994. If the Segment's success rate on these proposals is consistent with the rate experienced in 1993, backlog at the end of the first quarter will be restored to normal levels.

Gross Margin

Integration Segment gross margin as a percentage of revenue increased from 23.2% in 1992 to 25.6% in 1993. The following table summarizes the reasons for that increase.

(in millions)	
1992 Gross Margin	**$38**
Increased contribution from existing field office employees	19
Contribution from additional field office employees added during the year	8
Decrease due to higher supplies and material usage	(6)
Other	(6)
1993 Gross Margin	**$53**

The increase in gross margin is due to the factors relating to the increase in revenue previously discussed and improved workforce productivity. An important measure of productivity is field office employee utilization or the ratio of hours worked on client projects to the total number of hours available for such projects. That ratio increased from 72% in 1992 to 77% in 1993 due to the increase in system maintenance contracts which provide a steady flow of client service opportunities as well as concerted efforts to balance the size of the workforce with client projects. Average gross margin per field office employee, which increased from $30,000 in 1992 to $38,500 in 1993, did not vary significantly by geographic location in either 1993 or 1992. Although markets currently served are expected to become more crowded, the Segment believes that it will be able to maintain its margins at current levels in 1994.

Employee Utilization (%)

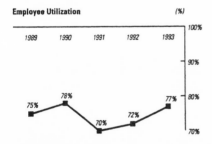

Cost of Revenue

Cost of revenue increased by $28.0 million or 22% over 1992 levels; however, such costs actually decreased as a percentage of revenue. As in any service business, the most significant portion of the Segment's costs relate to its workforce. The composition of the workforce shifted slightly from consultants to technicians as a result of the shift in revenue from design and installation to system maintenance. Administrative support staff remained unchanged

because of centralization of certain functions and productivity improvements. Average employee compensation and related expenses per employee increased due to normal rate increases and higher health care costs offset by the change in the composition of the work force. Average employee training costs increased by 18% to $6,500 due to the constantly changing environment.

The market for qualified consultants and technicians is extremely competitive; a situation that is expected to continue. In 1990, the Segment experienced employee turnover at an annual rate of 34%. In late 1991, the Segment introduced several innovative programs to retain valued employees and to identify individuals with long-term career prospects. These programs have been successful as annual turnover rates have declined to 31%, 27% and 22% in 1991, 1992 and 1993, respectively. The Segment's target annual turnover rate is 18%.

Employee Turnover (%)

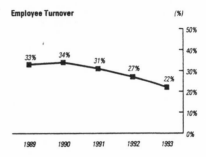

Supplies and materials represent a variety of direct costs incurred in the performance of design, installation and system maintenance services. Such costs increased at a rate which was slightly higher than the rate of revenue increase as a result of the increasing complexity of network systems. Occupancy costs remained unchanged between years as a result of cost controls instituted at the office level.

Operating Expenses

General and administrative expenses consist primarily of employee compensation and related expenses with such costs approximating $6.0 million and $5.0 million in 1993 and 1992, respectively. The increase in these costs is attributable to normal salary increases, incentive compensation awards and higher employee relocation costs. Sales and marketing expenses increased by 11% due to business expansion programs.

Changes in Financial Position

InfoSource, Inc., a Chicago-based consulting group, was acquired in January 1993 for $8 million or approximately 3 times its estimated 1993 pretax core earnings. InfoSource has offices in Chicago, Detroit, Milwaukee and Minneapolis and through this acquisition, the Segment was able to establish an immediate presence in cities where several of its existing clients have operations. In exchange for the purchase price, the Segment obtained $1.6 million in net current assets, $2.5 million in property and equipment and assumed lease liabilities of $0.9 million. Goodwill resulting from the acquisition totaled $4.8 million.

In January 1992, the Segment acquired WestNet, Inc., an eight-office practice based in Los Angeles, for $10 million or 2 1/2 times its estimated 1992 pretax core earnings. WestNet has offices in Los Angeles (2), San Diego, San Jose, San Francisco, Sacramento, Portland and Seattle and provided the Segment with entry to markets in the Western U.S. In exchange for the purchase price, the Segment obtained $7.6 million of property and equipment and assumed $2.9 million of liabilities including $.2 million of net current liabilities. Goodwill resulting from the acquisition totaled $5.3 million.

The Segment invested $4.1 million and $5.4 million in property and equipment in 1993 and 1992, respectively, excluding amounts obtained in the InfoSource and WestNet acquisitions described above. Additions consist primarily of computer equipment used in providing ID and SM services as well as equipment utilized in internal training programs. The Segment anticipates that property and equipment additions will approximate $7 million in 1994.

An average net working capital investment of 18.5¢ was required for each dollar of revenue in 1993 compared with 18¢ in 1992. This increase primarily resulted from the increase in the average number of days sales outstanding. The Segment expects that its working capital investment per dollar of revenue in 1994 will remain consistent with 1993 levels.

Corporate

The Company ended 1993 with $44 million in cash and equivalents; approximately the same amount with which it began the year. Cash generated from operating activities totaled $152 million or 18.8% of average stockholders' equity compared with $139 million or 19.4% in 1992. Current year operating cash flows enabled the Company to invest $124 million in property and equipment; lend $15 million to a major PC Segment supplier to facilitate the strategic expansion of the supplier's manufacturing facility; acquire the Chicago-based InfoSource consulting firm for $8 million and repay $23 million of outstanding borrowings. The Company's current ratio was 2.31 at year-end compared with 2.72 at the end of 1992. This decline resulted from the impact of higher accounts payable at year-end 1993 resulting from higher sales volumes coupled with the unusually large amount due from the U.S. Department of Justice at year-end 1992.

Long-term debt, including the current portion, totaled $146 million at December 31, 1993 and consisted of $139 million in borrowings against the Company's revolving line of credit as well as $7 million in capitalized lease obligations. The Company's debt to capitalization ratio improved from 18.2% at December 31, 1992 to 14.5% at year-end 1993. This improvement is due to strong operating results in 1993 and the reduction in outstanding borrowings. At December 31, 1993, the Company had over $100 million in borrowing capacity under its revolving line of credit.

The Company believes that it has adequate resources to meet its cash requirements through 1994.

Forward-Looking Information

PC Segment

Opportunities and Risks Including Those Resulting from Key Trends

The major opportunities and risks facing the Segment result from four key trends that are affecting the PC business. The following identifies and discusses those trends and the resulting opportunities and risks.

Trend 1 — Growth in unit sales. We expect continued growth in worldwide demand for PCs - roughly at a rate of about 12 percent in each of the next three years. We also expect that our share of that market will increase, from about 2.8 percent in 1993 to about 3.5 percent in 1996. Thus, we expect to sell about 1.9 million machines in 1996, up about 76 percent from the 1.1 million machines we sold in 1993.

Several factors could drive the growth in demand for PCs above our estimates: (1) falling prices open new markets of individuals and smaller businesses who otherwise would not purchase a PC, (2) emerging countries have just begun purchasing PCs, (3) advances in power and features enable new uses for PCs and make them an ever more effective substitute for mainframe systems, and (4) the number of PCs eligible for replacement is growing rapidly.

We are particularly uncertain about our share of the worldwide market because it is a complex function of (1) our prices relative to those of our competitors, (2) the market's perception of the performance, reliability, and service related to our products relative to those of our competitors, and (3) whether we are first-to-market with high performing products. In 1993, we captured market share from low-price competitors and maintained our market share of high-end PCs produced by leading PC makers. We expect those trends to continue in 1994.

There are several opportunities that result from the growth in unit sales trend. First, higher unit sales, even at somewhat lower margins, means higher total margin dollars and core earnings. Second, higher unit volume means less pressure on prices than would otherwise occur. Third, higher unit volume encourages distribution channels to handle our product.

We see little risk that the growth in PC units sold will slow in 1994. There is a greater risk that we will lose market share to competitors if, for example, we encounter serious quality problems that damage our reputation for quality and reliability, fail to introduce or are late in introducing high performance products, or overprice our products.

Trend 2 — Rapid innovation that improves the performance, features, and uses of the PC. We expect that dramatic improvements in performance and features that have characterized the PC industry will continue or accelerate in 1994. The following types of improvements are expected within the next few years.

Faster and more powerful PCs. Increases in the speed and power of PCs will (1) motivate current users of old PCs to upgrade to newer machines to save time and to run new applications, (2) make the PC a more effective substitute for centralized processing, (3) allow the use of new operating and applications software, and (4) enable PCs to be used for new purposes.

Improved features on PCs. Improvements such as larger, sharper color screens; smaller, lighter machines; machines that consume less power and have longer battery life; more flexible PCs that allow upgrades in microprocessors and additions to memory; PCs that communicate faster and more easily with other machines; and PCs that are physically easier to use are anticipated.

Advances in software. Dramatic advances in both operating and application software will make machines even more easy to use, speed the functions that PCs currently perform, open the way for entirely new functions, and improve the ability of PCs to communicate with other machines.

Technology that enables new uses for PCs. PCs will be at the heart of the expected merger of the computer, telecommunications, and entertainment industries. New uses will include electronic memo pads and mail, news and entertainment services, and interactive video for shopping and meetings.

Rapid innovation offers two opportunities for the Segment. First, the trend will continue to fuel the growth in the unit demand for PCs. With the right combination of price and functions, that growth could become explosive. Second, rapid innovation is consistent with the Segment's strategy to be first-to-market with innovative and technologically superior PC products.

However, rapid innovation also poses a significant risk for the Segment. Changes in technology could squeeze the Segment's ability to add value to the PC product. That risk results from two sources.

First, competitors could develop proprietary technology that the Segment would be precluded from incorporating into its products. In the current environment, PC makers generally have equal access to leading edge technology. However, several ventures involving competitors, vendors, and software companies seek to develop proprietary PC systems. If those ventures are successful, the superior features may not be able to be incorporated in the Segment's products. We are unable to predict the success of those ventures, and others that are sure to follow.

Second, component vendors could erode the Segment's ability to add value to the PC product by developing components that perform more functions. For example, vendors who build microprocessors could develop a microprocessor that performs some of the functions performed by the circuit boards now designed and built by the Segment. In the extreme case, an advanced microprocessor could eliminate the need for the Segment's circuit board. Thus, less of the PC would be produced by the Segment, and more would be embodied in the components purchased from suppliers.

In prior years, many component builders were new companies who needed the Segment's help in developing their components to assure the successful application and distribution of those products. However, many established component builders now see fewer advantages to a close association with the Segment. They prefer to make their leading edge components available to all PC makers at once to obtain the largest volume for their products. That policy undermines the Segment's ability to be first to market with leading products.

The rapid innovation trend could also result in the entry of new and powerful competitors into the PC industry. Potential new uses for PCs are already attracting large and powerful companies in the telecommunication and entertainment industry. Many of those companies, and the ventures created to exploit new technology, are many times larger than the Segment, and have considerable skills and resources.

We are unable to predict the long-term impact of rapid innovation on the PC industry and Segment. Within the next three years, however, we expect that the current industry structure will remain largely intact. We expect that technology will continue to fuel strong growth in unit sales. We also expect that we will have access to leading technology, and will quickly incorporate that technology into our products when available. We expect that the value we add will remain about the same percentage of sales as is currently the case. Finally, we do not expect major new competitors to have a major impact on the industry within the next three years.

Trend 3 — Falling prices. Average prices for our PCs declined 28 percent in 1992 and an additional 15 percent in 1993. Over the next three years, we expect that our average prices will decline at a more moderate rate of about 2 - 5 percent per year. That decline will result from the continuing shift in the mix of our products toward lower-priced products directed to the consumer retail market.

Prices could fall faster than the moderate pace that we expect. To maintain unit sales, low price competitors are motivated to lower prices even more. Our ability to charge premium prices over those of low price competitors is a function of our reputation with customers. If customers are unwilling to pay the current premium, we will lower prices to maintain our market share.

Falling prices offer both an opportunity and risk for the Segment. Falling prices help fuel the growth in unit volume because lower prices result in sales of PCs to individuals and businesses that otherwise would not buy a PC. However, falling prices may reduce the gross margin that we

can earn from the sale of our products, particularly if prices fall faster than we can increase our productivity.

Trend 4 - Better productivity. The Segment measures its overall productivity in terms of machines produced per employee. The Segment produced about 330 machines per employee in 1993, up from about 160 machines in 1992. The Segment expects that productivity will increase over the next three years so that we can expand our business while maintaining our workforce at about 3,300 employees. However, our primary competitors are also showing dramatic improvements in productivity. At a minimum, we must keep pace with increases in our competitors' productivity. Otherwise, prices will fall faster than productivity improves thereby negatively impacting operating results.

Management's Plans Including Critical Success Factors

Management believes that the Segment will be successful if it can effectively execute its business strategies. The following discussion of the Segment's plans is structured in terms of its activities and plans for implementing its strategies. The discussion of the plans for implementing each strategy concludes with a description of how that strategy correlates with the opportunities and risks identified in the preceding section.

First to Market with Innovative and Technologically Superior PC Products. The key to the Segment's success is to incorporate emerging technologies into its products in a timely manner. The Segment works closely with its suppliers to identify emerging technologies with requisite market appeal. It also devotes substantial resources to develop proprietary technologies through internal research and development and through participation with Predicta. The Segment must translate these efforts into high-quality, reliable products quickly to maximize advantage.

During 1993, the average length of time from when a product was determined to be commercially feasible to when it became available for sale approximated 12 months; a 3 month improvement from 1992. The Segment has established task forces both internally and with Predicta to reduce the average length of product development time to 9 months in 1994.

The timely introduction of high quality, innovative products will strengthen the Segment's reputation as a market leader and will enable it to maximize operating results. Failure to do so will relegate the Segment to the low value-added, commodity portion of the market.

Widest Distribution. The Segment seeks to maximize the distribution of its products through traditional channels such as dealers, value-added resellers and retail outlets. In 1993, the Segment embarked on a direct marketing program whereby users will be able to order products directly from the Segment using an 800-number. This program is being supported by direct mail and television advertising campaigns which are currently being developed.

Over 50% of the Segment's 1993 sales were centered in North America while Western Europe accounted for 33%.

The Segment will continue its aggressive marketing plans in those areas. The Segment is also focusing on emerging markets in Japan, South America and Asia which are not yet crowded and have potential for high unit volumes.

As product price declines are expected to continue it is essential for the Segment to increase its unit volumes. Direct marketing programs in its traditional markets as well as successful entry into emerging markets should provide the additional volumes necessary for continued profitable operations.

Service and Support. In 1991, the Segment introduced its user support telephone service in the U.S. which enables users to contact the Segment via an 800-number to have questions answered in a timely manner. The program was expanded to 24-hours in 1992. A similar program is currently being instituted in the Segment's major European markets.

In 1991, the Segment also began offering a 3-year unconditional warranty for parts and service. The Segment closely monitors warranty claim activity, including the performance of its authorized representatives, to ensure that service is provided quickly and to identify problems with specific products.

The Segment's service and support programs have proven to be cost effective ways to add value to its products. They also provide valuable information in terms of market research and help the Segment maintain its reputation for high quality, innovative products.

Image Marketing. The Segment reinforces its reputation through a variety of advertising programs. Prior to 1993, the Segment's advertising efforts focused on print media and were directed primarily toward product introductions. In 1993, print ads were introduced which were not product specific but rather focused on the broad themes of quality products and services. In late 1993, a prime-time television advertising campaign was directed at the home market with a focus on support services including the 24 hour user support line. Follow-on advertisements are currently being developed. The Segment intends to increase its television advertising campaigns in 1994.

Productivity Improvement. In 1992, the Segment established process improvement groups consisting of individuals from each of its functional areas. Improvements developed by these groups were largely responsible for the dramatic increase in productivity experienced in 1993. In 1994, a new incentive compensation program was introduced which rewards employees for developing suggestions for process improvements. Additionally, productivity improvements are becoming a larger component of management's individual incentive compensation goals.

Another factor impacting productivity is the Segment's manufacturing process which, except for the circuit board production line, is relatively unsophisticated. This lack of sophistication increases labor costs but enables the Segment to adjust its manufacturing lines quickly to accommodate new products or to meet changes in market demand for existing products.

The Segment's emphasis on productivity improvements will enable it to meet the anticipated growth in unit sales and will help maximize its gross margins.

Comparison of Actual Business Performance to Previously Disclosed Forward-Looking Information

The Segment's actual 1993 business performance differed from the forward-looking information disclosed in our 1992 report in the following areas.

PC unit volume and market share. Last year's report stated that we estimated 20 percent growth in PC unit volume and growth in market share from 1.7 to 1.9 percent in 1993. Instead, unit volume increased 85 percent and market share increased to 2.8 percent in 1993. We underestimated unit growth for two reasons, both having to do with the 15 percent decline in average unit prices. First, we underestimated the impact that the price decline would have on opening additional markets for PCs with businesses and retail consumers who otherwise would not purchase a PC. Second, we also underestimated the impact of our pricing strategy in taking market share from competitors who offer only low priced products.

Employee productivity. Our plans at the beginning of 1993 for improving employee productivity were made in the context of estimates for 20 percent growth in unit volume for 1993. The additional volumes experienced in 1993 was a challenge; however, manufacturing process improvements helped us expand capacity without increasing headcount.

Integration Segment

Opportunities and Risks Resulting from Key Trends

The major opportunities and risks facing the Segment result from four key trends affecting the industry. The following identifies and discusses those trends and the resulting opportunities and risks.

Trend 1 — Demand for services. Through the end of 1993, the Segment viewed itself as providing two types of services, integration services and systems maintenance. We now view integration services to design and install client-server networks as separable from consulting services to improve clients' business performance. Furthermore, trends in the demand for consulting, integration, and maintenance services differ. Each is separately discussed below.

The potential for continued growth in the demand for consulting services is substantial. There are two key factors giving rise to that demand. One factor is that PC technology already vastly exceeds organizations' ability to effectively use it, and the pace of innovations in PC technology shows no sign of abating. The other factor is the opportunity to use PC technology to improve business processes and thereby reduce inefficiency and redundancy and improve customer service.

The market for the design and installation of client-server networks, on the other hand, obviously is finite. Eventually, all that need them will have them. Also, improvements in technology might significantly reduce the complexities relating to network installation.

The market for systems maintenance presently is growing as more and more organizations install client-server networks. The market will reach a plateau and then continue in a more or less steady-state when most of the organizations that need client-server networks have them.

Opportunities resulting from trends in the demand for the Segment's services include:

a. The growth in the demand for consulting services provides the primary opportunity for achieving the Segment's goal of 15 percent growth in pretax core income during the next 3 years. It also provides an opportunity to use our reputation and referrals from existing clients to expand our client base. Our goal is 10 percent annual growth in the number of consulting service clients exclusive of mergers during the next 3 years.

b. Continuation of the market for the design and installation of client-server networks provides a window of opportunity to expand our client base for consulting services and systems maintenance. We expect 15 percent annual growth in the number of design and installation contracts for at least the next 3 years; however, we expect that profit margins on those contracts will decline during that period.

c. Systems maintenance work provides a stable revenue base and the opportunity to identify new consulting services needed by those clients. Our goal is to obtain systems maintenance contracts from 90 percent of each year's new integration clients and to obtain annual renewals from 90% of existing systems maintenance clients. We expect that profit margins on those contracts will decline over the next 3 years.

Risks include the following.

a. The rapid growth and profitability of consulting services is resulting in increased competition for providing those services as discussed below.

b. Innovations in software could eventually reduce the need for some of the types of consulting services presently provided. No such innovations are expected in the next 3 years.

c. A significant downturn in the general economy could cause clients to cancel or delay design and installation contracts.

Trend 2 — Intensity of competition. There presently is a considerable amount of competition between the providers of consulting, integration, and systems maintenance services to medium sized companies and prospects for the future are that the intensity of competition will increase. In addition, very large firms as well as some of the

smaller regional firms may attempt to encroach on our medium sized company market. The risks of increased competition include the possibilities of:

a. A reduction in the rate of growth of the Segment's client base

b. Downward pressure on prices causing reduced profit margins and net income.

Trend 3 — *Supply of people.* There has been a long-standing shortage of people with the requisite skills. Furthermore, college enrollment in the information systems field is down nationwide. Those two factors coupled with the increased demand for qualified people indicate that the shortage may become more severe. Risks to the Segment include the somewhat less than likely possibilities that:

a. Key people could depart in sufficient numbers and without replacement so that the quality of services provided suffers eroding our reputation.

b. The cost of salaries and benefits necessary to attract and retain qualified people could rise significantly thereby reducing profit margins and net income.

This industry-wide problem creates two opportunities for the Segment. They are:

a. The shortage of people and the high cost of training them could act as a barrier that prevents new competitors from entering the market.

b. The Segment's size, reputation, and training programs as well as other technical resources provide a competitive advantage in our college and other recruiting efforts.

Trend 4 — *Pace of merger activity.* The pace at which large providers of consulting services are acquiring small, regional providers of consulting services is increasing thereby shrinking the supply of attractive merger candidates. To date, this has not created a problem because the Segment finds that its size, reputation, and technical resources provide a competitive advantage when bidding to acquire a small, regional firm. Nevertheless, the shrinking supply of attractive merger candidates will at some point reduce our opportunity to use mergers to expand our client base, diversify into new geographic areas, and acquire more qualified professionals. We do not expect that to occur during the next three years.

Management's Plans Including Critical Success Factors

Management believes that the Segment will be successful if it is able to effectively execute its business strategies. The following discussion is structured in terms of our activities and plans for implementing our strategies. The discussion of plans for implementing each strategy concludes with a description of how that strategy correlates with the opportunities and risks identified in the section above.

Improve clients' business performance. The surest way for the Segment to be successful is by providing services that help our clients to prosper. The only credible judge of the value of our services is our clients. After a client has gained experience with a new system that we installed, we contact the client to determine their perception of the value of the services provided. Also, we closely monitor the amount of new business we receive from clients because that is an excellent indicator of their satisfaction with earlier services. Our peoples' performance is evaluated and their salaries and bonuses are determined based on clients' reports on the value of services received and on the amount of new business generated from those clients.

Successful implementation of our strategy to improve clients' business performance will help us to maximize opportunities resulting from increases in the demand for consulting services and minimize risks resulting from increased competition.

More services to existing clients. New work for existing clients helps to strengthen our relationships with our clients as well as to increase revenues and profits. Special activities to implement that strategy include:

a. We closely monitor each of our offices' progress towards the objective of increasing revenues at least 15 percent per year.

b. We closely monitor the level of services provided to each client.

c. Our people responsible for administering clients' accounts are periodically required to set goals for the amount of new business for each of their clients. Their performance evaluations are based on their success at meeting those goals.

d. Our client newsletter and seminars inform clients throughout the firm about the new types of innovative services that we can provide them.

This strategy helps us to maximize opportunities resulting from the increased demand for consulting services and to minimize risks resulting from increased competition.

Recruit, develop and retain the best people. Our firm's excellent reputation, size, and technical resources including training programs help our efforts to recruit the best people. We make maximum use of those selling points. Other activities include:

a. Our human resources department, with the help of consultants, develops and maintains state of the art compensation, fringe benefit, promotion, and family leave policies for our people.

b. New programs targeted to female employees include special arrangements for day care, part-time arrangements, and designating certain key people to ensure that qualified women employees are identified and promoted to local office and firm-wide management positions.

c. Our close relationships with certain professors at leading colleges and universities help to foster a favorable image of our firm on campus.

d. Because of our training programs, we hire outstanding college graduates who did not major in fields such as business processes or computer technology.

Although, the scarcity of qualified people is a risk for the industry, the Segment is confident that it will be successful in recruiting, developing and retaining highly-qualified individuals.

Mergers. We use mergers to enter new geographic markets, expand our client base, and acquire talented professional people. Special activities to identify attractive merger candidates include:

a. We use firms that act as brokers and specialize in matching firms for mergers.

b. We have developed special programs to help us determine whether a potential merger candidate would be a suitable addition to our firm.

c. We have developed a special program that facilitates the transition of people from merged firms to our Segment and reduces the risk of losing them during the transition period.

Although the pace of merger activity is increasing, the Segment is confident that the supply of attractive merger candidates will not dry up anytime soon. In fact, current merger negotiations with several attractive candidates are expected to result in at least one acquisition during each of the next 3 years.

Comparison of Actual Business Performance to Previously Disclosed Forward-Looking Information

The Segment's actual 1993 business performance was generally in line with the forward-looking information disclosed in our 1992 report. Three areas deserving special comment are discussed below.

Consulting services. Design and installation services and system maintenance services are the two broad types of activities discussed for the Segment in our reports for the current and prior years. Whenever we design and install client-server networks, we also provide consulting services for how to better use them. Until recently, however, we seldom provided consulting services unrelated to an ongoing installation of a client-server network, and we saw no need to separately accumulate revenues and costs for each type of service.

Towards the end of 1993 we decided to pursue, for the first time, contracts involving only consulting services. We expect that, eventually, consulting will become our primary service, and design and installation services will become an ever smaller percentage of our business. Because of the increasing role of consulting services, we instituted the necessary types of time reporting and bookkeeping procedures at the beginning of 1994 so that revenues and costs can be separately reported for design and installation services and for consulting services.

Merger activity. Last year's report discussed the possibility of a major acquisition that would have added offices in several cities where we do not now have a presence, increased annual revenue by more than 25 percent, and added a world-class expert to our staff in an industry for which we want to increase our business. In April, however, the Segment and the merger candidate both agreed to cease negotiations, and we have no plans to merge with that firm.

Utilization of employees. Last year's report discussed our goal to increase field office employee utilization to 80 percent from 72 percent in 1992. That goal was ambitious and we believe that we made excellent progress towards achieving it by increasing utilization to 77 percent in 1993. That improvement increased our gross margin by $19 million in 1993. Our gross margin would have increased by another $7 million if utilization had been 80 percent in 1993. We believe that employee utilization will be at approximately 80 percent in 1994.

Opportunities and Risks Managed at Corporate

Exposure to changes in foreign currency exchange rates is managed at Corporate. Forward exchange contracts are used to hedge portions of the consolidated Company's net monetary position in certain currencies. Forward exchange contracts also are sometimes used to hedge commitments for capital expenditures.

We believe that there is no cost-effective way to hedge against our biggest potential risk from changes in exchange rates. That potential risk stems from the PC Segment and the fact that most of its costs (including those of the plant in Ireland) are incurred in U.S. dollars and more than half of its revenues are received in foreign currencies, primarily those of Canada, the United Kingdom, France and Germany.

The risk resulting from U.S. dollar costs and foreign currency revenues to recover them is that the U.S. dollar will strengthen against the foreign currency. Absent an increase in the foreign currency sales prices of our products, either profits are reduced or our U.S. dollar costs are not recovered, that is, we suffer a loss on the sales of the product.

Given the downward trend in worldwide prices for PC products (other than high inflation countries), our ability to raise foreign currency sales prices is limited. In 1993, the Segment had approximately $1.2 billion of sales to foreign countries, primarily Canada, the United Kingdom, France and Germany. If the dollar were to strengthen against most or all of those foreign currencies all at the same time, the effect could be significant.

Information About Management and Shareholders

The Company's affairs are overseen by a ten-member Board of Directors who are elected by the shareholders at the annual meeting. Day-to-day operations are the responsibility of a five-person senior management team who are elected annually by the Board. Three members of senior management also serve as Directors. Brief biographical sketches of the Directors and members of the senior management team follow.

Nonemployee Directors

Dan Collins, age 58, is a retired U.S. Navy Admiral who has served as a director of the Company since 1988. He also serves as a director of Mardi Gras Cruise Lines and Tanque Verde Mutual Fund Group, Inc.

Russell Ford, age 45, is Chief Operating Officer of Boston Bancorp, the largest independent bank holding company in New England, where he has held various positions since 1975. He has served as a director of the Company since 1991 and also serves as a director of Saugatuck Gas and Electric Company and Oak Creek Communications.

Tom White, age 46, is President and Chief Executive Officer of Tubac Partners, Inc., a venture capital firm based in Tucson, Arizona. Prior to 1987, Mr. White served as a financial consultant to companies in the computer industry. He has served as a director of the Company since 1989 and also serves as a director of Amos Kempfert, an international real estate developer.

Julianne Folger, age 45, is the Dean of the College of Engineering at the University of New Mexico. She has served as a director of the Company since 1990 and also serves as a trustee of the Santa Fe Opera.

Robert Hoffman, age 55, is a partner with the San Francisco law firm of Parker, Barton and Mussman, where he specializes in intellectual property. He has served as a director of the Company since 1986 and also serves as Director of Caskin Oil Company and Biotech Applications, Inc.

Trent Weaver, age 60, is an international business consultant based in Washington, D.C. From 1980-1992, Mr. Weaver served in the U.S. House of Representatives. He was appointed as a director of the Company in February 1993 filling the vacancy created by the death of David Hughes who had served as a director since 1988.

Cal Cronin, age 40, is President, Chief Executive Officer and a Director of Micro Dynamics, Inc., a major component manufacturer that is one of the Company's primary suppliers of disc drives. He has served as a director of the Company since 1991.

Board Organization and Compensation

The Board of Directors met eight times during 1993 while the various Board Committees described below met thirteen times. Attendance at Board and Committee meetings averaged 95% in 1993. As required by Company policy, each Director attended at least 85% of the meetings of the Board and Committees on which they served. Non-employee directors receive a retainer of $30,000 as well as $1,000 for each committee meeting that they attend. The Company also reimburses each Director for out-of-pocket costs incurred in connection with their service to the Company.

The Audit Committee consists of four non-employee Directors and is responsible for overseeing the Company's system of internal accounting control, the preparation of the Company's consolidated financial statements and the engagement of the Company's independent accountants. Mr. Collins (Chairman), Mr. Ray, Ms. Folger, and Mr. Weaver served on this Committee which met four times during 1993.

The Compensation Committee also consists of four non-employee Directors and is responsible for making recommendations to the Board concerning annual compensation for members of senior management. Mr. Ford, (Chairman), Mr. Hoffman, Mr. Weaver and Mr. Cronin served on this Committee which met three times during 1993. Mr. Cronin was appointed to this Committee in 1992 as a result of his background in the computer industry. As previously mentioned, Mr. Ellis serves as director of MDI and currently serves as a member of its compensation committee.

The Nominating Committee consists of all non-employee Directors and is responsible for establishing procedures for the selection and retention of Board members, and evaluating and recommending nominees. Mr. Hoffman chaired this Committee which met three times during 1993.

Senior Management

Dale Ellis, age 50, President, Chief Executive Officer and Chairman of the Board. Currently serves as a director of Micro Dynamics, Inc., one of the Company's primary suppliers of disc drives.

Tony Mason, age 46, Senior Vice President-Personal Computers and member of the Board of Directors. He joined the Company as an engineer in 1989 and was responsible for the development and construction of the Company's Irish manufacturing facility.

Fred Snowden, age 45, joined the Company in 1989 as Senior Vice President-Integration Services. He previously had served as managing director of Network Solutions, Inc., the 400 person integration consulting firm acquired by the Company in 1989. He was appointed to the Board of Directors in 1991. He also serves as a director of Great Lakes Trading Company, a commodity brokerage firm.

Eleanor Peters, age 47, Senior Vice President-Research. Currently serves as a director of Predicta, the research and development partnership in which the Company is a participant.

Joseph Dulin, age 43, elected Chief Financial Officer and appointed to the Board in 1992 upon the retirement of Robert McBride. He served as the Company's Controller from 1987 to 1992.

Senior Management Compensation

The Company's senior management compensation program is designed to reward and retain individuals who have the ability to assist the Company in meeting its objectives in a challenging, dynamic industry. Each individual's annual compensation consists of three parts: base salary, incentive compensation awards and stock option awards. At the beginning of each year, an individual's base salary is established based upon his or her performance in the prior year as well as compensation practices at other similarly-sized computer companies . Under the incentive compensation portion of the program, a number of performance goals are established for each individual which are directly linked to the Company's objectives. Each goal requires the individual to achieve a minimum performance threshold in order to qualify for an award under the program. The amount of award applicable to each goal increases as an individual's performance exceeds the minimum performance threshold for each goal. If an individual achieves maximum performance for each goal, he or she is entitled to an aggregate incentive compensation award equivalent to 75% of his or her base salary. Stock options are granted to senior management as well as others throughout the Company to ensure that they are focused on enhancing shareholder value over the long term. The following table summarizes senior management compensation for 1993 as well as the number of shares owned by each individual at year end.

	Base Salary	Incentive Compensation Award	Stock Options	Common Shares Owned
Dale Ellis	$1,000,000	$410,000	100,000	315,000
Tony Mason	500,000	250,000	40,000	25,000
Fred Snowden	500,000	250,000	40,000	40,000
Eleanor Peters	350,000	175,000	20,000	35,000
Joseph Dulin	450,000	186,000	25,000	20,000

Criminal Convictions of Directors and Senior Management

None.

Major Shareholders

To the best of the Company's knowledge, the only shareholder who beneficially owns 5% or more of the Company's stock is Tanque Verde Mutual Fund Group, Inc. whose various funds hold approximately 12.9% of the Company's outstanding common stock. Mr. Collins, a Director of the Company, also serves as a director of Tanque Verde.

Transactions and Relationships Among Related Parties

The Company loaned its primary disc drive supplier, Micro Dynamics, Inc. (MDI), $15 million to finance the expansion of its manufacturing facility. MDI supplies the Company with approximately 90% of its disc drive requirements. Purchases from MDI approximated $235 million in 1993 and $149 million in 1992. Cal Cronin, a director of the Company is president and chief executive officer of MDI.

The Company is a participant in Predicta, a research and development partnership whose primary objective is to develop advanced PC technology. Participants include nine of the Company's primary component suppliers including MDI. Eleanor Peters, the Company's Senior Vice President of Research, is a director of Predicta.

Disagreements with Directors, Independent Accountants, Bankers, and Lead Counsel

None.

Report of Independent Accountants

This example illustrates the form of report which would be issued if the inde-
pendent accountant had been engaged to render an opinion on the entire
FauxCom annual report although this may not always be the case.

We have audited the accompanying consolidated balance sheet of FauxCom, Inc. as of December 31, 1993 and 1992, and the related consolidated statements of core earnings and net income, cash flows, and stockholders' equity for each of the two years in the period ended December 31, 1993. We also audited the five-year summary of business data, the description of information about management and shareholders, and the scope and description of the Company's businesses accompanying the financial statements. These financial statements, five-year summary and descriptions are the responsibility of the Company's management. Our responsibility is to express an opinion on these presentations based on our audits.

We conducted our audits in accordance with generally accepted auditing standards. Those standards require that we plan and perform the audit to obtain reasonable assurance about whether the information presented is free of material misstatement. An audit includes examining, on a test basis, evidence supporting the amounts and disclosures presented. An audit also includes assessing the accounting principles used and significant estimates made by management, as well as evaluating the overall presentation. We believe that our audits provide a reasonable basis for our opinion.

In our opinion, the financial statements referred to above present fairly, in all material respects, the financial position of FauxCom, Inc. as of December 31, 1993 and 1992, and the results of its operations and its cash flows for each of the two years in the period ended December 31, 1993, in conformity with generally accepted accounting

principles. It is also our opinion that the five-year summary and descriptions referred to above are fairly presented, in all material respects, in conformity with the applicable standards.

As part of the audit, we also performed such audit procedures as we considered necessary to evaluate management's assumptions and analyses and the preparation and presentation of the information in the following sections of the annual report.

- Current year review
- Management's analysis of financial and nonfinancial data
- Opportunities and risks including those resulting from key trends
- Management's plans including critical success factors
- Comparison of actual business performance to previously disclosed forward-looking information
- Broad objectives and strategies
- Impact of industry structure on the Company

In our opinion, the accompanying sections described above are presented in conformity with the respective standards of presentation, and management has a reasonable basis for the underlying assumptions and analyses reflected in the aforementioned sections.

February 15, 1994
Boston, Massachusetts

Background About the Company and Its Segments

Overview

FauxCom conducts business through its two business segments, the PC Segment and the Integration Segment. The PC Segment is a leader in the design, development, manufacture, and sale of personal computers. The Integration Segment helps clients design, acquire, and install personal computer networks, and provides maintenance services for those networks.

Most of the Company's business is decentralized at the segment level. Business functions controlled at the corporate level include treasury activities; legal, tax, accounting, and information processing services; investor relations; human resources; and the office of the chief executive. Information about those activities is presented for the Company as a whole.

The Company was incorporated in 1973. By 1979, we were a leader in the design, development, manufacture, sale, and service of dedicated word processing network systems. In 1985, we recognized the market potential for personal computers and, in 1986, acquired a leading personal computer maker. In 1987 the Company concluded that PC systems would ultimately replace dedicated word processing systems because of superior performance and flexibility. Thus, we exited the dedicated word processing business over a three year period to focus on expanding our PC business. We are currently among the leading PC makers in the world. The Company was among the first to recognize the trend and potential of client/server networks of PCs and, in 1989, acquired an integration services company. We have since expanded the Integration Segment, through both internal growth and acquisition.

PC Segment

Broad Objectives and Strategies

The Company evaluates the PC Segment's performance based on the degree to which it meets its primary objectives of increasing market share; maintaining its reputation for reliable, high performance personal computers; and achieving the highest gross margin percentage in the industry. In pursuing those objectives, we have adopted a strategy with the following primary components:

First to market with innovative products. Being first to market is critical for our reputation, and enables us to maximize margins and achieve the volumes necessary to increase market share.

Widest distribution. Utilize multiple distribution channels to make products available to as many customers in as many geographic markets as possible.

Service and support. Immediate attention to customer questions and warranty claims reinforce our reputation for quality and reliability.

Image marketing. Advertising programs must emphasize the leading technology, superior performance and reliability of our products.

Productivity improvement. Continuous productivity improvements are required to enable the Segment to compete effectively in an environment of falling prices and shrinking margins.

Scope and Description of Business

Description of industry. Companies in the industry design, develop, manufacture, and sell PC systems.

Principal products. The Segment's principal products are desktop, portable, and notebook PCs, including PCs that function as servers in PC networks. The Segment does not produce or market component parts, operating or application software, or computer peripherals such as printers.

Principal markets. Established markets exist in the U.S., Canada, Europe, and Japan. Markets are emerging in Africa, Asia, and South America. The Segment competes in all established markets, and is preparing to enter certain emerging markets. Users of the Segment's products include large and small businesses, educational institutions, and households.

Production process. The Segment manufactures circuit boards and assembles PCs using those circuit boards together with components purchased from suppliers. The production process for circuit boards is highly automated and capital intensive. The assembly process is primarily manual thereby avoiding the high fixed-costs of an automated assembly process and retaining flexibility to adjust for changes in technology as well as demand.

Properties. The Segment owns properties in Boston, Massachusetts, Dublin, Ireland, and Gorinchem, the Netherlands. The Boston property consists of 760,000 square feet of manufacturing space and 70,000 square feet of administrative space. The Dublin property provides 330,000 square feet of manufacturing space, while our products are distributed to European customers from a 150,000 square foot distribution facility in Gorinchem.

Key inputs. Inputs include purchased components, technology, people and capital assets.

Purchased components. Purchased components represent 85-90% of the cost of revenue. Components are frequently updated and improved. Quickly incorporating those improvements into the product line is critical to the Segment's success as state-of-the-art components are generally made available to all PC makers shortly after introduction.

Technology. Although most of the technology in a PC is embodied in purchased components, we use proprietary technology to get leading-edge components to work together with other components. Most of the Segment's technology is embodied in its circuit boards as well as in the highly automated process used to manufacture them.

People. We employ about 3,400 people, of whom 45% are in manufacturing, 30% percent are in marketing and distribution, 15% are in research and technical activities, and 10% are in general and administrative functions.

Tangible fixed assets. The Segment's tangible fixed assets are concentrated in its Boston and Dublin manufacturing plants. With the exception of the equipment to produce circuit boards, neither the buildings nor the equipment are specialized.

Distribution channels. We use multiple distribution channels including dealers, computer stores and superstores, value-added resellers. mass merchandisers, and mail order.

Seasonality and cyclicality. The Segment's revenue and earnings have not been seasonal. Sales of PCs have not been closely correlated with general economic activity. For example, the PC market continued to expand despite generally disappointing conditions in the general economy during 1992 and 1993.

Laws and regulations. The need for regulatory (e.g. FCC) approval may delay the introduction of new products. Compliance with environmental laws and regulations has not had a material effect on the Segment and none is anticipated.

Patents, trademarks, and licenses. The Segment and its suppliers and competitors all hold numerous patents. As competition has intensified, the number of cross-licensing and marketing agreements has increased. Patents and licenses have not prevented PC makers from quickly adopting the technology and product features offered by competitors' products. Our products enjoy a reputation for high-quality and performance and, therefore, we are able to compete effectively with other PC makers, particularly those who compete primarily on price.

Macroeconomic activity. Our growth has not been closely correlated with traditional macroeconomic measures. Rather, the growth in our business is due to the value of PCs in creating, analyzing, providing and communicating information relative to the value offered by competing products.

Contracts with customers and suppliers. The Segment has no long-term contracts with customers and suppliers. Dealers and other resellers order our product only when needed and unfilled purchase orders may be canceled at any time without penalty. We order materials and components in quantities sufficient for approximately three months of production. We work closely with many suppliers in the development of state-of-the-art components and sometimes provide financial support to key suppliers who offer

promising new components. We have also entered into a venture with certain suppliers and competitors relating to research in emerging technologies.

Impact of Industry Structure on the Company

Potential for technological and regulatory changes outside the industry. We are not aware of any technological or regulatory changes outside of the industry that pose a serious threat to displace the PC.

Bargaining power of resource providers. We assemble PCs using components and subassemblies purchased from many suppliers. There are generally an adequate number of suppliers for most components; however, certain key components are only available from a single source. The Segment has occasionally suffered significant cost increases and supply disruptions. Supply disruptions that cause the Segment to either delay the introduction of a new product or to not meet product demand could have a material adverse effect on the Segment's results of operations.

One supplier, ChipCo, supplies all of the advanced microprocessors used in our products as well as a dominant share of the advanced processors used in the PC industry. Leading PC makers immediately incorporate new generations of ChipCo's microprocessors into their products in response to market demand for more advanced machines. Because it sets the industry standard, ChipCo has substantial bargaining power over all leading PC makers. It has adopted a policy of making its microprocessors available to all PC makers at the same time and price; a policy that impacts the Segment's ability to be first to market with leading technology.

Bargaining power of customers. Most of our sales are to resellers (i.e., dealers, value-added resellers, and systems integrators that sell to large businesses and government as well as dealers, computer stores, superstores and mass merchandisers that sell to small businesses, the home, and education). The only customers that account for more than 5% of our sales are Techland Inc. at 8% of sales and Smart Machines, Inc. at 6% of sales.

Intensity of competition in the industry. Competition is intense and widespread. While 10 large companies account for approximately 50% of the worldwide market, none of the hundreds of other small companies accounts for more than 2% of the market. Large companies compete with small companies for the low end of the business and among themselves for sales of products that incorporate the latest technological advances in the industry. Higher initial prices and profit margins for new products quickly deteriorate during the 12 to 18 month life cycle of a product. Since our products can be used with competitors' products in the same network, customers can purchase competing products based on price alone.

Integration Segment

Broad Objectives and Strategies

The Company evaluates the Segment's performance based on the degree to which it meets its objectives of expanding its market share for consulting, integration and maintenance services in large cities in which it does not yet have offices; increasing revenues from existing offices by at least 15 percent per year; achieving pretax core earnings of at least 15 percent of revenue; and maintaining its reputation for improving clients' business performance through the use of client/server PC networks. In pursuing our objectives, the Segment has adopted a strategy consisting of the following primary components:

Improve clients' business performance. Create value for our clients by helping them apply the information technology in client/server networks to improve their business performance.

More services to existing clients. Our presence at existing clients provides an ideal vantage point from which to see opportunities for additional services.

Recruit, develop and retain the best people. The Segment competes against well known and respected competitors and organizations in other industries and professions for the best people. The Segment must provide new recruits with necessary technical skills and knowledge in its business approach. It must also continually develop seasoned professionals to add value in increasingly complex business and technical environments.

Mergers. Acquire high-quality integration businesses, if available at acceptable cost, as a means to enter geographic locations that offer attractive opportunities for growth and profitability.

Scope and Description of the Business

Description of industry. Integration, consulting, and outsourcing are the three broad categories of services provided by the industry. Integration services enable computers to work together, consulting services improve business processes using computer technology, and outsourcing is performing the data processing and information technology chores for a client. The Segment provides integration and consulting services but does not currently provide outsourcing services.

Principal services. Integration services involve the design and installation of local area networks (LANs) and servers in groups known as client/server networks. Those services include designing the networking strategy, identifying the technologies needed to implement such strategy, developing specifications and reviewing vendor proposals, and coordinating installation of hardware, operating systems, and software. Our system maintenance services quickly isolate and correct network problems thereby relieving clients of the burden of carrying high-priced, technical experts on their staffs. Consulting services include strategic planning, feasibility studies and needs analysis, performance analysis, contingency and disaster planning, and customized education programs.

Principal markets served. The integration services business is less than six years old. Estimated annual worldwide demand for such services approximates $50 billion of which

about one third is in the United States. We expect the demand for client/server networks will continue to grow because of the advantages of networks relative to traditional mainframe systems. As with other PC products, however, networks may become more like a commodity and networking may eventually become almost as easy as hooking up a telephone.

The size of the Segment's system maintenance market is closely related to the number of clients for whom we have provided integration services because those clients are our primary targets for maintenance contracts. The potential market for consulting services, on the other hand, is substantial as client/server technology is advancing faster than an organization's ability to effectively use it.

The Segment's client's are mostly medium to smaller sized businesses engaged in many different types of industries and not-for-profit organizations. Most of our clients are located in American, Canadian, and European cities where we have offices.

Processes for rendering services. Because of the diverse skills required, nearly all of our work is performed in project teams, consisting of both Segment and client personnel. The service process usually involves the following steps:

Project team — form the team aligning skills with client's needs

Needs analysis — understand the business environment and identify the role of a network system in improving the client's business processes

Planning and system design — plan for and design the system to meet the client's needs

Client understanding and buy-in — the client must work closely with the design team to insure that the network will improve the client's business processes

Implementation — oversee and coordinate the purchase and installation of hardware, operating systems and application software, and the realignment of business processes

Testing — ensure that the network operates as designed

Training — ensure that the client thoroughly understands the system, and the ways that the system can improve business processes

Follow-up — ensure that the client is realizing the benefits that the system was designed to achieve

System maintenance — ensure efficient and uninterrupted service from the network

Consulting — identify and implement additional ways to improve the clients business processes through the network.

Although certain steps are common to most assignments, the service delivered is tailored to the client's specific circumstances. The delivery process often involves frequent starts and stops as the assignment progresses through the steps described above.

Properties. The Segment shares administrative space with the PC Segment in the Boston facility. The Segment's field offices occupy 195,000 square feet of leased space.

Key inputs. Inputs include people, technical resources, and purchased hardware and software.

People. The nature of the services we provide requires people of exceptional ability. Some are generalists while others are experts in specific industries, business processes, change management, or the technical aspects of network design and installation.

Technical resources. We supply the following technical resources that enable our service teams to render high-quality services and to bring the Segment's collective knowledge to bear on improving clients' business processes:

- Unified approach - extensive training programs and documented procedures create a standardized approach to analyzing client situations and devising creative solutions that best meet the needs of our clients.

- Ready access to experts - our size, over 1,000 consultants, allows us to develop world-class experts in every aspect of our work.

- Extensive data bank - our data bank containing the work experience and skills of each of our people enables us to quickly assemble a project team that aligns skills with client needs. We also maintain a database of best practices for key business processes and network features that allows our people in every office to bring the best of the Segment's thinking to each engagement.

Purchased hardware and software. Our project teams develop system specifications, review vendor proposals and coordinate the installation of hardware and software at client locations. We do so as an agent for the client and thus the purchase price of the hardware and software is not reflected in our financial statements. The PC Segment is a major supplier of PCs for use in client/server systems; however, our policy is to recommend the best value in hardware and software to our clients, regardless of the supplier.

Distribution methods. We sell our services directly to clients. Prospective clients generally request proposals from 3 or 4 suppliers. Projects teams perform the majority of the work at the client's premises.

Seasonality and cyclicality. The Segment's business is not seasonal and general economic cycles have not had a great effect on the demand for our services. A recent downturn in the economy may have caused some clients or potential clients to decide that they cannot afford our services; however, the same downturn has also caused others to seek our assistance in finding ways to use network technology to eliminate redundancy and inefficiency and to improve customer service.

Laws and regulations. Management is not aware of any existing or proposed laws or regulations that could have a significant effect on the Segment.

Patents, trademarks, and licenses. The Segment does not hold patents, trademarks or licenses. To management's knowledge, competitors have no advantage over the Segment because of patents, trademarks or licenses held.

Macroeconomic activity. We have a wide range of clients in many industries and as a result, our revenue and expenses are not closely correlated to any particular type of macroeconomic activity. However, demand for consulting services is sensitive to macroeconomic activity.

Contractual relationships. Most of the Segment's integration and consulting assignments are covered by engagement letters that are equivalent to contracts. Most assignments have a fixed fee for professional services, reimbursement of expenses, and often a caveat for additional professional fees if unforeseen problems arise. Some assignments call for billing professional services at agreed upon hourly rates. Most assignments have arrangements for progress billings but we sometimes allow extended payment terms.

Maintenance services are covered by one-year contracts. The contracts call for an annual retainer that pays for an agreed number of hours of professional services. Additional hours, if needed, are billed at agreed rates. Expenses are reimbursed.

As a group, the Segment's employees are its largest supplier. The employees are not unionized and the Segment does not have employment contracts with its employees.

Impact of Industry Structure on the Company

Potential for technological and regulatory changes outside the industry. We are not aware of any technological or regulatory changes outside of the industry that pose a serious threat to reduce the demand for integration services. Bargaining power of resource providers. There is a scarcity of employees with the requisite skills for providing the types of services offered by the Segment. Thus, our individual employees have significant bargaining power, even though they are not represented by a union. Purchased hardware and software is another significant input. The hardware and software markets are intensely competitive, products are readily available, and suppliers have little bargaining power.

Bargaining power of customers. Our client base consists of medium to smaller sized businesses most of whom are located in the cities in which we have offices. Our clients are sensitive to the amount of our fees; however, the critical factor is their perception about the relative value of our services compared to those of our competitors.

Intensity of competition. Competition is intense and growing. Our competitors are large firms and are often large international and regional CPA firms. One advantage held by those firms is that they audit nearly all of the medium size companies that are potential clients for our consulting services. On the other hand, we often have superior resources to bring to bear to solve clients' business problems.

Stockholder Information

Corporate Address
2500 Patriot Parkway
Boston, Massachustts 02110
(617) 990-2580

Counsel
Barkley, Jordon & Malone
250 Federal Street
(617) 439-9000

Independent Accountants
Smalley Perkins & Kush
175 Central Street
Boston, Massachusetts 02110
(617) 520-1000

FauxCom Common Shares
are located on the American
Stock Exchange; the ticket
tape symbol for the shares
is FXC.

APPENDIX 3.B:
COSTS AND BENEFITS OF BUSINESS
INFORMATION DISCLOSURE

Robert K. Elliott and Peter D. Jacobson

Robert K. Elliott and Peter D. Jacobson are members of the Executive Office of KPMG Peat Marwick in New York.

This article analyzes the costs and benefits of disclosures of information by profit-making enterprises. It excludes the costs and benefits of disclosure by governmental entities and private-sector, not-for-profit entities. Entirely different issues arise when disclosure must be related to the goals and effective functioning of democracy and charitable undertakings.

Even when narrowed, however, the range of enterprise disclosure to be considered is enormous. It can vary from none to complete. None is a total right of privacy. Complete disclosure is a public right to see anything and everything.

Some parties might benefit and others might suffer from any disclosure, though it is also true that some disclosure is immaterial in cost and in effect. The types of costs and benefits are economic, political, social, and ethical. Parties may be affected by both costs and benefits. For example, the costs of corporate disclosure are borne by owners, but they are also beneficiaries of the disclosure they pay for. Financial report users do not neatly share in costs and benefits. Although owners pay for corporate disclosure, stock market investors considering ownership are free riders who pay nothing at all.

These kinds of complexities are one reason this article does not circumscribe the range of costs and benefits it considers. There is another. There are no agreed-upon measures of the dollar value of costs and benefits

from disclosure. The appropriate starting place for a consideration of costs and benefits is therefore to identify their range and nature and to explore their relationships.

The costs and benefits treated in this article are categorized by interests. The categories are:

- The entity's interests.

- Nonowner investors' interests.

- The national interest.

The analysis of these three sets of costs and benefits in sections I through III below is followed by a section that assesses future changes in the costs and benefits (section IV) and a concluding section on the limits of cost-benefit analysis.

The article makes an assumption throughout that must be understood in order to follow what is being said. All references to disclosure pertain only to "informative disclosure." Informative disclosure is useful for decision making, even if it involves costs that outweigh its usefulness. It is unbiased and untarnished by misleading omissions. Moreover, informative disclosure provides an opportu-

This article is a modified version of a paper prepared for the AICPA Special Committee on Financial Reporting, and the authors acknowledge the helpful suggestions and advice of committee members. However, the views expressed in the article are solely those of the authors.

Source: Elliott, R. K., and P. D. Jacobson, "Costs and Benefits of Business Information Disclosure," *Accounting Horizons* (December 1994), pp. 80–96. Reprinted with permission.

nity for a decision maker to obtain an incremental improvement in assessing the real prospects of an enterprise. Thus informative disclosure, as used in this article, is an ideal concept created to illustrate the costs and benefits of disclosure. (The appendix presents a more formal definition of informative disclosure.)

There is, however, a practical side to this approach. Frivolous and misleading disclosures by definition entail more costs than benefits. Investigating the costs and benefits of such disclosures is therefore not a very constructive enterprise.

I. THE ENTITY'S INTERESTS

For our purposes the entity will be treated as owners and employees, including managerial employees. Owners, of course, are a class of investors and share interests with the nonowner investors in the next section. The separation is justified because the entity's interests are hard to conceive of apart from those of owners. The interests of owners and employees can be different, but both share a dominating interest in maximizing long-term cash flow. The bigger the pie, the larger the shares to be divided, whether cooperatively or through conflict. "Long-term" presumes that the viability and earning power of the entity are not put at risk for the sake of short-term profits.

The remarks below treat "the entity" as an individual business entity, not as the collected set of "entities," which creates a group. Thus, what is in "the entity's" interest need not be in the interests of all entities as a group or in the interests of all entities in the subset represented by an industry. The "entity" is also the average entity. Differences in circumstances are sometimes addressed, but when they are not, assume the average entity.

Cost of Capital

The entity benefits when disclosure leads to a lower cost of capital. Disclosure accomplishes this by helping investors and creditors understand the economic risk of the investment. Inadequacy and incompleteness of in-

formation are reflected in the cost of capital as a premium above the risk-free rate of return plus the economic risk premium. Low disclosure generally results in a high information risk premium, and high disclosure generally results in a low information risk premium.

The way reduced information risk works to lower the cost of capital is illustrated in figure 1, a point-in-time graph that varies extent of informative disclosure against three costs of capital. However, because this is a point-in-time graph, two costs are fixed and therefore shown as constants. The risk-free rate of return—in our economy usually considered to be the yield on Treasury bills—is fixed at the graph's point in time, even though it would otherwise vary as market transactions changed the yield on Treasury bills. Similarly, the risk from economic factors is shown as a premium fixed at the graph's point in time, even though it otherwise varies as the entity's conditions and prospects vary. The third cost, the information risk premium (the cost of transacting without full informative disclosure), naturally decreases as informative disclosure increases.

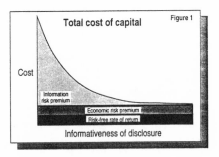

Figure 1

The key to the graph is the relationship between information risk, economic risk, and disclosure. The ideal, minimum cost of capital is the risk-free rate of return plus the premium for economic risk. However, the only way the investor or creditor can assess economic risk is through information. Therefore, the informativeness of disclosure is the route for the investor to arrive at the economic risk of the transfer of capital. With no information to assess economic risk, the capital supplier will charge a high (but not infinite) price for the capital, a price approximating the "loan shark" rate. As the company provides more informative disclosure, the demanded rates decline, because the capital supplier has a better and better understanding of the enterprise's economic risk. These events are shown by a curve for the information risk premium that declines as informativeness of disclosure increases and thereby approaches the risk-free plus economic-risk rate of return.

In understanding the graph, it is important to keep in mind the relationship between the information risk premium and economic risk premium. Information about a company can give either positive or negative impressions of a company's prospects, and the combination of such types of information contributes to learning the economic risk of the business. Thus when the information indicates poor prospects, it means that the economic risk premium is high, not that the information is functioning to raise the cost of capital. Ignorance of a company's risks (the highest level of information risk premium) is still an increment above the risk-free rate of return plus the economic risk premium. Getting a better understanding of the true economic risk would still lower the cost of capital.

The curve is based on the definition of informative disclosure given above and is otherwise illustrative only. It does not, for example, include the risk of misinterpretation of informative disclosure, and it does not include the investor's uncertainty as to the reliability of the informative disclosure. Nor does it take into account prior experiences with such factors. For these reasons, as well as because we are talking about the average entity, the curve cannot be expected to accord with every entity's cost-of-capital experience. For example, if the market misinterpreted informative disclosure and underestimated the economic risk, a company's securities would be overpriced. In that situation, additional informative disclosure accompanying an issue

of new shares could correct the overestimate of the company's prospects and thereby raise the company's cost of capital. Only if it is assumed that informative disclosure is misinterpreted this way most of the time would the illustrative value of the graph be undermined. But it is far more reasonable to assume that misinterpretations distribute normally between under- and overestimates of economic risk, with the net result for all entities that informative disclosure reduces the cost of capital.

It is difficult to prove empirically that the cost of capital is lowered by informative disclosure, even though it is logically and practically impossible to assess an entity's economic riskiness without relevant information. There is abundant evidence that prices are influenced by disclosure (efficient markets research), but that is not the same as empirical evidence that informative disclosure lowers the cost of capital. We also know that capital suppliers request and sometimes demand disclosures — that is, they sometimes make disclosure a condition of the transaction. Presumably the desired information is considered relevant to their decision making, but, again, this is not the same as empirical evidence that informative disclosure lowers the cost of capital. Finally, there is anecdotal evidence, such as the recent article by Sweeney (1994) in the *New York Times*, which argued that many companies "realize that institutional investors prefer to put money into companies that provide lots of information and that good investor relations can help their stock price."

Apart from the fact that the disclosure selected for testing must indeed be informative, practical problems have prevented empirical study. Dhaliwal (1978), however, took advantage of voluntary reporting of line-of-business information prior to the SEC's requirement to report it. Using three surrogate measures to compare the cost of equity capital for two populations (a control group unaffected by the requirement and a group that would disclose the information for the first time), his findings were consistent with the lower-cost-of-capital thesis.

More recently Conover and Wallace (1994) found that greater extent of disaggregated disclosure for geographical segments correlated with higher stock prices. Their research analyzed the disclosures for the year 1983 by 230 multinational companies listed on the New York or American stock exchanges. The year 1983 was chosen because it was the first year that FASB Statements 14 (on segments) and 52 (on foreign currency translation) were both applicable. As compared to the market as a whole, the firms' market performance was better in relation to the extent of their geographic segment disclosures by a statistically significant margin.

Cost of Developing and Presenting Disclosure

Owners alone ultimately pay for the cost of disclosure, just as they ultimately bear all entity costs. Disclosure costs include the cost of gathering, processing, auditing (if the information is audited), and disseminating the information. However, since costs affect cash flows, employees, as parts of the entity with an interest in its cash flows, have an interest in minimizing the cost of disclosure.

The cost of developing and presenting information that is also used by or needed by management must be excluded from the cost of developing such information for external disclosure. To the degree that the work has already been done or would be done for managerial purposes, there would be no need to duplicate it. Other disclosure costs (formatting, packaging, and disseminating information), however, would be unaffected by the overlap between costs incurred for managerial purposes and costs incurred for purposes of external disclosure.

Litigation Costs

Litigation can arise from allegations of insufficient informative disclosure or from allegations of misleading disclosure. All suits that arise from insufficient informative disclosure support the thesis that litigation costs decrease with extent of disclosure.

Litigation arising from disclosure that is alleged to be misleading requires closer analysis. Cases of genuinely misleading disclosure are not relevant, because they cannot tell us about the costs of informative disclosure, which we have defined as unbiased and helpful to financial report users. Suits alleging that informative disclosure is misleading are meritless, that is, they are unjust. But we know that such suits occur and that they can impose costs on the entity.

The costs of such suits can vary from minor to very significant. Although litigation cost arising from increased informative disclosure is not a regular cost for all companies, directors and officers insurance is a widespread cost that is arguably attributable in significant measure to meritless suits. For those sued, apart from the legal fees, court awards, and the costs of settlements made strictly as business decisions (the lesser of two cost evils), there is a cost in public relations and in the distraction of executives from productive activities in the entity's interests.

It may be held that litigation costs increase with the extent of informative disclosure, but it is unlikely that this is true overall. The case for increase lies in instances where voluntary disclosure, particularly of forward-looking information, followed by share-price declines, have led to allegations of fraudulently misleading disclosure. Such suits have been widely protested by the financial-reporting community and cited in Congressional hearings. Their existence raises the question of the relationship between the population of meritless suits and the population of voluntary informative disclosures that did not result in suits. The latter population is presumably by far the larger, and it weighs against the thesis that litigation costs increase with extent of informative disclosure increases. In addition, four other perspectives must be brought to bear:

- First, fuller disclosure should lead to smaller claims because the stock market would have more realistic expectations of the company's prospects. The smaller the discrepancy between the valuation implicit in the market price and the valuation based on the company's true prospects, the smaller declines in share prices from disappointed expectations. Since damages are based on the extent of the decline, the smaller declines would lead to smaller damage claims.

- Second, defendants would have better defenses. Assume, for example, richer disclosure of enterprise risks. Defense attorneys could point to such disclosures to argue that the plaintiffs were adequately informed of the potential decline in share prices. This would increase the proportion of cases won by defendants and reduce the settlement amounts. The more important effect is the reduction in settlement amounts, because the cost of pursuing litigation leads to the settlement of most securities class actions.

- Third, there would be fewer suits as a consequence of the two conditions just cited. A higher proportion of the share price declines would be too small to justify a suit. Better defenses from richer disclosure would warn class-action attorneys that they would have a more difficult time winning and gain less in settlement. This would also be factored into class-action attorneys' decisions to bring suit.

- Fourth, the relationship between share price volatility and meritless suits raises the question of the degree to which the nature of the business rather than extent of disclosure is the reason for a given suit. In instances where companies volunteered forward-looking information and were subsequently sued after share-price declines for allegedly misleading investors, extent of disclosure is causative, if not the only cause. However, because of the way in which these suits occur, triggered by declines in share prices, the nature of the business is a major factor.

For these reasons, we can conclude that considered in full context, litigation costs caused by meritless suits decrease, rather than increase, with increasing extent of disclosure.

Competitive Disadvantage

Disclosure that would weaken a company's ability to generate future cash flows by aiding its competition is not in the interests of that company's employees and owners. Public companies have traditionally been very sensitive about disclosing information that might create competitive disadvantage, and private companies, though not faced with public disclosure obligations, sometimes show similar concern (for example, about whether a supplier who receives disclosure reveals such information to the disclosing company's competitor who is also the supplier's customer).

The types of information that might create competitive disadvantage are:

- Information about technological and managerial innovation (e.g., production processes, more effective quality-improvement techniques, marketing approaches).

- Strategies, plans, and tactics (e.g., planned product development, new market targeting).

- Information about operations (e.g., segment sales and production-cost figures, workforce statistics).[1]

The level of potential competitive disadvantage from disclosure in the categories above varies considerably, from zero to very high. Some operational data create no competitive disadvantage. However, segment profitability data could allow competitors to concentrate on the most profitable areas of the disclosing entity's business. A potential competitor could learn something about the capital investment required to enter into competition. Disclosing product development plans could lead a competitor to develop the same kind of product, with a race to the marketplace, or it could lead to counter-product development that would render a planned product either less attractive when it was released or soon to be leap-frogged. Information on targeting new markets could lead to defensive

---

[1]Stevenson (1980, 9–11) provides these categories and gives some examples within the categories. More are available in Mautz and May (1978), for example, on pp. 95–96

measures, such as increased advertising. Information on technological innovation could help lead competitors to improvements of their own.

The key factor in determining whether information in the categories above creates competitive disadvantage is timing. Products in development eventually come to market. Strategies become obvious from actions, and information about them can then no longer lead to competitive disadvantage. At some age disclosure simply loses its capacity to create competitive disadvantage. A given category of disclosure can be competitively disadvantageous or competitively meaningless depending on when the disclosure is made.

The role of timing suggests the possibility of differential disclosure based on estimated risks of competitive disadvantage. For example, capital suppliers might receive disclosures promptly under agreement with the disclosing entity to keep the disclosures confidential. The disclosure would be released publicly only when time has reduced or eliminated the estimated risks of competitive disadvantage.

Timing is not the only factor that determines the level of competitive disadvantage from disclosure. Other factors implicit in the examples above are the type of information, the level of detail, and the audience for the disclosure. We have already noted that routine operating data is less likely to cause competitive disadvantage than information on product development. But the greater the level of detail about new product plans—for example, including all unique features and the reasons for their potential appeal—the greater the likelihood of competitive disadvantage. Finally, as shown by the example of restricting disclosure to capital suppliers under confidentiality agreements, the parties with access to a disclosure determine its influence on competitive disadvantage.

Even with awareness of the factors just cited, it is difficult to generalize or be certain about the effect of particular disclosures on competitiveness. For example, the potential competitor determining the investment hurdle to enter an industry might as likely be dissuaded by the disclosures as convinced to become a competitor. Japanese companies' lead in analog HDTV would have suggested that almost any information about their technology was competitively disadvantageous, but the absence of such information was probably a factor in the move to a digital approach that appears to have given U.S. companies a technological lead.

There is also disclosure behavior that runs counter to the notion of competitive disadvantage. New products are sometimes announced early in order to convince competitors the market has been taken and to give the product a headstart in name recognition. Announcements of new products and planned products are also a form of public relations, keeping a corporate name in the public mind associated with progress. Finally, product plans are often revealed to capital suppliers in order to keep or win their support.

There is a vast difference between the purpose of disclosure to investors and creditors, on the one hand, and competitors' purposes, on the other. The purpose of disclosure to investors is to help them to estimate the amount, timing, and certainty of future cash flows from investing in the disclosing entity. Competitors are not trying to predict the enterprise's future cash flows, and information solely of use in that endeavor is not of use in obtaining competitive advantage. Overlap between information designed to meet investors' needs and information designed to further the purposes of a competitor is therefore coincidental.

Every entity that could suffer competitive disadvantage from disclosure could gain competitive advantage from comparable disclosure by competitors. There cannot be competitive disadvantage to one entity without one or more others gaining competitive advantage. Assuming it is required, competitors would have access to each other's disclosures. This suggests a net equality of competitive advantage and disadvantage for each enterprise. However, individual circumstances would undoubtedly differ. A technological leader would presumably have more to lose in reciprocated technological disclosure than a technological laggard. And those subject to direct competition from foreign companies with lower levels of disclosure could suffer competitive disadvantage from disclosures used by those competitors without access to the reciprocal disclosure that could bring offsetting competitive advantage. Nevertheless, for any given entity, competitive advantage from others' disclosures or the potential for such advantage must be counted along with whatever competitive disadvantage stems from that entity's own disclosures.

This creates the concept of *net* competitive disadvantage from disclosure. It would vary from entity to entity and from time to time, could be positive or negative, and could therefore also be called net competitive *advantage* from disclosure.

At least one distinguished CFO believes that disclosure of research ideas to competitors benefits the entity because it enhances research productivity. Here is the way Judy Lewent, CFO of Merck, explained her thought.

> We know that in order to advance swiftly toward successful research, it is often necessary to have our competitors working very closely in the same area. For example, I'm convinced that our research productivity is enhanced because so few boundaries exist among scientists at different companies and universities and at government-sponsored research at the National Institutes of Health. Tremendous spillover benefits arise as a result of scientists' propensity to publish and exchange ideas, particularly at the discovery stage; yet this in no way diminishes the highly competitive nature of the research process. (Nichols 1994, 97-98)

Put another way, reciprocal disclosure can be mutually beneficial because of the fillip it gives to the rate of technological progress. The improved rate brings advantages sooner.

There is some interaction between competitive disadvantage and other costs and benefits of disclosure. The cost of developing and presenting disclosure reduces competitiveness to the degree that it exceeds competitors' similar costs. The same is true of any litigation costs arising from disclosure. A lower cost of capital from disclosure improves competitiveness, and good relations with capital suppliers could help do the same.

Entity Behavior

Entities sometimes alter their behavior in response to disclosure requirements or the information that is disclosed, and the behavior can lead to costs or benefits. Today, there is talk of developing substitutes for stock options in the event the FASB requires that the costs of such options be recognized. The FASB's pronouncement on postretirement benefits other than pensions acknowledged the argument that preparers would change the designs of their postretirement benefit plans or the way the plans were financed (FASB 1990, par. 130).

However, disclosure-responsive economic behavior may decrease as well as increase costs. Developing new approaches to remuneration to replace stock options is a cost that would be borne by the entity. The postretirement benefits statement, on the other hand, contributed to an increasing appreciation of the dimensions and growth of health benefits costs and the need to control them.

It is very difficult to predict the results of disclosure on enterprise behavior. The imminent adoption of the FASB's pronouncement on contingencies in 1975 led to predictions that corporate risk and insurance management would be changed (e.g., increased limits on insured exposures, increased legal expenditures, changed coverages to accommodate increased exposures from the disclosure requirements, revised insurance and reinsurance contracts by captive insurance companies). There was concern about adverse consequences. In a study performed after the Statement was issued, however, Goshay (1978) found that there were no impressive differences between the risk management decisions of the companies he studied and those of a control group.

The FASB's first statement on foreign currency translation in 1975 evoked controversy over potential costs in enterprise behavior. A post-issuance study three years later did find behavioral changes in foreign exchange risk management as a result of the new requirement. However, some of the changes were beneficial (for example, companies became more aware of exchange risk and more sophisticated in evaluating the cost of foreign currency loan transactions). The researchers could not conclude either that the increased level of resources devoted to exchange risk management resulted in significant cash flow benefits or that the disclosure requirement's effects were of overall benefit or detriment to entities or society at large (Evans et al. 1978, 15-20).

There seems no basis for concluding that extent of disclosure results either in net damage from enterprise behavior or net benefits. Each case is unique. However, if new disclosure is truly informative and previously underappreciated by enterprise management, as was the case with the costs of postretirement medical benefits, there is likely to be a net economic benefit.

An important element of entity behavior is the exercise of corporate suffrage and decisions by directors. Information prepared for external reporting also contributes to corporate suffrage and directorial decisions.[2] To the degree that informative disclosure to investors and creditors serves the health of a corporate entity by enabling those who participate in corporate governance as shareholders or directors to make wise decisions that affect the entity's future economic success, it is a benefit.

Public Relations

Disclosure can have public relations benefits. For our purposes, the primary public-relations issue is relations with the investment community.

Investors and creditors get impressions of companies' openness and forthrightness. A more formal assessment is the annual evaluation of corporate financial reporting by the Association for Investment Management and Research. Each year the Association's Corporate Information Committee rates the quality of reporting in 31 industries. Financial analysts aware of the companies that received awards for excellence are likely to have a more favorable impression of those companies because of it.

Corporate citizenship is another aspect of public relations served by disclosure. Businesses discharge some part of their accountability obligations to the community through disclosure.

Cost Summary

The major entity costs from informative disclosure that have been discussed in this section are summarized in figures 2, 3, and 4. These treat in sequence the total cost of increasing disclosure for a public company assuming positive net competitive costs, for a public company assuming negative net competitive costs, and for a private company, where competitive disadvantage and litigation are omitted as, relatively speaking, insignificant cost risks.

As with figure 1, these graphs reflect costs at a point in time, hypothetically varying only extent of disclosure and describing by the curves estimated cost changes from those variations. (Future cost changes from other circumstances are treated in section IV below.) Again the graphs are illustrative only. The curves are estimates.

In figure 2, two costs decrease with more informative disclosure (information risk premium and litigation cost) and two increase (information cost and net competitive cost). The

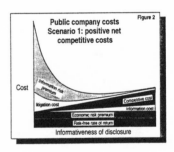

Figure 2

Public company costs
Scenario 1: positive net competitive costs

Cost

Informativeness of disclosure

---

[2]Statement of Financial Accounting Concepts No. 1 notes: "Financial reporting should provide information about how management of an enterprise has discharged its stewardship responsibility to owners (stockholders) for the use of enterprise resources entrusted to it. Management of an enterprise is periodically accountable to the owners …. Financial reporting should provide information that is useful to managers and directors in making decisions in the interests of owners." (FASB 1978, pars. 50, 52)

graph reflects the assumption that the entity suffers positive net competitive costs (net competitive disadvantage). The total cost curve has its minimum (the entity's optimal level of disclosure) in the valley at some level of informative disclosure that is greater than zero but less than complete. It is the task of those responsible for informative disclosure to determine in light of existing circumstances where on the curve we are today and how to respond to that determination.

Figure 3 is the same as figure 2 except in one very influential respect. It assumes negative net competitive costs (net competitive advantage) to an extent that exceeds information cost. This is shown by pulling the other curves toward and even beneath the horizontal axis, which is hidden but still represents informativeness of disclosure. With this assumption, the curve's "valley" disappears, and there is no real limit to the entity's disclosure consistent with its interests.

Figure 4, which describes the costs for a

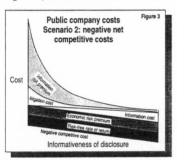

private company, differs from figures 2 and 3 by omitting litigation cost and net competitive cost. Only the cost of producing and presenting the disclosure rises with increasing disclosure. The resulting curve descends rapidly and then becomes a gradually rising plain, with the optimal level of disclosure being the lowest point on that curve. To imagine how this would function, consider the relationship between a private company and its banker. If the banker wants additional disclosure, the disclosure would not be expected to be distrib-

uted beyond that banker. There would then be no competitive disadvantage and minimal litigation risk. The advantage in cost of capital would have to be weighed only against the cost of producing and presenting the disclosure.

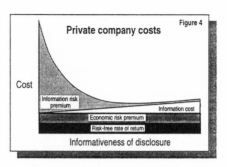

II. NONOWNER INVESTORS' INTERESTS

This category refers to the interests of investors and creditors who are not included in category 1—those in the marketplace who might invest in the entity. The category therefore excludes all owners, who have been defined as part of the entity, and also those potential owners who are employees of the enterprise.

Reduced Information Risk

Nonowner investors benefit from the lowered risk of making an error in allocating their resources. The way in which this occurs has already been described in section I under the entity's "Cost of Capital." It was described there because the two benefits are interdependent. The entity's benefit from a lower cost of capital is a consequence of nonowner investors' benefit from the lowered risk of making errors in their decisions: The investors' lowered risk leads them to lower the price for capital.

Reduced information risk is not automatically or equally available to every nonowner investor, because each is subject to the risk of misinterpreting informative disclosure. In addition, depending on the type of new information provided, there will be a learning curve in taking advantage of it. Nevertheless, the basic relationship between informative disclosure and nonowner investors remains that investors' likelihood of allocating their capital unprofitably diminishes with the increase of informative disclosure.

The benefit of lower information risk accruing to nonowner investors generates benefits to other interests. In fact, it is a great engine of such benefits. We have already noted the interdependence between the entity's lower cost of capital and investors' reduced information risk. In addition, the national interest in effective capital allocation and market liquidity depends on nonowner investors and creditors acting on disclosure in their decision making. Similarly, reduced information risk is integral to the social benefit of consumer protection.

Costs

Potential owners obtain the benefits of disclosure without the costs. They are free riders, not paying the costs of litigation, competitive disadvantage, or developing and presenting disclosure. However, they would pay these costs if they became owners in the sense that the stream of cash flows to the entity would be curtailed by the costs the potential owners had previously avoided as free riders.

III. THE NATIONAL INTEREST

Some may question whether the costs and benefits to the national interest should be weighed in evaluating disclosure, taking the position that accounting should be neutral in the sense of not being entwined with issues of public policy. However, neutrality in accounting in the sense of focusing on effective economic measurement is consistent with the national interest, and such accounting need not be entwined with narrower issues of public policy. There is no question that the full range of costs and benefits from disclosure includes those that fall to the national interest. Interpretations of the national interest in specific accounting issues are cited in public

debate; the FASB's mission statement contains a national-interest paragraph;[3] and the securities laws' establishment of a statutory disclosure system is Congressional testimony to the fact that corporate disclosure is a matter of national interest. These reasons and citations suggest that the national interest should not be excluded in considering the costs and benefits of informative disclosure.

The U.S. national interest is lodged in the concept of the greatest good for the greatest number. As with individuals, there is a difference between enlightened and unenlightened interests. On the national level it consists primarily of short-term (unenlightened) as opposed to long-term (enlightened) interests. The remarks below refer to long-term interests.

Cost of Capital

To the degree that disclosure contributes to lower capital costs, it is in the national interest. Low capital costs are desirable for their contribution to economic growth, jobs, and an improved standard of living. All these follow from the fact that low capital costs increase the rate of investment by entities.

The exception to the generalization that low capital costs are in the national interest is when inflation is being fought by higher capital costs. Even then, the national interest is served by the lowest cost of capital consistent with controlling inflation. More importantly, disclosure is not a useful technique in raising capital costs. Such a course (temporarily decreasing informative disclosure) is more likely to lead to chaos than macroeconomic benefits. Federal Reserve and fiscal policy, the accepted tools, are unquestionably more efficient and effective.

---

[3]"Accounting standards are essential to the efficient functioning of the economy because decisions about the allocation of resources rely heavily on credible, concise, and understandable financial information. Financial information about the operations and financial position of individual entities also is used by the public in making various other kinds of decisions." (FASB 1987, par. 2)

Effective Allocation of Capital

The national interest in effective allocation of capital cannot be underestimated. It has been of concern in recent years, with increased international competition. That is one of the explanations for "industrial policy" and studies on building competitiveness. Rich disclosure contributes to effective allocation of capital by enabling investors and creditors to identify the most productive enterprises. Unwise investments are bad for economic growth and national competitiveness. Apart from the obvious case of an investment that quickly ends in bankruptcy, companies capable of high level performance should have adequate supplies of capital.

The effective allocation of capital refers to more than the allocation of financial capital. It also includes human capital because human capital tends to flow to the best opportunities and informative disclosure helps talented people identify the best opportunities. With the increasing rate at which financial capital flows across borders, human capital, which crosses borders at a much slower rate, is widely recognized for its contribution to national competitiveness.

Liquidity

Disclosure contributes to the liquidity of the capital markets, also a benefit to the national economy. A more liquid market assists the effective allocation of capital. Liquidity varies according to the bid-ask spread. The wider the bid-ask spread the less liquidity (i.e., fewer transactions take place), and the narrower the bid-ask spread the greater the liquidity (i.e., more transactions take place). Two principal determinants of the bid-ask spread are the degree of information asymmetry between the buyer and seller and the degree of uncertainty of the buyer and the seller. Both larger asymmetry and greater uncertainty widen the spread, but lower asymmetry and less uncertainty—two products of broad, public disclosure—diminish it, thereby increasing liquidity.

National Competition Among Businesses

If there are indeed competitive advantages and disadvantages from entity disclosure, there must be a resulting increase in the intensity of competition. To the degree that disclosure adds to competition among U.S. businesses, other things being equal, it serves the national interest.

Vigorous competition among businesses leads to greater efficiency and national competitiveness. This has been part of our national political ideology and law for generations (e.g., the anti-trust laws and the FTC's mandate to fight restraints on trade). Economists and public policy-makers support the idea that competition is needed for long-term economic growth, and anticompetitive features in other societies are widely cited to explain slow growth and difficulties in emerging from recession.

The U.S. is not, of course, a land of unfettered competition. There are types of trade protection and subsidies that reduce the vigor of marketplace competition. Although these inconsistencies often reflect the power of relatively narrow interests or concern for their plight, rather than the national interest in its full breadth, there is also a set of inconsistencies based on national security needs and a smaller set based on the economic policy of assisting research-and-development projects considered underfunded and promising. However, national policy and our economy, on balance, are heavily weighted toward market-determined economic decisions, which means free and fair competition.

Apart from the exceptions just cited, there are specific devices to give monopoly advantages to companies and other economic agents. These are patents, copyrights, and trade secret law.[4] Their economic rationale is that a

---

[4]The subject matter of a trade secret may be a formula, machine, process, or compilation of information that confers competitive advantage and that is known only to its owner and employees (Stevenson 1980, 15–16).

certain level of anticompetitive advantage is necessary to encourage innovation and risk taking. Other justifications can be made based on notions of fairness and ideas of property, but only the economic rationale is of interest here.

Three conclusions follow from the existence of these devices and their economic rationale. First, our society recognizes that there should be limits on competition. Second, in the case of trade secret law, our society recognizes that there must be some protection against unauthorized disclosure even if it is anticompetitive. (Patents and copyrights are not limits on disclosure; they are forms of disclosure that are accompanied by monopoly rights to protect competitive advantage.) Third, discussions of competitive disadvantage from disclosure must consider that these devices protect competitive advantage that otherwise might be lost from disclosure.

There are limits to the need for anti-competitive devices to encourage innovation and risk taking. First, in our economy most innovation and risk taking is encouraged by the profit motive functioning apart from anticompetitive devices and, ironically, by competition. Innovation enables one competitor to stay ahead of another as does risk-taking investment in cost-lowering technology. Second, once conferred or otherwise in hand, monopoly rights function as a drag, rather than a spur, to innovation and risk taking. They are a spur only when they are a profit-protecting prize to be sought.

We can conclude that the existence of anticompetitive devices does not alter the generalization that, other things being equal, disclosure's encouragement of competition is in the national interest.

International Competition

Foreign corporations selling to the U.S. market do not have in their home countries the same disclosure requirements that U.S. corporations have here. It is typically more costly for U.S. firms to prepare disclosure under the U.S. requirements, a competitive disadvantage. Another potential competitive disadvantage is that U.S. disclosures allow foreign competitors to know more about publicly traded U.S. firms than such firms know about competitors from abroad.

The competitive advantage overseas firms have from lower disclosure requirements in their home countries could be cured by tariffs or other forms of trade restriction. Although the debate over free trade is beyond the scope of this article, the context puts the competitive-cost issue in a different light.[5] The difference in costs of disclosure can be seen as one of many cost differences that go into the economics of international trade. U.S. spending per pupil in excess of competitors', for example, could be considered a subsidy to the businesses that pay more for disclosure than their foreign competitors. Such cost differences are ingredients in the mix of comparative advantages that drives trade.

U.S. firms also compete with foreign corporations in third-country markets. Again, the competitive advantage derived from disclosure is one of the full set of cost differences that go into the economics of international trade. Trade restrictions, however, are not an option in such cases.

One mentioned remedy, assuming it were available, is the so-called level playing field, a U.S. level of disclosure identical to the levels in foreign competitors' home countries. However, equality of disclosure by itself is not a rational approach to the national interest. It ignores the quality and sufficiency of disclosure. No disclosure, foreign or domestic, creates a playing field as level as any other. An approach that totally ignores the objectives of effective capital allocation and the interests of investors cannot be considered rational. The benefits of informative disclosure obviously weigh against leveling by reduced disclosure. Moreover, the U.S. has long had a distinction between public-company disclosure requirements and private-company disclosure requirements that is inconsistent with a purely level playing field on disclosure.

[5]For a concise modern statement of free trade arguments, in the context of a rebuttal, see Bhagwhati (1988).

There is also the question of what is meant by a "playing field." A disclosure system is only part of a capital allocation system and cannot be understood out of that context. This point is made in the study on national competitiveness by Michael Porter of Harvard Business School for the Council on Competitiveness (1980, 83, 85). Porter notes that German and Japanese enterprises have fewer external reporting requirements, but have closer, long-term relationships with dominant owners, who are informed by other mechanisms. In this way Porter justifies recommending more and better disclosure in the U.S. to improve capital allocation in the interest of national competitiveness. For our purposes, the differences among national capital allocation systems means that comparisons based on disclosure alone must be considered incomplete.

Globally harmonized disclosure standards that adequately serve users' needs and meet cost-benefit tests would end the problem of international differences in disclosure. But that is down the road. For the present, it is important to note that U.S. companies can raise capital abroad if they choose to or engage in private placements in the U.S. Their decisions to stay in the U.S. public market suggest its advantages outweigh its disadvantages. The advantages include low cost and liquidity that are partly attributable to disclosure.

The U.S. also has an interest in attracting overseas firms to its capital markets. However, the arguments that apply to the national interest in the disclosures of domestic issuers apply to foreign issuers. It is again in the national interest, for example, that the stock of U.S. capital be effectively allocated and for the markets to be liquid. If attracting foreign issuers is in the national interest, the benefit of lower capital costs from fuller disclosure serves that interest.

Litigation Costs

Litigation arising from informative disclosure—i.e., meritless suits—creates a social cost. There is evidence that high-tech companies, with high share-price volatility, have been particular targets, sued when their shares decline. Thus it is arguable that meritless suits have their greatest influence on the smaller, cutting-edge firms that contribute disproportionately to economic growth and job creation.

As described in section I, there are various components to the costs of litigation, but in sum they weaken enterprises financially and distract them from their economic missions. The national cost is a less effective economy. There are also costs in economic growth from a higher cost of capital (since the threat of litigation has curtailed disclosure) and from less effective corporate governance (since independent directors, fearing liability, are harder to obtain).

Consumer Protection

Disclosure plays a major role in the government's consumer protection efforts. This includes regulated disclosures on product labels, in advertising, and in lending. For our purposes, the important element is the consumer-protection aspect of corporate financial disclosure. The SEC regulates corporate financial disclosure largely to protect the interests of investors and creditors, the consumers of corporate securities. To the degree that informative disclosure provides needed consumer protection, other things equal, it is a benefit in the national interest.

Externalities

Society has an interest in the externalities of business operations (e.g., environmental pollution and effects on communities). Federal and local governments have acted in all sorts of ways to regulate externalities and remedy their effects. Measurement and disclosure have been a key part of these efforts (e.g., the environmental impact statement). To the degree that public disclosure by business entities (e.g., risks and uncertainties) assists governments in assessing problems caused by externalities and making socially useful decisions in response, disclosure is in the national interest.

IV. LOOKING TO THE FUTURE

A full consideration of costs and benefits includes how they could change in the future. The objective is to contribute some perspective on long-term, net costs and benefits. Many of the generalizations below depend on the conclusions reached above, but only major factors are considered.

For the entity, the lowered cost of capital would continue to be a benefit. If we presume additional informative disclosure, the benefit should increase. The rate of increase depends on the degree of informativeness of current disclosure. If it is very high, only marginal improvements are available. Research on the needs of financial report users would clarify this.

The cost of developing and presenting today's disclosure will decrease in the future primarily because of advances in information technology. A greater overlap between managerial information needs and those of investors and creditors should have a similar, if smaller, effect. If we postulate increasing disclosure, there would still be a cost-of-preparation decline in the long term. In the future, information technology will totally transform the economics of developing and presenting disclosure.

Litigation cost is extraordinarily difficult to predict because of possible changes in laws and regulations. Additional safe harbors for forward-looking information, for example, are a genuine possibility. An extrapolation from today's litigation costs suggests significant increases in the future, but such increases would not bear a one-to-one relationship with litigation costs from increased informative disclosure. Today's costs derive from meritorious as well as meritless suits, and many meritless suits originate in business volatility that precipitates drops in stock prices, not increased extent of disclosure. When considered in full context, increased informative disclosure, as we have seen, should reduce litigation exposure.

Greater informative disclosure would increase competitive disadvantage for public entities, but not sharply. The mitigating circumstances cited above would continue to limit the level of disadvantage. Competitors will improve their ability to learn from informative disclosure, which would help to maximize competitive disadvantage for disclosing companies, but this would be partly offset by the increasing dependence of business on science and technology and the advantage of more rapid fruition of profitable ideas from mutual disclosure. If the level of disclosure by U.S. public companies increases faster than that of foreign companies, competitive disadvantage from foreign competitors' use of increased disclosure by U.S. companies will grow. However, if the reverse occurs (the level of disclosure by foreign competitors increases faster than that of U.S. companies), competitive disadvantage to U.S. public companies from added disclosure will decrease.

Nonowner investors' benefits from informative disclosure would increase in the future as those disclosures increased. Again, the rate of increase depends on the degree of informativeness of current disclosure.

Information overload has long been an important concern, but the analytical power of investors and creditors, assisted by computers and software, should keep pace with any likely increase in informative disclosure. At the moment, institutional investors and creditors have access to greater analytical power than is necessary for current levels of disclosure. The only potential caveat in this scenario applies to individual investors. As a group, they would be less well prepared to benefit by processing additional disclosure than institutional investors, but should nevertheless. Efficient market research shows that securities prices reflect all publicly available information, which means that individual investors would benefit from information analyzed by institutional investors. In addition, many individual investors rely on investment advisors who would either perform or have access to analyses of additional informative disclosure. Finally, any substantial market demand for simplified analytical software is likely to be filled, making it possible for an increasing number of individual investors to perform their own analyses of increased informative disclosure.

The national interest in informative disclosure will continue and will become stronger. The advantages of lower cost of capital, market liquidity, increased competition in the business world, and, most importantly, effective allocation of capital would improve with greater informative disclosure. The national interest in consumer protection and corporate externalities should grow only moderately, in part because they are, in the circumstances, rather high at the moment. Their standing is masked by the difficulty in getting any issue at the top of the national agenda and by the paramountcy of economic growth and job creation.

Summary

In light of the trends just discussed and recalling figures 2, 3, and 4, we can ask, first, whether the optimal level of informative disclosure is likely to increase or decrease in the future when viewed solely from the entity's perspective. However, unlike figures 2, 3, and 4, the costs would be changing over time, rather than responsive to hypothetical increases in disclosure as of today.

The dominant trend appears to be the rapidly decreasing costs of preparing and communicating disclosure. This would increase the optimal disclosure level for private companies. For public companies, unless competitors develop the capability to impose significantly greater competitive disadvantages through use of the information or litigation costs become more perverse, the most likely result is that the optimal level of disclosure will increase in the future. This applies both to public companies with negative net competitive cost from increased disclosure (competitive advantage) and for those with positive net competitive cost.

The second information-technology trend, users' greater power to access and interpret information, will increase all users' benefits. Users' interests in increased disclosure are consistent with an increase in the optimal level of disclosure from the entity's perspective.

These changes would be consistent with the national interest. From the perspective of the national interest, an increase in the optimal level of disclosure would be a long-term benefit.

V. THE LIMITS OF COST-BENEFIT ANALYSIS

Cost-benefit analysis of disclosure is limited in its effectiveness by the nature of social decision making, which certainly includes setting accounting standards. Nobel-laureate Kenneth J. Arrow's studies of collective decision making found that ideal outcomes could never be a direct aggregation of constituent preferences (Arrow 1983). Thus, assuming, fanciful though it may be, that decision-makers determining business disclosure had absolute knowledge of every individual and organizational self-interest in terms of dollar-denominated costs and benefits, it would be impossible to reach a decision that gave those preferences equal treatment. No social preference can directly reflect the rank ordering of all constituents' diverse preferences.

These constraints suggest that mechanisms for social decision making need to do more to achieve socially desirable ends than tote up representations of constituents' interests or their preferences, even if they claim backing in cost-benefit data. The constraints also suggest that judgments must be brought to bear to make tradeoffs. Public-interest objectives can help, and so can procedures to ensure due consideration of the interests of all relevant parties, including those interests not vehemently expressed or even unexpressed.

The limited use of cost-benefit information suggests the FASB was wise to add this qualification to its mission-statement precept on weighing the views of constituents: "The ultimate determinant of concepts and standards, however, must be the FASB's judgment, based on research, public input, and careful deliberation, about the usefulness of the resulting information" (FASB 1987, 3).

Even if it cannot be decisive by itself, additional academic research on the costs and benefits of disclosure could be very helpful. Research could advance our knowledge and improve cost-benefit evaluations. The authority of credentialed researchers can drive home finally the fact that a full set of dollar-denominated costs and benefits is a hopeless quest. Ideally, research on costs and benefits would have balance. Increases in studies of costs or benefits alone, or a population of studies heavily weighted toward one of the two, could have a one-sided effect on the public dialog. That would be unfortunate, because one of the potential contributions of cost-benefit research is to help ensure that all parties with a stake in disclosure decisions receive the attention worthy of that stake.

APPENDIX
Informativeness of Disclosure

Although the text and graphics in this article are heuristic, it is possible to take a more formal, information-theoretic view of the informativeness of disclosure. Under this approach, the information content of a message is defined as its capacity to reduce uncertainty (i.e., increasing informativeness of disclosure equates to decreasing investor uncertainty which leads to a decreasing information risk premium demanded by investors). Uncertainty reduction is inversely related to the *ex ante* probability of receiving a particular true[6] and relevant[7] message: the more improbable the message *ex ante*, the more informative. For example, the reliable message that a particle moved faster than the speed of light has zero probability *ex ante*, thus infinite information value to a theoretical physicist (but not a teeny bopper). The reliable message that a building is on fire has very low *ex ante* probability, thus very high informativeness to an occupant. The response "fine" to the question "how are you?" has very high *ex ante* probability, thus very low information content. It is well known, for example, that stock prices do not respond to earnings-per-share announcements that equal the expected amounts, but do respond to surprising earnings-per-share announcements.

To express the idea formally, the information content, I_M, of a reliable, relevant message, M, equals the logarithm of the reciprocal of the *ex ante* probability of receiving the message ($I_M = \log_2(1/p(M))$).[8] The information content of multiple, nonredundant messages is the sum of the contents of the individual messages. Nonredundancy is expressed as a conditional probability:

$$p(M_1 \cap M_2) = p(M_1) \bullet p(M_2 | M_1) = p(M_2) \bullet p(M_1 | M_2)$$

Thus x values in figures 1 through 4 in this article can be defined as

$$x = \log_2\left(1/p\left(M_1\right)\right) + \sum_{i=2}^{n} \log_2\left(1/p\left(M_i \,|\, M_1, \,...,\, M_{i-1}\right)\right)$$

where n is the number of messages disclosed.

---

[6]If messages were dichotomized as true or false, then true messages would have information content and false messages would not. Of course, real messages are not generally dichotomous with respect to truth. Rather, they have degrees of reliability, which might be measured, for example, by their standard errors of estimate: the smaller (larger) the standard error, the greater (lesser) the reliability. For simplicity, this appendix assumes highly reliable (i.e., essentially true) messages.

[7]Investor uncertainty does not refer to a generalized state of mind, but rather to a specific decision problem, such as how much shares of company X are worth. Only information that reduces uncertainty with respect to that estimate is relevant for purposes. If an investor were trying to decide the worth of shares of company X, the receipt of reliable news that a fish flew through the sky might be very informative generally, but would shed no light on the worth of company X, would be irrelevant to the investor's decision, and would have no information content for that decision.

[8]If message M can take any of n values and the *ex ante* probability of the ith value is p_i, then the expected information content, $E(I)$, of the message (also known as the entropy of the message) is

$$E(I) = \sum_{i=1}^{n} p_i \log_2(1/p_i)$$

For a primer in information theory, see Cover and Thomas (1991).

Note that x is independent of the order in which the n messages are disclosed, because each probability is conditional on all prior messages. Also note a caveat: managers may have a bias to present good news and withhold bad news. To the extent investors suspect such a bias, they discount the news. However, there are at least four mitigating factors to this tendency: (1) accounting and disclosure standards are structured to produce unbiased presentations[9] (e.g., a company must disclose not only assets, revenues, and opportunities, but also liabilities, costs, and risks), (2) independent audits of information reduce bias, (3) managers' (long run) employment potentials are affected by their reputations for integrity, and (4) biased reports may be punished by criminal and civil litigation.

Thus the x axis in the figures in this article assumes that information is unbiased. And, by definition, redundant information has no informative value (i.e., the information content of company reports is not proportionate to their mere volume, but to their capacity to reduce uncertainty to investors).

---

[9]In this context, unbiased means that companies cannot elect to disclose only the favorable information under generally accepted accounting principles, but must report all the information. Although accounting standards do include some biases (such as conservatism and nonrecognition of research and development assets), they relate to matters that are not under management's discretion, and users—aware of the biases—can adjust for them.

REFERENCES

Arrow, K. J. 1983. *Collected Papers of Kenneth J. Arrow*. vol. 1, *Social Choice and Justice*. Cambridge, MA: The Belknap Press of Harvard University Press.

Bhagwhati, J. 1988. *Protectionism*. Cambridge, MA: The MIT Press.

Conover, T. L., and W. A. Wallace. 1994. Equity Market Benefits to Disclosure of Geographic Segment Information: An Argument for Decreased Uncertainty. Working paper.

Cover, T. M., and J. A. Thomas. 1991. *Elements of Information Theory*. John Wiley & Sons, Inc.

Dhaliwal, D. S. 1978. The Impact of Disclosure Regulations on the Cost of Capital. *Economic Consequences of Financial Accounting Standards: Selected Papers*. Stamford, CT: FASB: 73–100.

Evans, T. G., W. R. Folks, Jr., and M. Jilling. 1978. *The Impact of Statement of Financial Accounting Standards No. 8 on the Foreign Exchange Risk Management Practices of American Multinationals: An Economic Impact Study*. Stamford, CT: FASB.

Financial Accounting Standards Board. 1978. *Statement of Financial Accounting Concepts No. 1: Objectives of Financial Reporting by Business Enterprises*. Stamford, CT: FASB.

———. 1987. *Rules of Procedure, Amended and Restated Effective January 1, 1987*. Stamford, CT: FASB.

———. 1990. *Statement of Financial Accounting Standards No. 106: Employers' Accounting for Postretirement Benefits Other Than Pensions*. Stamford, CT: FASB.

Goshay, R. C. 1978. *Statement of Financial Accounting Standards No. 5: Impact on Corporate Risk and Insurance Management*. Stamford, CT: FASB.

Mautz, R. K., and W. G. May. 1978. *Financial Disclosure in a Competitive Economy*. New York, NY: Financial Executives Research Foundation.

Nichols, N. A. 1994. Scientific Management at Merck: An Interview with CFO Judy Lewent. *Harvard Business Review* (January–February): 89–99.

Porter, M. E. 1992. *Capital Choices: Changing the Way America Invests in Industry*. Council on Competitiveness and Harvard Business School.

Stevenson, Jr., R. B. 1980. *Corporations and Information: Secrecy, Access, and Disclosure*. Baltimore, MD: The Johns Hopkins University Press.

Sweeney, P. 1994. Polishing the Tarnished Image of Investor Relations Executives. *New York Times* (April 3).

4

Entitlements, Rights, and Fairness in Intrafirm Resource Allocation

The previous chapter focused on fairness in financial accounting as it affects consideration of presentation, distribution, and disclosure. This chapter focuses on the problems of fairness in management accounting in general and intrafirm resource allocation in particular. Consideration of fairness in distribution may have a differential impact on intrafirm resource allocation. Accordingly this chapter elaborates on the different ways of modeling the fairness assumption in intrafirm resource allocation and reports on an experiment examining the effects of entitlements, rights, and fairness on unit manager behavior in intrafirm resource allocation.

MODELING THE FAIRNESS ASSUMPTION

The concept of fairness is very much a determinant of economic transactions. But the nature of what determines behavior in economic models is *homo economicus:* "the selfish brute who devotes himself single-mindedly to maximizing the present value of his measurable wealth."[1] It is a behavior dominated by rational responses to economic incentives.[2] D. Kahneman et al. questioned the traditional assumption that fairness is irrelevant to economic analysis.[3] They argued that even profit-maximizing firms will resort to fairness if their potential customers are likely to resist the unfairness and use punishment mechanisms against the firms at some cost to themselves. Those transactions (customers, tenants, employees) are assumed to have the following traits: "(1) They care about being treated fairly and treating others fairly. (2) They are willing to resist unfair firms even at a positive cost.

(3) They have systematic implicit rules that specify which actions of firms are considered unfair."[4] Their experiments showed the presence of a willingness to enforce fairness, helping to explain some anomalous market phenomena.

Several other economists have also used a notion of fairness in their interpretations of regulation[5] and of the market phenomena of price and wage stickiness.[6] The demands of customers and employees for fair treatment and the role of perceived unfairness triggering the search for alternative suppliers were also examined by Arthur Okun.[7] It can explain the hostility of customers to price increases that are not justified by matching cost increases. W. J. Baumol showed that the fairness criterion is operational and can be applied to concrete problems such as the issue of rationing of commodities:

> Persons who design public policy are, typically, at least as concerned with issues of equity as with allocative efficiency. The economist's influence is therefore impeded by his inability to deal with issues of fairness in applied problems. Fairness theory, perhaps for the first time, provides an analytic instrument for the purpose. Inevitably, it must, of course rest upon value judgements as well as observable relationships. But what is remarkable about fairness theory is that both the behavioral relationships and the value judgements on which it is based are, essentially, those used in the standard welfare analysis of resource allocation. In both, the basic data are consumer preferences and production relationships, and in both the basic value judgement is that the desires of the affected individuals, rather than those of some superior arbitrator, must count.[8]

The absence of fairness considerations in economic models is equivalent to a self-interest assumption. Self-interest is assumed to dominate all motives. Various studies, however, attempted to demonstrate how nonselfinterested behavior, envy or, usually, altruism, can be incorporated into microeconomic models.[9,10,11,12,13,14] Gary Becker justifies his model of altruism as follows:

> Sociologists have explained the strong survival throughout most of the biological world of altruism toward children and other kin by group selection operating through the common genes of kin. Using an economic model of altruism, I have explained its survival by the advantages of altruism when there is physical and social interaction: kin have had much interaction with each other because they have usually lived with or near each other. Since the economic model requires interaction, not common genes, it can also explain the survival of some altruism towards unrelated neighbors or co-workers, and these are not explained by the kin selection models of sociologists.[15]

Various studies attempted to challenge the self-interest assumptions in economics in experimental nonmarket-like situations involving real payoffs.[16,17,18] Most of the subjects appeared willing to consider the welfare of others by taking lesser payoffs and acting as if altruism or fairness was an important factor in their preference structures. N. Frohlich and J. Oppenheimer explicitly tested for altruistic, egalitarian, and difference maximizing behaviors.[19] Their interactive preferences were defined as follows:

> Intuitively, altruistic preferences are those by which individuals are willing to give up some things to increase the welfare of another person . . .
>
> Egalitarian preferences involve a concern for the degree of equality of income, wealth, or payoff associated with the outcomes; hence they involve some form of fairness. Conceptually, difference maximizing behavior is akin to malice. It reflects a preference for outcomes that maximize the difference between what one gets and what some other person gets (with the latter getting the lesser amount, of course).[20]

The results showed that nonmaximizing or nonself-interested behavior occurs consistently. The results are very much compatible with the social sciences assumption of a *homo sociologicus,* with human behavior determined not so much by rational responses to economic incentives but by "social forces" such as norms and customs.[21]

The situation in accounting is more akin to *homo economicus* than *homo sociologicus.* For intrafirm resource allocation, as well as for cases involving asymmetric information between parties to a contract, agency theory predicts unconstrained opportunistic behavior.[22] It ignores, however, various social and psychological factors which may reduce misrepresentations in firms. The opportunistic behaviors are due to a behavior in accord with the self-regarding utilitarian theory of fairness, where resources are perceived as rights by one of the parties to the contract. However, where other theories of distributive justice are instituted, a more egalitarian behavior is expected. Accordingly, the remainder of this chapter examines the issues of theories of distributive justice and intrafirm resource allocation.

To illustrate, consider the case of a decentralized firm with two related units. A common resource given to (or produced by) the first unit can also be used by the second unit. The two unit managers have opposing payoff functions and full information on one another's payoffs.[23] The reward schemes of each unit manager are strictly increasing functions of divisional profits.[24] The first unit manager, given (or producing) the common resource, is entitled by central management to distribute the common resource between him/herself and the unit manager of the second unit. The first unit manager's offer to the second unit manager, following the need for intrafirm resource allocation, is concurrent with one of three concepts of fairness or justice in distribution.[25]

Utilitarian Theory of Distributive Justice

This asserts that people ought to act so as to maximize some function which is monotonically increasing the utility of each of the members of society.[26] One version of utilitarianism used in accounting research is that each person's utility is independent of any other person's utility and each person maximizes his own utility. In the context of the intrafirm resource allocation described in this study, if the first unit manager perceives the resources entrusted to him or her as rights and behaves in accord with a utilitarian theory of fairness, the allocations are expected to be non-Pareto optimal, which is also an unequal split. This is the opportunistic behavior predicted by agency theory and observed in some experimental settings.[27]

Egalitarian Theory of Distributive Justice

This asserts that a just distribution gives everyone an equal share of resources based on equality of needs,[28] assessments of dignity,[29] or satisfaction of minimum needs.[30] In the context of intrafirm resource allocation described in this study, if the first unit manager perceives the organizational (experimental) institutions as triggering instead an egalitarian theory of distributive justice, the allocation is expected to be Pareto-optimal, which is also an equal split. It follows from both theory and experimental evidence that subjects who hold beliefs favoring equality or payment according to need would always split payoffs equally.[31]

Lockean Theory of Distributive Justice

Natural law/desert theories maintain that, as a matter of law, someone or other deserves resources. One such theory, the Lockean theory, asserts that an individual deserves, as a matter of law, a property entitlement in resources that have been accumulated or developed through the individual's expenditure of effort.[32,33] In the context of intrafirm resource allocation described in this study, if the first unit manager perceives the organizational (experimental) institutions as triggering instead a Lockean theory of distributive justice, the allocation is expected to be Pareto-optimal, which is also an equal split, or a split more proportional to the returns generated by each unit. Accordingly:

H_1: *The intrafirm resource allocation decision, as expressed by the greed index, will be different and in accord with either the self-*

regarding utilitarian theory, the egalitarian theory of distributive justice, or the Lockean theory of earned desert.

The hypothesis implies that the greed index, the amount in excess of an equal split received by the first manager, will be different for the three groups of subjects perceiving the experimental institutions as triggering one of three particular concepts of distributive justice.

The experimental design described below uses a mechanism that creates a right by telling the subjects that they have "earned" their entitlements, and a treatment variable that motivates subjects about relying on utilitarian, egalitarian, or Lockean theories of distributive justice. Following related research, the study controls for age, ethnic affiliation,[34,35] political orientation,[36] and gender.[37,38,39,40,41]

EXPERIMENTAL DESIGN

General

The experiment involved face-to-face bargaining between a team of two people. The bargaining was face to face. The two people were informed of each other's capital, return, and payoffs as well as the whole team return. Contracts were in writing and strictly enforced. Subjects were given motivational instructions about relying on either utilitarian, egalitarian, or Lockean principles of fairness in choosing numbers or in forming contracts.

Experimental Instructions

Game-Trigger, Utilitarian Moral Authority

The subjects were assigned randomly the letters A and B and were placed in separate rooms with a monitor. The monitor instructed each subject to read silently the following set of instructions, then read them aloud again.

INSTRUCTIONS

General

You are about to participate in an experiment in decision making. The purpose of the experiment is to gain insight into certain features of complex economic processes. If you follow the instructions carefully, you might earn a considerable amount of money. You will be paid in cash at the end of the experiment.

Specific Instructions to Participants

You are person _____. The other participant is person _____.
The experiment includes two stages. Stage 1 involves a game where the winner earns the right to become the controller. Stage 2 requires a decision to be made.

Stage 1

Both participants A and B will play a game. Whoever wins this game earns the right to be designated "controller" for the decision in the next stage. The rules of this preliminary game are as follows:

| | | | | | | | | | | | | | | | | | | | | | | | | | | | | | | | |

Above here is a picture of 17 vertical hatch marks. Each player must, on each turn, cross out 1, 2, 3, or 4 hatch marks. After a player has crossed out as many marks as he or she wishes, it is the other player's turn to cross out 1, 2, 3, or 4 hatch marks. The game continues until all marks have been crossed out. The person who crosses out the last mark loses the game. A will go first on the first decision, B will go first on the second decision.

Example: A goes first and crosses out 4 marks:

𝕏 𝕏 𝕏 𝕏 | | | | | | | | | | | | |

Then B crosses out 4 marks:

𝕏 𝕏 𝕏 𝕏 𝕏 𝕏 𝕏 𝕏 | | | | | | | | |

Then A crosses out 4 marks:

𝕏 𝕏 𝕏 𝕏 𝕏 𝕏 𝕏 𝕏 𝕏 𝕏 𝕏 𝕏 | | | | |

Then B crosses out 4 marks:

𝕏 𝕏 𝕏 𝕏 𝕏 𝕏 𝕏 𝕏 𝕏 𝕏 𝕏 𝕏 𝕏 𝕏 𝕏 𝕏 |

A must cross out the last mark on his or her turn, so A loses the game and B has earned the position of the controller.

Stage 2

The decision involves choosing a number. The number will correspond to the actual dollar amount to be allocated to A and B for investment of the team's capital. The rate of return on capital for A is 20 percent and for B is

40 percent. Both A and B are entitled to a fixed salary of $3 plus 10 percent of their respective return generated. The total return of the team will also be compared to the return of other teams.

Whoever wins the game in stage 1 *earns the right* to become "controller" for that decision. If you win the game and are designated the controller, you may, if you wish, choose any number you like by filling out the form on page _____ and giving it to the monitor. However, if you lose the preliminary game and are not designated controller, you may still attempt to influence the controller to form a *joint agreement* and choose some other number. In order to induce the controller to choose an acceptable *joint agreement,* you may offer to give part of your capital to the controller.

Example: Assume that A wins the game and is designated controller for the decision. Also assume the following payoffs for A and B:

Number	A's Capital	B's Capital	A's Return (20%)	B's Return (40%)	Total Return	A's Payoff (10%)	B's Payoff (10%)
1	$4	$1	$0.8	$0.4	$1.2	$0.08	$0.04
2	5	2	1.0	0.8	1.8	0.10	0.08
3	3	5	0.6	2.0	0.8	0.06	0.20

Once A has become a controller, he or she may choose any number without consulting B. However, B may attempt to persuade A to join in a joint decision to choose another number and/or a different division of capital and payoffs. If a joint agreement is reached, *both* parties must sign the agreement form on page _____, stating both what the chosen number will be and how much money will be transferred from one participant's capital to the other participant's capital. For example, A may choose number 2 because it maximizes his or her salary ($3 + $0.10). B may convince A to sign an agreement choosing number 3 and directing $2 of capital to be transferred from B to A. The outcome of such scenario is as follows:

Number	A's Capital	B's Capital	A's Return (20%)	B's Return (40%)	Total Return	A's Payoff	B's Payoff
3a	$5	%3	$1.0	$1.2	$2.2	$0.10	$0.12

Questions (Refer to your payoffs on page _____)

1. Number _____ makes me the most money. Number _____ makes me the least money.

2. If I become the controller, I can make $____ even if the other person doesn't agree.

3. If I am the controller, I may choose the number which corresponds to my maximum payoff without making a joint agreement with the other participant, True or False? ____

4. Which of the following do you prefer? ____
    (a) $1.50 for sure
    (b) A fair coin toss which pays $0 for heads and $11 for tails

Payoff Sheet

Number	A			B			Total
	A's Capital	A's Return (20%)	A's Payoff (10%)	B's Capital	B's Return (40%)	B's Payoff (10%)	Return
1	$ 0.00	$ 0.00	$0.00	$120.0	$48.00	$4.80	$48.0
2	40.00	8.00	0.80	100.00	40.00	4.00	48.00
3	60.00	12.00	1.20	60.00	24.00	2.40	36.00
4	75.00	15.00	1.50	37.50	15.00	1.50	30.00
5	90.00	18.00	1.80	25.00	10.00	1.00	28.00
6	105.00	21.00	2.10	10.00	4.00	0.40	25.00
7	120.00	24.00	2.40	0.00	0.00	0.00	24.00

Agreement Form

Number Chosen ____

$____ to be paid from the capital of ____ to the capital of ____

Signed: _____
A

Signed: _____
B

In essence, these instructions told subjects that they had to choose a number between 1 and 7 and that they would be paid in cash according to the discrete payoff functions given on page ____ of the instructions. In addition, one subject won, through a game, the right to choose the number unilaterally and was told that he had *earned* that right by winning the game. Information was also collected on the subject's age, gender, race-ethnicity, and political orientation.

Game-Trigger, Egalitarian Moral Authority

This set of instructions resembled the previous experiments in all respects save one. The difference is that whenever the moral authority instructions say "earns the right" to become "controller for that decision," it is followed by the following new instructions: *"Each participant in the experiment has an equal need for the amount of payoffs."*

Game-Trigger, Lockean Moral Authority

This set of instructions resembled the previous experiments in all respects save one. The difference is that whenever the moral authority instructions say "earns the right" to become "controller for that decision," it is followed by the following new instructions: *"Each participant in the experiment deserves a property entitlement in payoffs that reflect the return they generate for the whole team."*

Properties of the Experimental Design

The first property of the experimental design is to create entitlements as rights. By winning the game and being explicitly told that they have earned the right to become a controller, the subjects would feel justified in treating the entitlements of the controller's position as a right.

The second property of the experimental design is to create experimental institutions (treatment variables) that motivate subjects about relying on utilitarian, egalitarian, or Lockean theories of distributive justice. This is accomplished by telling nothing, leaving the subjects to rely on utilitarianism, or explicitly reminding them that each participant in the experiment has an equal need for the amount of payoffs (triggering an egalitarian theory of justice), or that each participant in the experiment deserves a property entitlement in payoffs that reflect the return they generate for the whole team (triggering a Lockean theory of distributive justice).

The third property of the experimental design is to create three types of capital distributions: (a) capital distributions that provide B with higher payoffs (numbers 1–3), (b) capital distributions that provide equal payoffs for A and B (number 4), and (c) capital distributions that provide A with higher payoffs (numbers 5–7).

Subjects

The subjects were sixty undergraduate accounting majors. Thirty of them became controllers as a result of winning the game. They were randomly assigned to each of the three experimental groups. They were paid $3 per session plus their earnings.[42]

Exhibit 4.1
Results of the Analysis of Variance on the Greed Index

Source	DF	Sum of Squares	Mean Square	F Value	Pr > F
A. Model	6	2.9298	0.4883	3.62	0.0044*
1. Fairness Treatment	2	1.4023		5.19	0.0087*
2. Gender	1	0.6789		5.03	0.0291**
3. Age	1	0.6117		4.53	0.0380**
4. Ethnic Affiliation	1	0.0322		0.24	0.6269
5. Political Orientation	1	0.2045		1.52	0.2238
B. Error	53	7.1550	0.1350		
C. Corrected Total	59	10.0858			

*Significant at = 0.01
**Significant at = 0.05

EXPERIMENTAL RESULTS

To test the overall relationship between the greed index and the fairness (or theories of justice) treatments, an analysis of variance was used. Gender, age, ethnic affiliation, and political orientation are control variables.[43]

Exhibit 4.1 presents the results of the analysis of variance on the subjects' greed index, the amount in excess of an equal split. These results are highly significant. The hypothesis of this study is verified in the sense that the intrafirm resource allocation decision, as expressed by the greed index, is different among subjects adhering to different theories of justice, namely, the self-regarding utility theory, the egalitarian theory of justice, and the Lockean theory of earned desert. As shown in Exhibit 4.2, the greed index of the subjects adhering to the self-regarding utilitarian theory is the highest, and the greed index of the subjects instructed about the egalitarian theory of distributive justice is the lowest. Utilitarian subjects behaved in a greedy fashion, whereas the egalitarian subjects tended toward an equal split. Lockean subjects were less greedy than utilitarian subjects and not as egalitarian as the egalitarian subjects.

The results are consistent with the thesis that where theories of justice are instituted as part of the unit policy on fairness, a more egalitarian behavior is expected than when no such institutions are introduced.

The subjects viewed the entitlements as rights, but the exposure to a particular value-oriented theory of fairness affected their intrafirm resource allocation and their payoffs. In the absence of a moral authority, subjects

Exhibit 4.2
Greed Index Measures, Means and Standard Deviation by Fairness Treatment

Fairness Treatment	Means	Standard Deviation
1. Self-Regarding Utilitarian Theory	0.5100	0.4363
2. Egalitarian Theory of Distributive Justice	0.1400	0.3925
3. Lockean Theory of Earned Desert	0.3750	0.3354

behaved in a utilitarian fashion and maximized their payoffs regardless of the potential negative impact on the total return of the firm. In the presence of a moral authority advocating either an egalitarian theory of distributive justice or a Lockean theory of earned desert, subjects behaved in a less greedy fashion, tending toward an equal split of payoffs.

CONCLUSIONS

This study reports on an experiment examining the effects of entitlements, rights, and fairness on unit manager behavior in intrafirm resource allocation. Experimental institutions are used to trigger a particular concept of justice, indicating which distribution or set of distributions is fair within that experiment. An experimental setting was used. The decentralized firm consists of two related units. A common resource given to a first unit can also be used by the other unit. The first unit is entitled by central management to distribute the common resource between him/herself and the unit manager of the second unit. The distribution could be unilateral or involve bargains struck between the two unit managers who have opposing payoff functions and full information of one another's payoffs. The experiment focuses on the amount in excess of an equal split received by the first manager, called a "greed index," under experimental institutions triggering three concepts of fairness in distribution: (1) utilitarian theory of distributive justice; (2) egalitarian theory of distributive justice; and (3) Lockean theory of distributive justice. In the experiment, students served as subjects. As predicted, utilitarian subjects behaved in a greedy fashion, whereas egalitarian subjects tended toward an equal split. Lockean subjects were less greedy than utilitarian subjects and not as egalitarian as egalitarian subjects.

The evidence shows that the presence of a moral authority advocating either an egalitarian theory of distributive justice or a Lockean theory of earned desert reduced drastically the unconstrained opportunistic behavior predicted by agency theory. The opportunistic behaviors, in accord with the self-regarding utility theory of fairness where resources are perceived as rights by one of the parties to a contract, change to a more egalitarian behavior when other theories of justice, that is, egalitarian theory of distributive justice or a Lockean theory of earned desert, are instituted. While some subjects, left on their own, appear unreservedly opportunistic, others do constrain their own behavior out of a compliance to an instituted ethical code. As suggested by E. Noreen,[44] the simple fact of instruction is successful in reducing agency costs by moderating certain self-seeking behavior. This is not surprising given the experimental evidence that people who understand the benefits of cooperation are more likely to cooperate,[45] and apparently some sermonizing may even help.[46] The sermonizing in this experiment helped. All we need to do is teach some ethics and instill a commitment of ethical behavior. As stated by Noreen:

> To a large extent, we conduct our research by grubbing around in the underbrush of business looking for evidence of opportunistic behavior and of contractual counter-measures against such behavior. We need to keep in mind that while our models presume that businessmen are opportunistic and that we can find (statistically significant) examples of such opportunism and of counter-measures taken against such opportunism, it does not follow that businessmen generally are or should be opportunistic. It would be a mistake to wittingly or unwittingly inculcate in the next generation of accountants and managers the notion that it is foolish, naive or abnormal for businessmen to feel constrained in their actions by ethical considerations. At least some varieties of ethical behavior are not to be scorned; they are a necessary lubricant for the functioning of markets.[47]

NOTES

1. Brennan, Geoffrey, and James Buchanan, *The Power to Tax* (Cambridge: Cambridge University Press, 1980), 16.

2. Elster, Jon, "Social Norms and Economic Theory," *Journal of Economic Perspectives* 3, no. 4 (1989): 99–117.

3. Kahneman, D., J. L. Knetsch, and R. H. Thaler, "Fairness and the Assumptions of Economics," *Journal of Business* 59 (1986): 285–300.

4. Ibid., 299.

5. Zayac, E. E., *Fairness or Efficiency: An Introduction to Public Utility Pricing* (Cambridge, Mass.: Ballinger, 1978).

6. Arrow, K., "Social Responsibility and Economic Efficiency," *Public Policy* 21 (1973): 303–317.

7. Okun, Arthur, *Price and Quantities: A Macroeconomic Analysis* (Washington, D.C.: Brookings, 1981).

8. Baumol, William J., "Applied Fairness Theory and Rationing Policy," *The American Economic Review* (September 1982): 639.

9. Valanvanis, S., "The Resolution of Conflict When Utilities Interact," *Journal of Conflict Resolution* 2 (1958): 156–169.

10. Sen, A. K., "Rational Fools: A Critique of the Behavioral Foundations of Economic Theory," *Philosophy and Public Affairs* 6, no. 4 (1977): 317–344.

11. Hochman, H., and J. Rodgers, "Pareto Optimality Redistribution," *American Economic Review* 59, no. 4 (1969): 542–557.

12. Frohlich, N., "Self-Interest or Altruism: What Difference?" *Journal of Conflict Resolution* 18 (1974): 55–73.

13. Margolis, H., *Selfishness, Altruism and Rationality* (New York: Cambridge University Press, 1982).

14. Becker, Gary, "Altruism, Egoism, and Genetic Fitness: Economics and Sociology," *Journal of Economic Literature* (September 1976): 817–826.

15. Ibid., 825–826.

16. Marwell, G., and R. Ames, "Experiments in the Provision of Public Goods II," *American Journal of Sociology* 85 (1980): 926–937.

17. Miller, G., and J. Oppenheimer, "Universalism in Experimental Committees," *American Political Science Review* 76 (1982): 561–574.

18. Marwell, G., and R. Ames, "Experiments in the Provision of Public Goods I," *American Journal of Sociology* 86 (1979): 1335–60.

19. Frohlich, Norman, and Joe Oppenheimer, "Beyond Economic Man: Altruism, Egalitarianism, and Difference Maximizing," *Journal of Conflict Resolution* 28, no. 1 (1984): 3–24.

20. Ibid., 5–6.

21. Eckel, Catherine C., and Philip Grossman, "The Price of Fairness: Gender Differences in Punishment Games," *working paper, Wayne State University* (1995).

22. Watts, R., and J. Zimmerman, *Positive Accounting Theory* (Englewood Cliffs, N.J.: Prentice-Hall, 1986).

23. Various studies expanded the accounting discussion of fairness in financial reporting by introducing the main philosophical concepts of distributive justice in the accounting context.

24. This study assumes that unit managers' utility depends on pay and bonus only. It is also more realistic to assume that unit managers value the personal consumption of resources as well as pay.

25. The three classes of theories of distributive justice represent value-oriented explanations. Nonvalue-oriented theory, such as sociobiological theory, maintains that behavior is genetically determined. Our experiment does not rely on any sociobiological explanation given that the tasks do not involve life-or-death decisions.

26. Hoffman, Elizabeth, and Matthew L. Spitzer, "Entitlements, Rights and Fairness: An Experimental Examination of Subjects' Concepts of Distributive Justice," *Journal of Legal Studies* 14 (1985): 259–297.

27. Waller, W. S., and R. A. Bishop, "An Experimental Study of Incentive Pay Schemes, Communication, and Intrafirm Resource Allocation," *The Accounting Review* 65 (1990): 812–836.

28. Maslow, A., *Motivation and Personality* (New York: Harper and Row, 1970).

29. Yale Divinity School, "Moral Claims, Human Rights and Population Choices," *Theological Studies* 35 (1974): 100.

30. Rawls, J., *A Theory of Justice* (Cambridge, Mass.: Harvard University Press, 1971).

31. Deutsch, M., "Equity, Equality and Needs: What Determines Which Value Will Be Used as a Basis of Distributive Justice?" *Journal of Social Issues* 31 (1975): 137–150.

32. MacPherson, C. B., *The Political Theory of Possessive Individualism: Hobbes to Locke* (New York: Clarendon Press, 1962).

33. Locke, John, *Second Treatise of Government* (New York: Blackwell, 1966).

34. Kachelmeier, S. J., and M. Shehata, "Culture and Competition: A Laboratory Market Comparison between China and the West," *Journal of Economic Behavior and Organizations* 19 (1992): 145–168.

35. Kim, K. I., H. J. Park, and N. Suzuki, "Reward Allocations in the United States, Japan, and Korea: A Comparison of Individualistic and Collective Cultures," *Academy of Management Journal* 33 (1990): 188–198.

36. Frohlich and Oppenheimer, "Beyond Economic Man."

37. Carment, D. W., "Effects of Sex Roles in a Maximizing Difference Game," *Journal of Conflict Resolution* 18 (1974): 433–443.

38. Ibid.

39. Hartman, E. A., "Motivational Bases of Sex Differences in China," *Journal of Conflict Resolution* 24 (1980): 455–475.

40. Ingram, Barbara Lichner, and Stephen E. Berger, "Sex-Role Orientation, Defensiveness, and Competitiveness in Women," *Journal of Conflict Resolution* 21 (1977): 501–518.

41. Skotko, V., D. Langmeyer, and D. Lundgren, "Sex Differences as Artifact in the Prisoner's Dilemma Game," *Journal of Conflict Resolution* 18 (1974): 707–713.

42. After each experiment, the subjects were informed about the nature of the experiment and the need not to tell their friends about it, in order to eliminate any time trend in the results. Later subjects appeared as naive about the experiment as earlier subjects had been.

43. The risk preferences of the subjects were gauged by the following question: Which of the following do you prefer?
   (a) $1.50 for sure
   (b) A fair coin toss which pays $0 for heads and $11 for tails
The overwhelming majority of the subjects, over 95 percent, chose (b) over (a), indicating that they were not extremely risk averse.

44. Noreen, E., "The Economics of Ethics: A New Perspective on Agency Theory," *Accounting, Organizations and Society* 13, no. 4 (1988): 359–370.

45. Dawes, R. M., "Social Dilemmas," *Annual Review of Psychology* 2 (1980): 169–193.

46. Ibid.

47. Noreen, "The Economics of Ethics," 368.

REFERENCES

Abdel-Khalik, A., and E. Lusk. "Transfer Pricing: A Synthesis." *The Accounting Review* 1 (1974): 8–13.

Bolnick, B. "Toward a Behavioral Theory of Philanthropic Activity." In E. S. Phelps, ed., *Altruism, Morality, and Economic Theory.* New York: Russell Sage Foundation, 1975, pp. 13–28.

Buchanan, James M. "The Samaritan's Dilemma." In E. S. Phelps, ed., *Altruism, Morality and Economic Theory.* New York: Russell Sage Foundation, 1975, pp. 71–86.

Carment, D. W. "Effects of Sex Role in a Maximizing Difference Game." *Journal of Conflict Resolution* 18 (1974): 433–443.

Cyert, R., and J. March. *A Behavioral Theory of the Firm.* Englewood Cliffs, N.J.: Prentice-Hall, 1963.

Dawes, R. M. "Social Dilemmas." *Annual Review of Psychology* 2 (1980): 169–193.

Deutsch, Morton. "Equity, Equality, and Needs: What Determines Which Value Will Be Used as a Basis of Distributive Justice." *Journal of Social Issues* 31 (1975): 137–150.

Frohlich, Norman, and Joe Oppenheimer. "Beyond Economic Man: Altruism, Egalitarianism and Difference Maximizing." *Journal of Conflict Resolution* 28, no. 1 (1984): 3–24.

Gould, J. R. "Internal Pricing in Firms When There Are Costs of Using an Outside Market." *Journal of Business* 1 (1964): 61–67.

Groves, T. "Incentive Compatible Control of Decentralized Organizations." In *Directions in Large Scale Systems: Many-Person Optimization and Decentralized Control,* ed. Y. Ho and S. Mitters. New York: Plenum, 1976, 16–32.

Groves, T., and M. Loeb. "Incentives in a Divisionalized Firm." *Management Science* 25 (March 1979): 221–230.

Harris, M., C. H. Kriebel, and A. Raviv. "Asymmetric Information, Incentives and Intrafirm Resource Allocation." *Management Science* 28 (June 1982): 604–620.

Hartman, E. Alan. "Motivational Bases of Sex Differences in Choice Behavior." *Journal of Conflict Resolution* 24 (1980): 455–475.

Hirshleifer, J. "Economics of the Divisionalized Firm." *Journal of Business* 20 (1975): 96–108.

Hoffman, Elizabeth, and Matthew L. Spitzer. "Entitlements, Rights, and Fairness: An Experimental Examination of Subjects' Concepts of Distributive Justice." *Journal of Legal Studies* 14 (1985): 259–297.

———. "The Coase Theorem: Some Experimental Tests." *Journal of Law and Economics* 25 (1982): 73–98.

Ingram, Barbara Lichner, and Stephen E. Berger. "Sex-Role Orientation, Defensiveness, and Competitiveness in Women." *Journal of Conflict Resolution* 21 (1977): 501–518.

Jensen, M. C., and W. H. Meckling. "Theory of the Firm: Managerial Behavior, Agency Costs and Ownership Structure." *Journal of Financial Economics* 3 (October 1976): 305–360.

Kachelmeier, Steven J., and Mohamed Shehata. "Culture and Competition: A Laboratory Market Comparison between China and the West." *Journal of Economic Behavior and Organizations* 19 (1992): 145–168.

Kanodia, C. "Risk Sharing and Transfer Price Systems under Certainty." *Journal of Accounting Research* 17 (1979): 74–98.

Kim, Ken I., Hun-Joon Park, and Nori Suzuki. "Reward Allocations in the United

States, Japan, and Korea: A Comparison of Individualistic and Collectivistic Cultures." *Academy of Management Journal* 33 (1990): 188–198.

Lev, Baruch. "Toward a Theory of Equitable and Efficient Accounting Policy." *The Accounting Review* 1 (1988): 1–22.

Locke, John. *Second Treatise of Government*. New York: Blackwell, 1966.

Loeb, M., and W. A. Magat. "Soviet Success Indicators and the Evaluation of Divisional Management." *Journal of Accounting Research* 16 (1978): 103–121.

MacPherson, C. B. *The Political Theory of Possessive Individualism: Hobbes to Locke*. New York: Clarendon Press, 1962.

Maslow, A. *Motivation and Personality*. New York: Harper and Row, 1970.

McKean, R. N. "Economics of Trust, Altruism, and Corporate Responsibility." In E. S. Phelps, ed., *Altruism, Morality, and Economic Theory*. New York: Russell Sage Foundation, 1975, pp. 29–44.

Mill, John Stuart. *Utilitarianism*. Indianapolis: Bobbs-Merrill, 1957.

Noreen, E. "The Economics of Ethics: A New Perspective on Agency Theory." *Accounting, Organizations and Society* 13, no. 4 (1988): 359–370.

Pallot, June. "The Legitimate Concern with Fairness: A Comment." *Accounting, Organizations and Society* 16 (1991): 201–208.

Rawls, J. *A Theory of Justice*. Cambridge, Mass.: Harvard University Press, 1971.

Ruland, Robert G. "Duty, Obligation, and Responsibility in Accounting Policy Making." *Journal of Accounting and Public Policy* 3 (1984): 223–237.

Schiff, M., and A. Y. Lewin. "The Impact of People on Budgets." *The Accounting Review* 45 (April 1970): 259–268.

Skotko, Vincent, Daniel Langmeyer, and David Lundgren. "Sex Differences as Artifact in the Prisoner's Dilemma Game." *Journal of Conflict Resolution* 18 (1974): 707–713.

Waller, William S., and Rachel A. Bishop. "An Experimental Study of Incentive Pay Schemes, Communication, and Intrafirm Resource Allocation." *The Accounting Review* 65 (1990): 812–836.

Watts, R., and J. Zimmerman. *Positive Accounting Theory*. Englewood Cliffs, N.J.: Prentice-Hall, 1986.

Williams, Paul F. "The Legitimate Concern with Fairness." *Accounting, Organizations and Society* 12 (1987): 169–192.

Yale Divinity School. "Moral Claims, Human Rights and Population Choices." *Theological Studies* 35 (1974): 100

Selected Readings

Arrow, K. "Social Responsibility and Economic Efficiency." *Public Policy* 21 (1973): 303–317.

Baumol, William J. "Applied Fairness Theory and Rationing Policy." *The American Economic Review* (September 1982): 639–651.

Becker, Gary. "Altruism, Egoism and Genetic Fitness: Economics and Sociology." *Journal of Economic Literature* (September 1976): 817–826.

Brennan, Geoffrey, and James Buchanan. *The Power to Tax.* Cambridge: Cambridge University Press, 1980.

Elster, Jon. "Social Norms and Economic Theory." *Journal of Economic Perspectives* 3, no. 4 (1989): 99–117.

Frohlich, Norman. "Self-Interest or Altruism: What Difference?" *Journal of Conflict Resolution* 18 (1974): 55–73.

Frohlich, Norman, and Joe Oppenheimer. "Beyond Economic Man: Altruism, Egalitarianism, and Difference Maximizing." *Journal of Conflict Resolution* 28, no. 1 (1984): 3–24.

Hochman, H., and J. Rodgers. "Pareto Optimality Redistribution." *American Economic Review* 59, no. 4 (1969): 542–557.

Kahneman, D., J. L. Knetsch, and R. H. Thaler. "Fairness and the Assumptions of Economics." *Journal of Business* 59 (1986): 285–300.

Margolis, H. *Selfishness, Altruism and Rationality.* New York: Cambridge University Press, 1982.

Marwell, G., and R. Ames. "Experiments in the Provision of Goods I." *American Journal of Sociology* 84 (1979): 1335–1360.

———. "Experiments in the Provision of Goods II." *American Journal of Sociology* 85 (1980): 926–937.

Miller, G., and J. Oppenheimer. "Universalism in Experimental Committees." *American Political Science Review* 76 (1982): 561–574.

Okun, Arthur. *Price and Quantities: A Macroeconomic Analysis.* Washington, D.C.: Brookings, 1981.

Sen, A. K. "Rational Fools: A Critique of the Behavioral Foundations of Economic Theory." *Philosophy of Public Affairs* 6, no. 4 (1977): 317–344.

Valanvanis, S. "The Resolution of Conflict When Utilities Interact." *Journal of Conflict Resolution* 2 (1958): 150–169.

Zayac, E. E. *Fairness or Efficiency: An Introduction to Public Utility Pricing.* Cambridge, Mass.: Ballinger, 1978.

Index

Accounting measurements, expansion of, 71–72

Accrual basis of accounting, 92–93

American Institute of Certified Public Accountants (AICPA): and auditor's report revisions, 9–12; and fairness concept, 3, 9–12; issuing of SASs, 17–18; Special Committee on Financial Reporting (Jenkins Committee), 76–77

Annual report to employees, 84–85

Arthur Andersen & Co., 1–2, 52–53

Arthur Young & Co., 55

Auditor's standard report: adverse opinion in, 22; content of, 17–21; disclaimer of opinion in, 22; emphasis paragraph in, 22–23; format and content changes in, 7–12; meaning of "fair presentation in conformity with GAAP" in, 10–17; origins of, 5–7; qualified opinion in, 21–22

Budgetary information disclosures, 90–92

Canadian Institute of Public Accountants (CICA), 15

Cash flow accounting, 93–94

Chase Manhattan Bank, Inc., 51–52

CICA Handbook, 15

Cohen Report, 7–9

Continental Vending decision, 13–14

Contract theory (Rawls), 62

Corporate social reporting, 87–90

Disclosures, proposed expansions of, 71–80

Distributive justice, 161–170; egalitarian theory of, 162; entitlement principle of, 63; and intrafirm resource allocation, 161–170; and justice in acquisition and transfer, 63–65; Lockean theory of, 162–163; Rawls' theory of, 59–62; utilitarian theory of, 162; and value added reporting, 66–67

Drysdale Government Securities, Inc., 51–53

Economic models, self-interest assumptions in, 159–161

Egalitarian theory of distributive justice, 162

Employee reporting, 83–85
Entitlement theory (Nozick), 62–65, 89
Equitable and efficient accounting pol-
  icy theory (Lev), 74–75
Ethics of accounting, 58
External reporting, 76–77

Fair presentation in conformity with
  GAAP, meaning of, 10–17
Fairness: and conformance with GAAP,
  13–14; as moral concept of justice,
  59–67; as neutrality of accountant,
  1–3
Fairness in disclosure: and Bedford's
  disclosure proposals, 71–74; and
  budgetary information disclosures,
  90–92; and employee reporting, 83–
  85; and equity concept, 74–75; and
  external reporting, 76–77; and human resource accounting, 85–86; and
  proposed new disclosures, 80; and
  recognition vs. disclosure, 77–79;
  and social accounting and reporting,
  86–90; and user primacy principle,
  75–76; and value added reporting,
  80–81
Fairness in distribution, 57–68; and
  Gerwith's theory of justice, 66–67;
  and Nozickean libertarian view of accounting, 64–65; and Rawls' contract
  theory, 62. See also Distributive justice
Fairness in presentation (fairness doctrine), 1–23; and concept of conservatism, 2; and fairness in disclosure,
  23; and fairness in distribution, 23;
  fraud cases resulting from, 51–56; as
  implicit ethical norm, 2–3; and management of earnings and income
  smoothing, 23; and recognition vs.
  disclosure, 77–79
Financial Accounting Standards Board
  (FASB), 77
Financial forecasts, disclosure of, 90–
  92
Financial statements, stewardship function of, 92–94
Fraud, accountants' liability in, 51–56

Gaa's user primacy, 75–76
Generally accepted accounting principles (GAAP); and auditor's private
  standard of fair presentation, 10–15;
  and "present fairly," 10–17; as sole
  standard of reference, 15–16
Generally accepted auditing standards
  (GAAS), 11–12, 13, 16, 18, 19–21
Gerwith's theory of justice, 62, 65–67,
  89
Great Britain: financial disclosure requirements, 90–91; true and fair doctrine in, 3–5

Healy, Paul, 50
Human resource accounting, 85–86;
  proposed models for, 86
Hurdman, Main, 53–54

Income smoothing, 49–50
Information overload theory, 73–74
Intrafirm resource allocation: and
  agency theory, 161; and egalitarian
  theory of distributive justice, 162;
  and greed index, 163, 168–169; and
  Lockean theory of distributive justice, 162–163; and utilitarian theory
  of fairness, 162

Jenkins Committee, 76–77

KMG (auditing firm), 53, 54

Libertarian view ofaccounting, 64–65
Lockean theory of distributive justice,
  162–163

Managerial and cost accounting, 3
Manufacturers Hanover Trust, 52, 53

Nozick's Theory of Justice, 62–64, 89

Peat, Marwick, Mitchell & Co., 55–56
Penn Square, 54–56
Percentage of completion accounting,
  54
Preciseness theory, 74

Principle of Generic Consistency (Gerwith), 66

Rawls' contract theory, 62
Rawls' theory of justice, 59–62, 88
Relevance theory, 74
Retrieved systems theory, 74
Right to know theory, 73

Social accounting and reporting, 58–59, 62, 86–90; social contract argument for, 88; social investment decisions, 89–90; social justice argument for, 88–89; and tracking of environmental risk, 88; and users' needs, 89
Social indicators accounting, 87

Social investments, 86–90
Social responsibility accounting activities, 87
Socioeconomic accounting, 87

Total impact accounting (TIA), 87
Touche Ross, 54
True and fair doctrine, 1, 27–48; lack of comprehensive definition, 3–5

User primacy principle, 75–76
Utilitarian theory of distributive justice, 162

Value added reporting, 66–67, 80–81

Wedtech Corp., 53–54

About the Authors

JANICE MONTI-BELKAOUI is Professor of Sociology at Rosary College, River Forest, Illinois, and Chair of the Department of Sociology, History, and American Studies. She writes frequently for scholarly journals and is coauthor of *Accounting in the Dual Economy* (Quorum, 1991).

AHMED RIAHI-BELKAOUI is Professor of Accounting at the College of Business Administration, University of Illinois at Chicago. At last count, he has published more than 100 articles in various refereed journals and other publications and authored or coauthored more than 24 academic and professional books for Quorum.